The Reminiscences Of

Captain Herbert E. Hetu
U.S. Navy (Retired)

INTERVIEWED BY

Paul Stillwell

U.S. Naval Institute • Annapolis, Maryland

Copyright © 2003

Preface

In 1986 a delegation of three retired naval officers visited the Naval Institute on behalf of the newly formed United States Navy Public Affairs Alumni Association. The group included Captain Herb Hetu, Captain Ed Castillo, and Captain Bob Jones. As part of their effort to document the history of Navy public affairs, they were looking for suggestions on how to start an oral history program.

In the course of getting acquainted with them, I concluded that Captain Hetu, the president of the new organization, would be a great candidate for the Naval Institute's program because of the variety of billets he'd held in the field. During his career he had been on the public affairs staffs of the Chief of Naval Operations, two Secretaries of the Navy, Commander in Chief Pacific Fleet, Commander in Chief U.S. Naval Forces Europe, with the Seventh Fleet detachment in Vietnam, and with the Central Intelligence Agency. He had also worked with a variety of news media people and had been involved with books, magazines, radio, and television. It was a broad background worth documenting. The bonus, as I discovered during the interviews that followed, was that Hetu was a gifted storyteller. As a result, the narrative that follows is not only informative but also highly readable and often entertaining.

As Captain Hetu progressed through a series of jobs, it became apparent that he had been assigned to a number of high-visibility billets because of demonstrated ability. On the one hand, his approach was proactive in telling the Navy's story, and on the other it was frequently imaginative. He had the ability to think outside the box, as the current saying has it. In his dealings with the media, he was able to capture attention for positive developments and to ensure that the unfavorable events were handled in a professional, responsive way. Though he didn't attempt to manage the news per se, he made sure that reporters knew and understood the Navy's point of view. In the process he and the media developed a sense of mutual respect that benefited both. One of the things that aided him in the process was that he had served as a line officer before specializing in public affairs and thus well understood the operational aspects of the Navy. His work in the aftermath of two 1969 tragedies—the loss of an EC-121 aircraft and a collision between the destroyer Frank E. Evans and the carrier Melbourne—can serve as case studies for public affairs professionals.

Because of the jobs in which he served, Captain Hetu's recollections provided candid insights into a number of well-known individuals: Admiral David McDonald, Admiral Stansfield Turner, Admiral John McCain, Jr., and Secretaries of the Navy John Chafee and John Warner. Then there is the fun part of the story. Hetu was blessed with a sense of humor and enjoyment of a good time. Two examples of that are his work in providing Navy support for the Hollywood movies South Pacific and In Harm's Way. Many other examples appear throughout the transcript.

Ms. Carolyn Zimmer did the initial transcription of the interview tapes. Captain Hetu received a copy of the transcript but unfortunately did not submit any inputs prior to his death. In his stead, I have done some light editing in the interests of accuracy, smoothness, and clarity. In addition, I have inserted footnotes to provide further information for readers who use the volume.

Ms. Ann Hassinger of the Naval Institute's history division has made a significant contribution through her diligence in the overall process of printing, proofreading, and overseeing the binding of the completed volumes.

Finally, the Naval Institute expresses its gratitude to the Tawani Foundations and the Pritzker Military Library for their generous financial support of the oral history program that produced this memoir.

Paul Stillwell

Paul Stillwell
Director, History Division
U.S. Naval Institute
August 2003

CAPTAIN HERBERT EDMOND HETU
UNITED STATES NAVY (RETIRED)

Personal Data

Born: November 25, 1929, Sharon, Pennsylvania
Died: April 7, 2003, Alexandria, Virginia
Parents: Herbert E. and Susan E. (Donnelly) Hetu
Married: Margaret Ann Petros, October 30, 1954; divorced in 1985
         Kathryn A. Black, December 28, 1991
Children: Michael A. Hetu, born September 16, 1955
         Deborah J. Echard, born September 22, 1956
         Susan L. Beyer, born August 26, 1957
         Patricia A. Hetu, born October 20, 1960
         Jacqueline M. Barber, born March 5, 1963
Education: John Carroll University, Cleveland, Ohio, bachelor of science, 1952
         Boston University, Boston, Massachusetts, master of science, 1965

Dates of Rank

Ensign:	October 30, 1952
Lieutenant (j.g.)	December 30, 1953
Lieutenant	September 1, 1956
Lieutenant Commander	July 1, 1962
Commander	July 1, 1966
Captain	July 1, 1972
Retired	July 1, 1975

Chronological Record of Service

Enlisted: August 8, 1948

Aug 1948-Nov 1948	Recruit Training, Naval Training Center, Great Lakes, Illinois
Nov 1948-Jan 1949	Hospital Corps School, Great Lakes, Illinois
Feb 1949-Aug 1949	Naval Hospital, Philadelphia, Pennsylvania
Jun 1952-Oct 1952	Officer Candidate School, Newport, Rhode Island
Nov 1952-Nov 1954	Deck Officer, USS <u>Salem</u> (CA-139)
Dec 1954-Jul 1956	Chief, Magazine and Book Branch, Office of Information, Navy Department, Washington, D.C.

Sep 1956-Jul 1958	Assistant Public Information Officer, Staff, Commander in Chief Pacific Fleet
Jul 1958-Nov 1959	Public Information Officer, Staff, Commander Service Force Pacific Fleet
Nov 1959-Dec 1960	Assistant Officer in Charge, Armed Forces Public Information Office, Los Angeles, California
Jan 1961-Apr 1962	Navy Press Officer, Office of the Assistant Secretary of Defense (Public Affairs), Washington, D.C.
May 1962-Aug 1964	Chief, Audio-Visual Branch, Office of Information, Navy Department, Washington, D.C.
Sep 1964-Aug 1965	Postgraduate Student, Boston University
Sep 1965-Jun 1966	Public Affairs Officer, Tenth Naval District/Caribbean Sea Frontier, San Juan, Puerto Rico
Jun 1966-Oct 1967	Special Assistant for Public Affairs, Staff of the Chief of Naval Operations, Washington, D.C.
Nov 1967-Apr 1969	Public Affairs Officer, Staff, Commander in Chief U.S. Naval Forces Europe, London, England
Apr 1969-Dec 1969	Officer in Charge, Public Affairs, Seventh Fleet Detachment Charlie, Saigon, South Vietnam
Jan 1970-Apr 1974	Special Assistant for Public Affairs, Staff of the Secretary of the Navy, Washington, D.C.
Apr 1974-March 1977	Assistant Administrator for Communications, American Revolution Bicentennial Administration, Washington, D.C. (including a period after official retirement from active duty)

Civilian Employment

Mar 1977-Aug 1981	Director of Public Affairs, Central Intelligence Agency, Langley, Virginia
Aug 1981-Dec 1985	President, Hetu & Lukstat, Inc., Public Relations, Washington, D.C.

Jan 1986-Oct 1986	Senior Vice President and General Manager, Carl Byoir & Associates, Washington, D.C.
Oct 1986-Apr 1987	Senior Vice President, Hill & Knowlton, Washington, D.C.
Apr 1987-1995	Vice President, Communications, Aerospace Industries Association, Washington, D.C.
1996-2000	President, LHC Communications

Presidential Commissions

President's Commission on Strategic Forces, chaired by Lieutenant General Brent Scowcroft (1983)

National Bipartisan Commission on Central America, chaired by Henry Kissinger (1983-84)

President's Blue Ribbon Commission on Defense Management, chaired by David Packard (1985-86)

President's Commission to Investigate the Space Shuttle Challenger Accident, chaired by William Rogers, 1986

President's Special Review Board investigating the Iran-Contra affair, chaired by Senator John Tower, 1987

Captain Hetu was a founding member and first president of the United States Navy Public Affairs Alumni Association. He was a member of the National Press Club, The Army and Navy Club, National Aviation Club, The National Aeronautic Association, and the Aviation/Space Writers Association. He was awarded Boston University's Distinguished Alumni Award for outstanding achievement in the field of public relations.

Authorization

The U.S. Naval Institute is hereby authorized to make available to individuals, libraries, and other repositories of its choosing the transcripts of four oral history interviews concerning the life and naval career of the undersigned. The interviews were recorded on 9 May 1996, 17 May 1996, 5 June 1996, and 20 June 1996 in collaboration with Paul Stillwell for the U.S. Naval Institute.

The undersigned does hereby release and assign to the U.S. Naval Institute the rights and title to these interviews, with the exception that the undersigned retains the right to use the material for his own purposes, as he sees fit. The copyright in both the oral and transcribed versions shall be the sole property of the U.S. Naval Institute. The tape recordings of the interviews are and will remain the property of the U.S. Naval Institute.

Signed and sealed this __15TH__ day of __JULY__ 1996.

_____
Captain Herbert E. Hetu, USN (Ret.)

Interview Number 1 with Captain Herbert E. Hetu, U.S. Navy (Retired)

Place: Captain Hetu's home, Alexandria, Virginia

Date: Thursday, 9 May 1996

Interviewer: Paul Stillwell

Paul Stillwell: Well, it's a pleasure to see you again, Captain, and to begin this series. The proper place to begin is with when and where you were born, and we can go from there.

Captain Hetu: Yes. Born in a little town in western Pennsylvania, Sharon, Pennsylvania, on November 25, 1929. My parents had moved there from Massachusetts, and that's where I spent most of my life, except for World War II, when my dad was in the Navy. We can talk about that.

Paul Stillwell: Please tell me more about your parents.

Captain Hetu: Well, I'm an only child. My dad was from Southbridge, Massachusetts, which is up near north of Boston, near Worcester. He came from a French-speaking town—Hetu is French—in Brittany, and he spoke French and English. They taught them in English, I think, in the morning, in the Catholic schools and French in the afternoon they spoke. So he was fluent in French.

He had quit high school, I think, in his freshman year to work, to support the family. He came from a poor family. Then later he became interested in accounting and was the bookkeeper at the American Optical Company, which is still in Southbridge. Then he went to Boston and went to accounting school—without a high school degree, remember.

Paul Stillwell: About what period would that have been?

Captain Hetu: Nineteen twenty-five, something like that, '22, '23. And he graduated from this accounting school, Morgan Accounting School, as I recall, and got a CPA, certified public accountant, which in those days was a pretty big deal. I guess it's still important.

One of the people that he met in the course of doing business in Boston came to Pennsylvania and started an accounting company, wrote to my father, and asked him to come to Pennsylvania and be his partner. In the meantime, my father had met my mother, who lived in East Boston. My mother was born in Ireland and came over with her father, who was a first mate on a freighter. In fact, it's that freighter there, the SS Sandwich, which I've been on as a child. Anyhow, my mother came; they got married and moved to Sharon, Pennsylvania.

In 1935, the Navy was looking for Supply Corps officers and sent out a letter apparently to all CPAs in the country, is my understanding, asking if they were interested in a reserve commission in the Navy. And my dad said, "Yes." He got a direct commission in 1935 as full lieutenant. And remember, still no high school education.

Paul Stillwell: Do you have any idea why the Navy felt this need to beef up the Supply Corps?

Captain Hetu: I don't know. I would like to look into that. I've thought about it, but I haven't taken the opportunity to do that. I don't know. That always sort of puzzled me, because he was then called to active duty before Pearl Harbor, in, I think, April of 1941, which was interesting, because nobody was predicting war then. Not really, I don't think, not imminently, anyway.

Paul Stillwell: What sort of participation did he have between 1935 and 1941?

Captain Hetu: I remember him taking a lot of courses by mail and going to reserve meetings in Pittsburgh, which was about 60 miles from Sharon.

Oh, in the meantime, between '35 and when he was called up, we lived in Sharon, across the back alley from the superintendent of schools. And so over a lawn mower one

Saturday, I guess, my dad and the superintendent of schools talked. My dad confided in him, and said, "You know, I don't have a high school diploma. I'd love to—how can we work that out?"

So the superintendent of schools said, "I'll make up a test for you." And this must be the first high equivalency diploma certainly ever granted in Sharon, Pennsylvania.

Anyway, I remember my dad studying when I was a kid, on the front porch in the summertime. He took his test and passed. And so it was kind of interesting, my father and I graduated from the same high school, not at the same time. [Laughter] So he was a heck of a guy. And this is sort a long-winded way of saying that's really why I ended up in the Navy.

Paul Stillwell: Please tell me about your mother.

Captain Hetu: Mother, who is still alive, living close by, is almost 89 years old. She was born in Belfast, Ireland, ended up with, I think, two sisters that lived; there were a bunch that died. Her dad was on a freighter out of Belfast and ended up spending more time in the eastern United States than he did in Ireland, so he decided to move the family to Boston. She came in through Ellis Island and that whole business when she was ten years old, so that's almost 80 years ago—before World War I.[*]

Paul Stillwell: Did she talk about the old country?

Captain Hetu: What she remembered. Her memories are pretty dim now about that, because she was pretty young when she came over.

Paul Stillwell: Well, I was thinking more of when you were growing up.

Captain Hetu: Yes, a little bit. Really more about Boston than about the old country. My grandfather was quite a character.

---

[*] Ellis Island, in New York Harbor, was the processing center through which more than 12 million immigrants to the United States passed between 1892 and 1954.

Paul Stillwell: Was there a sense of gratitude about the opportunities in this country?

Captain Hetu: Oh, yes. I think so, yes. The house that they lived in is still in the family, which boggles my mind. It's a small little house in East Boston, not far from Logan Airport. And, you know, Boston, there's all three-deckers. They had this little house in the midst of all these three-deckers; I can see it in my mind now. I went there as a kid and visited my grandfather's ship, in fact, the SS <u>Sandwich</u>, which was a small freighter. And my mother met my dad there and so forth. For two people that came from very humble beginnings, I think they did quite well.

Paul Stillwell: What were your interests as a boy growing up in Pennsylvania?

Captain Hetu: Oh, goodness. I suppose what all kids do. I think one of my biggest recollections from being a kid, a small child, was getting my first bike, because of the independence. All of a sudden, I was able to go places and do things. One of my strong recollections as a child was getting my first bike and being able to get a basket for that bike and put things in it and go places. Boy, was that ever great.

Paul Stillwell: Did you play sports?

Captain Hetu: Baseball and football. I didn't play varsity sports in either high school or college. Loved to play football. You wouldn't know it to look at me now, but I was too small in high school and college to play, but I loved to play. I played in a sandlot league and that sort of thing. Even in the early days, we had our uniforms, and we had a lot of fun.

My dad went in the Navy in April of 1941—was called up, and then we started to move. He didn't really go very far. He was a Supply Corps officer and a specialist as a supervisory cost inspector. So they sent him to Pittsburgh, which wasn't very far away and he took over—they had some shipbuilding companies there, Dravo.

Paul Stillwell: Built LSTs.*

Captain Hetu: Exactly. Yes, my mother was sponsor of one.

Paul Stillwell: How did that come about, just because of her connection with a naval officer?

Captain Hetu: Yes, yes. Daddy was then the supervisory cost inspector, and in those days, they were kicking them out so fast that they were looking for people. You know, to sponsor a ship now is quite special. It was then, too, but I mean, a commander's wife acting as a sponsor was pretty junior. Right behind you is a model of it.

Paul Stillwell: LST-836.†

Captain Hetu: Yep, Holmes County, and, in fact, I ran into that ship in Vietnam, which was pretty unusual.

Paul Stillwell: I'm pretty sure I saw her over there also.

Captain Hetu: Well, I went aboard. That's a story, but I was a commander in Vietnam and I went aboard. I had to go up to Danang for something, and I saw it sitting there, and I couldn't resist. I went over, and I think an ensign or jaygee was the senior officer aboard.‡ I went up; there was a chief on the quarterdeck. I was a commander. And he said, "What command?"

I said, "Well, I'm from the Seventh Fleet staff in Saigon." Oh, my God, you know.

---

* LST—tank landing ship, an amphibious warfare ship capable of putting her bow directly onto a beach, opening bow doors, and lowering a bow ramp to permit vehicles to exit.
† The LST-836 was laid down 11 September 1944 at the American Bridge Company, Ambridge, Pennsylvania. The ship was launched 29 October 1944, with Mrs. Herbert E. Hetu as sponsor, and was commissioned 25 November 1944. She served until decommissioned in 1971. On 1 July of that year she was loaned to the Singapore Navy, where she was renamed Endurance. Singapore bought the ship from the United States in December 1975.
‡ Jaygee—lieutenant (junior grade).

This ensign came running, "What's wrong?" You know, that's the first reaction, "What happened?"

I said, "No, no, no. Look, my mother sponsored this ship, and this is a nostalgic visit. I'd like to go down to your wardroom, and you probably have pictures from the launching." And they did. They had a picture from the day she sponsored the ship. I said, "See the little fat kid there? That's me." And so we had a good laugh and a cup of coffee.

Paul Stillwell: What a wonderful experience that must have been.

Captain Hetu: It really was, because I had been on it that day. They launched the ships in Pittsburgh sideways.

Paul Stillwell: I've seen pictures of that.

Captain Hetu: Because if they didn't, they'd end up in Ohio someplace. They launched them into the river, and they went in. It was extraordinary. I remember it vividly.

Paul Stillwell: What were some of your strong points in school?

Captain Hetu: Well, leadership. That's a terrible thing to say; that sounds unhumble. Because academics was not my strong suit until later. But my dad went into the Navy, and I went my first two years of high school in Pittsburgh, to North Catholic High School, which was a brand-new school. I worked there as a janitor after school as a young kid to make some money, which was great experience; I loved it.

Then we moved to Philadelphia, and I went to West Philadelphia Catholic High School for one year. Then we moved back when the war was over and went back to Sharon, Pennsylvania. I ended up my senior year at Sharon High School with all my old pals from grade school that I hadn't seen for several years.

Paul Stillwell: So the extent of your dad's wartime experience was in Pennsylvania?

Captain Hetu: Yes.

Paul Stillwell: That's unusual.

Captain Hetu: Pittsburgh, and then he went to Philadelphia to be the supervisory cost inspector for the Fourth Naval District, and he made captain. Yes, never got out of Pennsylvania, which I think sort of broke his heart. He really wanted to do something a little more special than that. The Navy thought it was important. He tried, I remember once, to go to the Pacific, and it fell through. He wanted to at least hear a gun go off.

Paul Stillwell: That's a pretty rapid rise from lieutenant to captain in ten years.

Captain Hetu: Yes, yes. Well, and he was a lieutenant, I think, when he went in in '41, made lieutenant commander quite quickly.

Paul Stillwell: That's even more remarkable.

Captain Hetu: Yes. And I say, for really a self-made man. My pop was a special, special guy.

Paul Stillwell: What can you say about values that you got from your parents?

Captain Hetu: Oh, well, you know, certainly my dad—as you can tell, I have great admiration for him, and I didn't probably realize that till I was in college, what a really special guy he was. As I said, academics were not my strong point in high school, and I suppose changing schools every year or so didn't help that along. You're a teenager trying to make new friends in strange cities and stuff. Your goals become skewed trying to make friends rather than worry about algebra and stuff.

So I graduated high school in 1947 and didn't do particularly well. I really graduated by the skin of my teeth. I had trouble with physics and took a special course and passed it. I mean, when I put my mind to it, I could do it, but it was getting my mind to it. You asked me what special qualities, leadership I said, and I'll tell you quickly why.

In our high school in Sharon, Pennsylvania, on class night, which was the night two nights before graduation—I don't think that's done in other localities that I know of, but they had a—the seniors all got costumes. I mean, the whole senior class bought a costume. We went to an amusement park on class day and took it over and had a big party. But the night before that, it had become traditional, I think back in the '30s, for the junior and senior class to fight—crazy.

Paul Stillwell: You mean physical violence?

Captain Hetu: Yes, yes. I mean, riot, police, and so forth. This is a nice settled western Pennsylvania town, a lot of values—steel mills, where I worked in the summertime in college. The kids would beat the hell out of each other. The year before my senior year, a guy almost got killed, got run over by a car, and they were terrible, and they were stupid.

So two of my friends and I, Chuck Ferry, Bob Hess, and I were called, for whatever reason, "the big three" in our senior class. We were not class officers, but we kind of were the leaders of the class, and we decided to stop this. So we called a meeting of the senior class in the big auditorium. This was a fairly large high school. I don't remember how many were in my class, 300 maybe. We said, "This is stupid. Why are we doing this?" It's because nobody wanted to stop it. I mean, nobody had the guts to say, "Look, I don't want to fight, okay? I don't want to get killed, and why are we doing this? Why are we hurting each other? We love each other all year long, we play football together, we do all kinds of stuff. There's this macho thing that you have to go out and fight on class night, crazy." And we stopped it.

The junior class came in, and they all agreed it was kind of dumb. They weren't looking forward to fighting, and we weren't looking forward to fighting. We had all our friends. We, for the first time ever, stopped it, and to my knowledge, it has never recurred. So I say leadership. It was kind of not an elected leadership, but we kind of took over the reins.

Paul Stillwell: De facto.

Captain Hetu: Yes.

Paul Stillwell: Did you have career objectives in mind at that point?

Captain Hetu: Yes, for a guy that didn't do very well in high school, I really thought I would like to be a doctor. I had always leaned in that direction; I liked medicine. I liked things about medicine, particularly the physical sciences, you know, biology and stuff like that where you had hands-on things.

So I went to John Carroll University, a Jesuit school in Cleveland. How I got in, I don't remember, but I guess I had some good grades. Went with one of the big three. Chuck Ferry and I went to John Carroll. I took premed for a year and, again, did not cover myself with academic glory in my first year of college.

Paul Stillwell: What year did you enter college?

Captain Hetu: Forty-seven. So at the end of my freshman year, and this starts my Navy business, there was a very short-lived stipulation under the draft law that you could enlist in the Navy for one year. It was called USNEV, enlisted volunteer. And then you could serve, I think it was, four years in the active reserve or six years in the inactive reserve and you took one year of active duty. Both my roommate and I thought this was a pretty good deal—to leave college for a year and take a little sabbatical. It was the best thing I ever did in my life.

Paul Stillwell: Did you have a predisposition because of your father's experience?

Captain Hetu: Oh, yes, oh, yes, oh, yes, absolutely. I wanted to be in the Navy. I tried to join the merchant marine when we lived in Philadelphia, as a kid, when I was what, 15. I looked 11. I was so funny. I forget where the merchant marine place was, and I went to try and sign up. That guy just about laughed at me, and I told him my dad was in the Navy and he said, "Well, we better call your dad and get him down here. Maybe next year, but don't quite think we can do it now." My dad, who was then a captain, walked in and just blew the place away. They thought this was great, and my dad did, too, but I obviously didn't make the merchant marine.

Paul Stillwell: Did you go through boot camp?[*]

Captain Hetu: Oh, yes. I enlisted in August of 1948, dropped out of school. I told my mother and dad I wanted to get my draft thing out of the way, and I really wanted to get out of college for a year anyway to sort of get my head together. I had always wanted to be in the Navy, and the lure of that sailor's uniform just was too strong. My roommate went in the Army, in fact; he didn't want to go in the Navy. So we both quit and enlisted under the same law, but I went to the Navy.

My object lessons started immediately. [Laughter] I went to Pittsburgh; they put us on a train to Great Lakes.[†] We arrived very late at night. My recollection is it was 11:00 o'clock or maybe midnight, a slow train from Pittsburgh. And took us into the great big drill halls they had up there at Great Lakes, and stood us—they had painted lines on the floor and put us each in a box.

But first we walked in, and they gave us a box and told us to make it up and tape it and so forth, write our names on the box, our home address. Stood us in these squares, and this chief got up and said, "Take off all your clothes."

I said, "I think I've made a big mistake here. This is not the glamour I thought this was going to be."

Took off all your clothes, and he said, "All your clothes." And we put them all in the box and taped them shut and stood there naked, holding these boxes of all our things.

I said, "Boy, talk about the Navy." You know, "Your butt belongs to me." It sure did. We were totally dependent on these guys. But, best thing that ever happened to me in my life. I went through boot camp.

---

[*] "Boot" is a slang term for a newly enlisted sailor or Marine. Recruit training is known as boot camp.
[†] Recruit training was conducted at the Naval Training Station, Great Lakes, Illinois, about 30 miles north of downtown Chicago on the shore of Lake Michigan.

Paul Stillwell: Please give me some details on the training and the camaraderie and so forth.

Captain Hetu: Yes. It's much different than college. It was a different group of people. I have my boot camp picture right there, and I'll show it to you. Yes, it was really a learning experience for me about getting along. Well, I sort of had a pretty good background in that by moving around. Moving high schools was a great help to me to get along in boot camp and learn who the boys were. You become very quickly a society unto yourself, and everybody's, of course, in it together. You want to get through the—I think it was 12 weeks when I went. Our two chiefs, whom I still very much remember, teaching us all the things we had to know. We wore boots; I guess they still do. I mean, actually laced the boots up.

Almost daily somebody would forget and lace them on the wrong side. You know, it was easier to lace them by crossing your feet so they'd lace them on the inside of the leg. Almost every day somebody did that. I did it. It was a wonderful experience.

Paul Stillwell: Did you have a position of leadership in your company?

Captain Hetu: No. I really wasn't a platoon leader or anything, no. I just wanted to survive. I was, I guess, sort of singled out, because I'd had a year of college, but no. I can vividly remember things like service week, and I worked in the mess hall as a garbage disposal technician, riding the garbage truck to the dump. I mean, it was an extraordinary experience; it really was. And it really started me on the right path in life; it did. And I don't mean this in a demeaning way, but it became obvious to me after not too many days there that I was taking orders, and my life was being directed by people who I didn't think were necessarily smarter than I was.

Paul Stillwell: But they had the power.

Captain Hetu: They had the power, and you had to—I guess my only leadership role in boot camp, for which I got in trouble occasionally, was trying to tell people, "You could do this standing on your head. I mean, don't lose your sense of humor. You've got to laugh at these people, you've got to see the humor in this and not get yourself crazy trying to take on somebody you can't take on. You're going to lose, so relax."

Paul Stillwell: That kind of attitude could get you labeled a Communist.

Captain Hetu: Yes, yes. "Enjoy it, you know."

Paul Stillwell: What do you remember about the life in the barracks?

Captain Hetu: Well, it the first time that I had ever lived with what—we had 120 people in our company, and living with all these guys, upper and lower bunks, showers. I can remember that; it was difficult for me.

Paul Stillwell: Washing your clothes.

Captain Hetu: Washing the clothes. Yes, we had to wash them. Yes, and confrontations. I remember I had a confrontation with a guy who said I had stolen his socks. I'll never forget that. I think I could probably even remember his name, in fact. Isn't that funny? I hadn't even thought about that for a while. But you washed your stuff in those mass sinks and so forth, and you had to hang them out on a line, but with clothes stops.* You remember the old clothes stops?

Paul Stillwell: I remember those.

---

* A clothes stop is a small cotton lanyard used for fastening parts of a uniform to a line after washing or for securing uniform items that are rolled up.

Captain Hetu: It was not easy, and somehow I guess I got one or two of his socks mixed in with mine. He had challenged me to a duel practically over this. He was going to kill me and all kind of stuff.

Paul Stillwell: And frequent inspections of your person and your locker.

Captain Hetu: Oh, yes. Well, what you learned immediately is that you had zero life of your own. Anybody could walk in at any time of the day or night and make you do things. But it was a good lesson.

Paul Stillwell: What do you remember about the curriculum that you covered?

Captain Hetu: Drilling, drilling, drilling, which I enjoyed; I really liked that. I got a kick out of that. I can remember the swimming, where we had to go the pool, jump off the tower, which we were all terrified. No suits. You know, hold your vitals, close your eyes, and jump. Yes, it was this mass education thing, which was interesting.

I think it was great, in fact, best I can remember. I remember the fire control training, where we had to go one day into the trainer with the hoses and all that stuff. I was looking forward to it. I was a hospital corpsman. I went to hospital corps school.

Paul Stillwell: At Great Lakes?

Captain Hetu: At Great Lakes, yes, because I had had a year of premed, and so I was a hospital corpsman and loved it to death. I had a good tour of duty as a hospital corpsman. Went to corps school at Great Lakes and then went to the Philadelphia Naval Hospital. I was fairly high in my class at corps school, and you picked your duty station by your ranking. You sat in a room, as I recall, and they called your name off, and they had all the hospitals or duty stations, and then they would check them off. They had so many billets in each place. I probably was dumb in picking Philadelphia because I had lived there, but I guess that's the reason I did it. It was relatively close to home. It was at the other end of the state, but I could get home if I wanted to.

Paul Stillwell: Did you make liberties in Chicago while you were at Great Lakes?

Captain Hetu: Oh, yes.

Paul Stillwell: What were some of the attractions?

Captain Hetu: Oh, boy. Oh, my gosh, downtown Chicago. When we were in corps school we did get to go off. I think we had to be back by—you had to make muster Monday morning. Muster in corps school was like 5:30, out on the grinder.* I mean, God, they'd break you out of the barracks at 5:30 in the morning, and you ran out onto this grinder, and this was in the wintertime. I went through corps school from October through December. Cold, very cold at Great Lakes. You'd go out and stand in your position out on a street, I remember, between the barracks and the headquarters building for the corps school. The chiefs would stand inside in plain sight. It was dark in the morning at Great Lakes, and cold, and they'd stand there drinking coffee and shooting the breeze and let us stand out there for what seemed like an hour and a half. It was probably about five minutes or so, and then they'd come out and take muster.

Then we would have to go back in and clean up the barracks, get into our work blues to go to class. We'd stand in line every Thursday morning, I think it was, to get new sheets. They wouldn't bring the sheets to the barracks; that was too easy. You had to take in your two sheets from your bunk, and pillowcase, I guess it was, and stand in an interminably long line forever, turn those in and get two new ones, and then go back and make up your bunk every Thursday morning. I just remember corps school as being cold all the time.

Paul Stillwell: I take it you were not squeamish with injuries and blood and that sort of thing?

---

* The term grinder refers to a large paved area at a shore facility, used for parades, drills, and inspections.

Captain Hetu: No, no, I wasn't. When I got to the naval hospital in Philadelphia, we first had a general assignment sort of to get familiar with the hospital, learn our way around and procedures. So you sort of did floating duty for a month or something like that. I remember I got two weeks on a ward that was called "Death Valley." It was Ward N, and it was where they had lots of old veterans.

Paul Stillwell: The Naval Home was there then.

Captain Hetu: Is that right? I guess maybe it was. These were older people, and all had severe heart conditions.

Paul Stillwell: Probably had some Spanish-American war veterans and what have you.

Captain Hetu: Well, they were old people, and you were sort of thrown into this situation. I mean, I was 18, and I was already learning how to tie off dead people. We call it tie off because you had to take care of their bodily fluids when they died. Eighteen is a little young to be doing stuff like that, but you learned in a hurry. Again, you had to keep your sense of humor, or you'd go crazy.

Paul Stillwell: Were you rated as a petty officer then?

Captain Hetu: No. I graduated from corps school as an HAS; it was a hospital apprentice, two stripes. Then I made seaman. I never did make third class; I wasn't in long enough. But ended up working in an eye ward, which was terribly interesting, and even at that young age became a scrub corpsman in the eye surgery. Scrub meaning I was part of the operating team; I didn't do much. Generally what I did for cataract operations was hold the ultraviolet light because, in those days, when they did cataracts, they had to open the eye up and go in and take the lens out. If they lost the vitreous humor on the eye, you could go blind. This is a long story, but occasionally the lens would break, and so you'd put the ultraviolet light on so they could see the pieces of the lens and get it out of the eye so it wouldn't be floating around.

Paul Stillwell: Was the clientele for that hospital mostly from the naval shipyard nearby?

Captain Hetu: A lot of sailors and Marines, young sailors and Marines with eye injuries and, you know, a piece of metal in their eye, and things like that.

Paul Stillwell: That's a hazard in an industrial area like that.

Captain Hetu: Yes. And lots of veterans, older people. We had lots of older, older than me, people for cataract operations, detached retinas, and things like that. In those days, when you had a cataract operation, you had to lay immobile for, I think it was, 24 to 30 hours, immobile. I mean, you could not move, and we put sandbags next to their head. Then we would take care of the patient like for an eight-hour shift, and these people could not see; it hurt. They couldn't get up for the bathroom or anything else. It had to be done with bedpans and urinals and so forth. They couldn't move.

Paul Stillwell: Was this after the operation?

Captain Hetu: After the operation, because they had to wait until that slit in the eye, where they took out the lens, healed. If they even sat up or something, they could lose that stuff, and it was dreadful. People had back pains, and we used to massage their backs and legs, and they'd get cramps. Now, my mother and dad had cataract operations, and I'd take them down in the morning and bring them home at noontime. Amazing.

Paul Stillwell: That's progress.

Captain Hetu: Yes, I'll say.

Paul Stillwell: Well, that was a time when retired personnel could depend much more on the naval hospital system than now.

Captain Hetu: I guess so, because a lot of the people were veterans and not even retired, just veterans, who came in, who had been in the Navy and were getting taken care of there.

Paul Stillwell: Were there enlisted quarters there for you to live?

Captain Hetu: Yes, oh, yes. Pretty nice, I mean, after boot camp and corps school, we lived in sort of cubicles. I forget what it was, eight to a cubicle or something. Had a pressing machine where you could press your uniforms, and it was quite nice, to my way of thinking. Now it would be like prison, I suppose, but it was pretty nice then.

Paul Stillwell: Well, it's a matter of expectations, and they're much higher now.

Captain Hetu: Sure, yes. I loved it. I enjoyed my time at the hospital. It was a great tour of duty.

Paul Stillwell: Well, you said, though, it was so short you didn't make third class. Why did you stay such a short time?

Captain Hetu: Well, I was under this one-year enlisted thing for the draft law. So by the time I really got rolling, I was ready to go home. You know, three months' boot camp, three months' corps school and then six months as a ward corpsman, and then I was out as a reserve.

Paul Stillwell: It's surprising they would send you to that long a boot camp when you had such a short obligated service.

Captain Hetu: I don't think there was any other way to do it. It was good. I'll tell you, it changed my life. That was the turning point of my life. I went back to school and did well.

Paul Stillwell: Again at John Carroll?

Captain Hetu: Yes. I went back to John Carroll. I decided in my sophomore year or junior year, that I was not—obviously, I didn't go through with medical school. The turning point in my life was organic chemistry, the second turning point. I was doing very well, getting A's in the other subjects, but I couldn't get organic chemistry, and I just never got along. I mean, the first time I took it, I went in after a month to the professor, and said, "I think I missed the magic word the first day of class, because I haven't understood a word you've said since then. I have no idea what you're talking about. I'm trying, but I just don't have any idea what you're talking about."

Well, we sat down, and he said, "Why don't you drop the course before you—it won't count, and then we'll pick it up, start again next semester."

I said, "That's a good idea. I'll pay attention the first day and find out what the key word is I missed because, man, I missed something."

Well, you know the end of this story. I tried it again, and I still missed the key word. I was never good in mathematics. There is a lot of math in organic chemistry, and I wasn't good in math, but I was good in biology. I liked the comparative anatomy classes and things like that. Anyhow, so end of my junior year, I said, "I'm not going to be a doctor, that's just kind of foolish. I don't want to be a teacher, and I don't want to be a researcher or anything. If I'm not in medicine, I don't want to go on with this." So I switched my major my senior year and took sociology.

Paul Stillwell: Why that?

Captain Hetu: Well, probably the path of least resistance, in the sense that it was one of the majors that I could take. I didn't want to be a chemistry major, obviously. I could have been a biology-anatomy major quite easily. In fact, that and philosophy were my two minors, but I didn't want to do that. I wanted something that would give me a little broader base if I wanted to go to law school or go into journalism or something else, that I would have some sort of a general-based course.

I took sociology, and I could do that by taking a lot of courses in the summertime. My last two years at school I stayed there and worked during the summer. I was a driving instructor for the AAA, for instance, which was a good course. I was quite an entrepreneur in college. I had a lot of jobs. I ran a flower service and pall-bearing service. We had pallbearers for the local funeral homes.

Paul Stillwell: I have never heard of a pall-bearing service before.

Captain Hetu: [Laughter] Well, there were some old people's homes close by, and I just fell into it, no pun intended. It's a long story, but I happened to be around the place in the summertime when one of the funeral homes came looking for pallbearers, and I said, "What's this all about?"

They said, "We have people from some of these retirement homes, [nursing homes that they had then, I guess], who don't have a lot of family, and they need pallbearers. They want pallbearers, but they don't have enough people in the family. The pay is $25.00 a carry or something."

I said, "Sounds good to me. All I need is a dark suit and a pair of black shoes." So I did that, and then I said, "Look, you know, anytime you need people, call me, and I'll come." So I did, and we didn't do it often, but maybe every couple months we'd get a job. And I ran a flower service, corsages for all the dances, and I was a barber in college. I ran the barbershop in the dorm, charged 50 cents a head. I made more money then than I make now, in real dollars.

Paul Stillwell: Were you drilling in the Naval Reserve at this time?

Captain Hetu: No. I was in the inactive reserve. No, I didn't do anything. I did get called up between my junior and senior year. In fact, I was technically a senior, because I was going to summer school, and I got called up, got orders to go to Lejeune, to go with the fleet Marines as a corpsman.[*]

---

[*] Marine Corps Base Camp Lejeune, Jacksonville, North Carolina.

Paul Stillwell: Was this because of the Korean War?

Captain Hetu: Korea, yes.* And that came sort of out of the blue.

Paul Stillwell: And not too welcome, I would suspect.

Captain Hetu: No. I wasn't looking forward to going to Korea, I must say, not as a corpsman with the Marines. In any case, I got notification that I was going to get orders and called up and so forth. And it said, "Well, you're in college."

I said, yes."

They said, "If you're starting your senior year, then we'll give you a deferment until the end of your senior year."

I said, "Well, I am technically a senior." So they deferred me, and I didn't go to Lejeune. Then college ended, and I was looking what to do next.

Paul Stillwell: What year did you graduate?

Captain Hetu: Fifty-two, because I had the one year in the Navy. I started in '47 and finished in '52. In looking for something to do, I almost joined the platoon leaders. The Marines in those days had a platoon leaders' thing for college people. Then I thought, "No, I really would like to go back in the Navy. I'd like to be a naval officer. My dad was a naval officer. I've seen the enlisted side; I enjoyed it, but I would like to be a naval officer."

Paul Stillwell: Did you talk this over with your dad?

Captain Hetu: Oh, yes. He was delighted.

Paul Stillwell: Naturally.

---

* The Korean War began in June 1950.

Captain Hetu: Very pleased. I said, "I don't have a job, I'm not engaged to be married, I don't have anything holding me." So I applied for OCS and got accepted, and that began the trail.* I loved OCS, I really did enjoy—well, I say I loved it. I don't know if I loved it, but it was a great experience, but I think I had a leg up on most people because of my enlisted time, boot camp, all that sort of thing that teaches you camaraderie and stuff.

Paul Stillwell: Was this at Newport?

Captain Hetu: Newport, yes.

Paul Stillwell: Probably still had the same buildings when I went through a dozen years later.

Captain Hetu: Oh, I'm sure. We lived in the old wooden barracks, and I was in Class 7, OCS. And we thought the people in Class 1 were probably all dead by the time we went through. [Laughter] But I was in the seventh class to go through OCS, and I'd love to go back there. People told me about the place now, and my name's on the honor roll or something because I got a Legion of Merit. But I don't know.

Paul Stillwell: Those barracks were torn down; they built some brick buildings.

Captain Hetu: Yes, yes. I've driven by them in later years. I did go in once. I think I was a captain when I stopped and went in one time just to say, "Hey, I just want to look around." It was like going on the LST. Everybody was running around and saying this guy from the Secretary of Navy's office is here, or some captain from the SecNav's office. Holy mackerel."

I said, "That's not why I'm here."

Paul Stillwell: Well, it struck me as sort of a glorified boot camp with a more demanding curriculum.

---

* OCS—Officer Candidate School.

Captain Hetu: Yes, yes. And there we learned another object lesson, a really good object lesson of banding together, because we all wanted to get through that place, and we all wanted to get commissions, especially me.

Paul Stillwell: What do you remember about the subjects that were covered in classes?

Captain Hetu: Well, we took an engineering course. It was a tough class. They did well, but the one that I enjoyed was maneuvering boards.[*] I remember once you got the hang of it, it was fun, but it took me a while. Relative motion was difficult.

Paul Stillwell: Did you have simulators for some of that maneuvering training?

Captain Hetu: Yes, we did. And once I got the hang of that, I did well and I really enjoyed it. I liked that a lot. We had courses in UCMJ where I caused, I guess—I was a seaman, you know.[†] I was an OCHN, so unlike virtually everybody in the company, I had previous service.[‡] So I was sort of the platoon leader and had a hash mark.

Paul Stillwell: What kind of uniforms did you wear?

Captain Hetu: Sailor suits.

Paul Stillwell: Okay.

Captain Hetu: Bell bottoms. The only difference between us and the real sailors was we had an OC patch on our shoulder.

---

[*] A maneuvering board is a sheet of paper containing a compass rose, concentric circles, and logarithmic scales. It is used for working out relative motion problems for ships that are maneuvering. In years past it was known as a "mooring board."
[†] Following the unification of the U.S. armed forces in 1947, a new Uniform Code of Military Justice (UCMJ) was enacted for all the services and put into effect on 31 May 1951.
[‡] Hetu's rate at the time was officer candidate hospitalman (OCHN).

Paul Stillwell: But you didn't have a dark stripe on your hat like the midshipmen?

Captain Hetu: No. The VD stripe.* [Laughter] No, we didn't; we had an OC on our uniform.

Paul Stillwell: Did you get anything in weaponry?

Captain Hetu: Oh, yes. I guess I was sort of, in sense, a little bit. I remember a lot of people had trouble with signal flags, learning the flags and the signals. So I held classes. I used to cut hair in Officer Candidate School, in the barracks, because I had cut it in college, and so it was a great adventure for people. They didn't have to go stand in line in the barbershop every week. They would just come to my room, and we would study while I cut hair. I had made up a study guide for the flags, and we made up stories for each of the flags. I can't even remember now.

Paul Stillwell: Mnemonic devices.

Captain Hetu: Yes. And so we all giggled and laughed about that, but we all passed.

Paul Stillwell: What do you remember about the disciplinary aspects of it?

Captain Hetu: I remember one of the great causes, a thing that really got us riled, was that they asked us the last week I think we were there, to rank the people in our section. Companies were made into four sections; I think there were 30 in a section. We were supposed to rank the people in our section for leadership and the people we didn't like and to write a comment on the drill people and all that. There was almost a revolution, at least in our section.

---

* For midshipmen from the Naval Academy or NROTC units their white hats had a dark blue stripe around the edge. Sailors who didn't like competition from midshipmen told potential dates that the dark stripe was used to denote sailors who had venereal disease and thus should be avoided. The stripe actually had nothing to do with VD.

Paul Stillwell: These were peer reviews?

Captain Hetu: Yes, that we didn't want to do. Nobody wanted to do them. I didn't want to do it.

Paul Stillwell: What was the outcome?

Captain Hetu: I guess we had to do it. As I recall, it was do that or go to the fleet, keep your white hats. This is part of the drill, and it's something that you have to do. I remember having long discussions in my barbershop about that, and there were a lot of very strong feelings about that, because these were people who had been in the Navy barely 12 weeks or so. We did it. I think we did it kicking and screaming and probably didn't do a very good job. I have no recollection of how I rated people. I think I rated them very blandly, and we just didn't like that.

Paul Stillwell: Well, it's uncomfortable inherently.

Captain Hetu: Yes, yes, yes. I know now the reasons, I guess, for it, but then we didn't. Because we had such a strong feeling of camaraderie, and we had worked so hard together to get through there and then to be asked at the end to—because we were really afraid that it would impact on people's graduation or their duty assignments, and we didn't want to hurt each other. We'd all made it, and we knew we were going to graduate, and nobody wanted to hurt anybody. So let bygones be bygones and petty differences—by then they were just washed away. We wanted to get that gold stripe and get out of there. [Laughter]

Paul Stillwell: Was there any attrition as the class went along?

Captain Hetu: Yes, some. I think our company did quite well. Out of 120, I don't think we lost more than six, and that was pretty low.

Paul Stillwell: The Navy was building up for the Korean War, and it needed bodies.

Captain Hetu: Yes, they were probably a little more liberal then. Anyway, I got an extraordinary assignment out of OCS.

Paul Stillwell: Before we get to that, I wonder if you could just talk about the Newport atmosphere and going on liberty there.

Captain Hetu: Oh, boy, yes. Well, there was a lot of weekend drinking, and I can't remember the names of the old hotels there, the bars.

Paul Stillwell: Viking Hotel.

Captain Hetu: The Viking, yes. Going there and drinking, probably drank too much, never did get in any trouble, but that was probably luck rather than anything else. But made some good, quick friends and lasting friendships at OCS. I still have my graduation book somewhere here, which I still look through, all those little notes on the pictures, and I sometimes wonder what happened to a lot of those guys.

I ran the class party, our section party. We had it at the hotel there, not the Viking, the other one. I looked the other day, and somewhere I have a box of Navy stuff that I can't find. We had a great party. I designed the invitation and all that stuff and put the party together. I went in and signed up the hotel and all that business. I was in the PR business even then, I guess.

I asked my dad, who was coming to the graduation, to wear his uniform. He was still in the reserves. He did and blew some of my instructors away. They had no idea that my dad was a naval officer, let alone a captain. Captain, I guess, was a pretty big thing then. So when he walked in the party, why, there was a lot of, "Yes, sir, you know, who may . . ." You know, your name and I told—well, we had most of our instructors, and it was kind of fun. I remember that, because I had never said a word. Why would you? No reason to. When they saw Dad was a captain, they said, "You're . . .

Paul Stillwell: I have a fond memory of going to this girls' school called Salve Regina in Newport.

Captain Hetu: Oh, yes.

Paul Stillwell: There were a bunch of girls that had been cloistered all week, put together with a bunch of guys that had been cloistered all week, and the inevitable results.

Captain Hetu: Bingo, yes. Let's see, I went to OCS in the summer. See, I graduated from college, spent, I think, only about two weeks at home, and went right in.

Paul Stillwell: Was it hard to get into OCS at that period?

Captain Hetu: I guess relatively, as I recall. My previous enlisted service certainly helped, and I did well in college my last three years and ended up on the dean's list, to my father's great surprise and joy.

Paul Stillwell: Well, that one year away probably helped you in terms of maturity.

Captain Hetu: Absolutely changed my life. The enlisted year in the Navy turned me around. Best thing I ever did, absolutely turned my life around. Credit the Navy for that.

Paul Stillwell: How much choice did you have in an assignment coming out of OCS?

Captain Hetu: Well, I remember when we knew we were going to make it, we had our interviews. I'm trying to remember whether it was the guy that interviewed me to go to OCS or for my duty. But I remember being interviewed by, obviously, a mustang, lieutenant, with lots of medals, and he had the Medal of Honor.[*] Being a Navy brat, in a sense, reserve junior, I knew the medals off by heart from World War II and everything.

---

[*] "Mustang" is Navy slang for a former enlisted man who has risen through the ranks to become an officer.

So I said to him, "My God, you got the Medal of Honor, Lieutenant. That's incredible." I had never seen anybody with the Medal of Honor. Wow.

He was, I guess, impressed that I knew what it was. Anyway, he said to me, "Well, what do you want to do? What's your preference when you graduate?"

I said, "Well, I want to go to sea."

He said, "What? You want to go to sea?"

And I said, "Yes, oh, yes, absolutely. That's why I'm here."

He said, "Oh, that's interesting. Most people want to go to intelligence school or communications school. What kind of ship do you want?"

I said, "Well, I'd really like to see the Navy. I'd like to get a destroyer, if I can."

He said, "Oh, that's doable. Yes, I can get you a destroyer." He said, "How would you like a cruiser? You know, in a cruiser you really see more of the Navy. You do steaming and you do things but you get some honors and old Navy stuff."

I said, "Hey, destroyer or cruiser, either one, whatever you think is best for me would be great."

He said, "This is too easy." [Laughter]

In any case, I don't know if that helped, but I ended up with orders to the Salem, which was a brand-new cruiser in those days.* The Salem had been commissioned in 1949, beautiful ship, gorgeous ship; it still is. It was the rotating flagship for the Sixth Fleet. The Des Moines, the Newport News, and the Salem were the rotating flagships, so I had an absolutely—the USS Salem Association, of which I'm a member, saved the ship. It's up in Massachusetts. It is a beautiful ship; it still is. It had lovely, gorgeous lines, and it was a flagship with teak decks and really two of the most wonderful years of my life on that ship. It was absolutely sensational.

Paul Stillwell: Well, that feeling of pride you've described before was probably magnified by that experience.

---

* USS Salem (CA-139), a Des Moines-class heavy cruiser, was commissioned 14 May 1949. She had a standard displacement of 17,255 tons, full-load displacement of 20,934 tons, was 717 feet long, 75 feet in the beam, and had a draft of 26 feet. Her top speed was 33 knots. She was armed with nine 8-inch main battery guns and twelve 5-inch dual-purpose guns. She served almost entirely in the Atlantic Fleet until eventually being decommissioned on 30 January 1959. In 1994 the Salem was moved Quincy, Massachusetts, where she had been built, and the following year opened as the centerpiece of the United States Naval and Shipbuilding Museum.

Captain Hetu: Oh, boy. I was a deck officer. Again, when I went aboard, there was sort of an interview and said, "What do you think you're best qualified to do?"

I said, "Well, I've never been on a cruiser, I don't know, but I'd really like to be a deck officer. I'd like to things on deck and be a gunnery officer and be a real naval officer."

They said, "Okay." So I got a deck division.

Paul Stillwell: You were in the gunnery department.

Captain Hetu: Yes, gunnery department. Sixth division—junior division officer, of course. I started standing bridge watches, and I'm extremely proud to say I qualified as OD under way very quickly, even ahead of several academy people, much to their consternation.[*] But I really loved doing that and ended up, before I left, as the OD for general quarters.[†] It was sensational, what a marvelous adventure. Those were the good old days. I'm showing a picture of myself in a sword and standing in-port deck watch. That's the way we stood our watches in the Mediterranean. We were really dressed up.

Paul Stillwell: It looks as if she might be in Istanbul there.

Captain Hetu: I think so, yes. What a great time.

Paul Stillwell: What do you remember of the skippers?

Captain Hetu: Brooke Schumm was my first skipper, who just died, I think, a couple of years ago.[‡] He was relieved by Captain Creighton.[§] We had another name for him.

---

[*] OD—officer of the deck. The cruise book for the Salem's 1953 Mediterranean deployment, which Hetu helped edit, includes a photo of him on the ship's bridge.
[†] General quarters is the condition of readiness in which the ship's crew is at battle stations.
[‡] Captain Brooke Schumm, USN, commanded the USS Salem (CA-139) from 9 October 1952 to 28 October 1953. He died 15 April 1985.
[§] Captain Liles W. Creighton, USN, commanded the Salem from 28 October 1953 to 14 January 1955. He died 30 December 1970.

Paul Stillwell: Why did you have another name for him?

Captain Hetu: Well, he was a rather large person, and we used to call him "J. Lawton Fatback." He died not long ago either. Neither of those guys made admiral. Both of them made tombstone admiral, but they didn't make admiral on active duty.* That was unusual, because in the flagships a lot of the former skippers had made admiral, Romoser, some of those people.†

    Well, I had so many opportunities on that ship, again, to move ahead. It was so much fun.

Paul Stillwell: What are examples of that?

Captain Hetu: The greatest thrill I had on that ship, and probably one of the greatest thrills in my life, which I still remember vividly, was we were down in Guantanamo at our annual refresher training down there, shooting and so forth.‡ There was a dogleg channel into Guantanamo, and the cruisers came all the way in and anchored relatively close in every night. I had the getting-under way watch, and if you remember what we used to do was get the anchor at short stay, turn the engines over and so forth, and try and get the ship pointed around to the channel before the captain even got up on the bridge.§ He came up and sat down in the chair, and I made my report, and said, "Ready in all respects to get under way, Captain."

    He said, "Very well, take her out." And I almost fainted.

Paul Stillwell: Which captain was this?

---

* From the mid-1920s onward, officers who had received combat decorations received a one-grade honorary promotion, widely referred to as a "tombstone promotion," at the time of retirement. Although the individual still received the retired pay of his actual rank, he was authorized to assume the title of the higher grade. The practice ended in 1959.
† Captain William K. Romoser, USN, commanded the Salem from 9 November 1951 to 9 October 1952.
‡ Guantanamo Bay, on the south coast of Cuba, near the eastern end of the island, for many years provided a fleet anchorage and training area for U.S. Navy ships.
§ Short stay refers to an anchor that has been heaved in to a point just short of breaking ground. In other words, the ship is ready to get under way on short notice.

Captain Hetu: That was Schumm. I said, "You want me to take your ship out?" And he did. I obviously blanched a little bit, but I thought, wow, great.

Paul Stillwell: It's a wonderful feeling of confidence.

Captain Hetu: Oh, man. He sort of gave me an aside and said, "You'll have help if you need it. Don't worry." And yes, I took that hummer out very slowly, because I knew we had to get around that corner, and that was worrying me, but I got her out and great, great thrill. Man, I was walking eight feet tall for about two days.

Paul Stillwell: How did that ship handle?

Captain Hetu: Beautifully. By then, I pretty well knew, and he obviously knew that I knew how to do it, and they had let me do some other things by then. I can't remember how much before that he had let me take it alongside in a replenishment operation. That was a big ship, a lot of ship, and he let me take it alongside an oiler and, as you know, you get pretty close.

Well, that was just such an extraordinary experience and one that gives you so much confidence. I liked Captain Schumm; he was a good guy. We had an exec named Wilson, who I really stayed in touch with for a long time, even after I left the ship, who was a very nice, a good leader.[*] A good guy, I mean, even after I got stationed in Washington, he had my then wife and me over for dinner. He had made captain by then, nice guy, helped me along. We had another executive officer on the ship; his name was J. L. P. McCallum, and he was a submariner, and he was a tough guy.[†]

Paul Stillwell: What were examples of that toughness?

---

[*] Commander Donald W. Wilson, USN, served as executive officer of the Salem from 9 January 1954 to 14 March 1955.
[†] Commander James L. P. McCallum, USN, served as executive officer of the Salem from 7 February 1953 to 9 January 1954.

Captain Hetu: Not well liked at all. Oh, just sort of a martinet, going around and getting sailors on report for having their hats on the back of their head while chipping paint and stuff like that, which we all thought was nuts.

Paul Stillwell: Well, the exec's expected to do some of that.

Captain Hetu: Yes, I guess so. But he was just a . . .

Paul Stillwell: Carried it too far.

Captain Hetu: . . . a horse's ass. He was walking around with this Marine, and we made fun of him. I was on the ship with P. X. Kelley, was one of my closest pals on the ship.*

Paul Stillwell: Was he the CO of the detachment?

Captain Hetu: No, he was the second in command; P. X. was a first lieutenant.

Paul Stillwell: What do you remember of him from those years?

Captain Hetu: Oh, God. Well, P. X. and I were liberty pals, and we did a lot of liberty and had a lot of fun.

Paul Stillwell: How was he on the beach?

Captain Hetu: Oh, well, terrific. To this day, when P. X. calls me on the phone, and he used to call—I did some work for him when he was Commandant, and I was out of the Navy by then. But I did a study for the Marine Corps on their public affairs once. When P.X. would call me on the phone, the secretary would come in smiling and saying, "Some guy on the phone keeps yelling, "Sandwich, Sandwich."

---

* First Lieutenant Paul X. Kelley, USMC. As a four-star general, Kelley served as Commandant of the Marine Corps from 1 July 1983 to 30 June 1987.

I said, "That's P. X. Kelley." Because at Villefranche, when we went back to get the liberty boat, the last boat at midnight, they would sell sandwiches and beer on the quay there.* We would always get a sandwich, so P. X., to this day, calls me up and yells "Sandwich" in the phone. He was a great guy. We used to do a circus act at bars and restaurants.

Paul Stillwell: What was your circus act? What did it consist of?

Captain Hetu: [Laughter] We used to do a lion tamer act, where, depending on who was the best able to stand, one would do be the lion and one would be the lion tamer. We used to get rave reviews, and if there was a piano player there, we would teach him how to play the circus music, you know, da-da, da-da-da-da, da-da-da.

Paul Stillwell: What was the stimulus that would bring on this act?

Captain Hetu: Gin. [Laughter]

Paul Stillwell: Was this for the benefit of the bar patrons?

Captain Hetu: Whoever. Got a lot of free drinks on the 02 level on Villefranche.

Paul Stillwell: What are some of your memories of other liberty ports in the Med?

Captain Hetu: Oh, Naples. We were on liberty one night in Naples, going down one of those streets. The cab drivers used to turn off their lights and turn off their engines going down the hills to save gasoline. We were in a cab with P. X. Kelly and Joe Taylor and I. Joe Taylor was a Marine captain, and he was head of the detachment on the ship.† Joe reached over and took the keys out of the cab and threw them out the window. The guy

---

* For many years the port of Villefranche, on the Mediterranean coast of France, served as homeport for the flagship of the U.S. Sixth Fleet.
† Captain Joseph Z. Taylor, USMC.

didn't see him, and he got down below and tried to start the cab and he couldn't do it. Silly. Now you'd go to jail, I suppose, for something like that.

Paul Stillwell: Were there receptions in these various ports for the local dignitaries?

Captain Hetu: Yes, yes, on board the ship. Yes, the ship was a gorgeous ship, and we would rig canvas every time we went in port, over the quarterdeck and had receptions. We stood around in the corral in our whites and squired young ladies around the ship and so forth. Not so bad.

Paul Stillwell: Very impressive appearance; I mean, it's like a movie set.

Captain Hetu: We went into Venice. We were there for, I think, ten days or two weeks. We were there a long, long time, right in the Grand Canal, in the summertime. I was able to secure permanent shore patrol duty. I was on the beach for about a week, living in a hotel, as a shore patrol officer, and almost had to be medically evacuated.

Paul Stillwell: What do you mean by that?

Captain Hetu: Oh, God. Well, the liberty parties came ashore usually at noontime and stayed until midnight. We used to divide up the watch so that we were not on for 12 hours, and I learned a lot in my shore patrol role. I did shore patrol in almost every port, did it in Haiti. I saw some strange things.

Paul Stillwell: What was the role of a shore patrol officer?

Captain Hetu: Just trying to keep everybody squared away. Certainly in my mind it was to try and get these kids back safely and not try and be a policeman so much as try to help them, because there were a lot of young sailors who had not been away from home. They hadn't had that kind of freedom and didn't know how to handle the booze. And I was a kid myself; I was only 22. Some of them got pretty drunk.

Paul Stillwell: Well, there was an ethic that that was the thing to do, rather than being the tourist and sightseeing and so forth.

Captain Hetu: Yes, oh, yes, yes. If you were the tourist, then you went with the chaplain on the tours, and the real men went to the bars and got drunk and disorderly.

Paul Stillwell: What did you see in Haiti?

Captain Hetu: Oh, Haiti was my first experience, because when I went aboard the ship from OCS, we left virtually in the next week for the Caribbean, for refresher training. I didn't even know my way around the ship yet and was assigned shore patrol duty in Haiti, Port-au-Prince. God, it was just dreadful.

Paul Stillwell: What did you see there?

Captain Hetu: Well, the place was very poor. I suppose it's still—I haven't been back for years. I don't have any idea. But I can remember going in bars with dirt floors and terribly scruffy awful bars and the black horrors and so forth and these kids getting drunk.

I guess it was in Guantanamo where I got the duty, and they had a bus that took enlisted men from the enlisted clubs over to the boat landing, and it was a zoo. I was an ensign, and I got duty riding the bus, which seemed like an endless journey with all these drunks—bedlam, like a movie. I was in this bus, I thought, "I'm never going to get out of here alive." Trying to keep order on the bus was crazy. That was like a school bus with 100 drunk kids on it. No way. All I wanted to do was stay near the door so I could get out of there. But I certainly learned lessons.

Paul Stillwell: What part of the ship did the sixth division have responsibility for?

Captain Hetu: The sixth division was amidships, on the port side. I didn't do that terribly long until I got the fifth division. I mean, I got my own division, which was a 5-inch division. The sixth division was a 3-inch division.

Paul Stillwell: I see.

Captain Hetu: I was a mount officer. Then, when I got the fifth division, I became head the after battery fire control, which was great fun.

Paul Stillwell: They have those sort of fire control towers.

Captain Hetu: Yes, up high, yes.

Paul Stillwell: What are your memories of gunnery practice?

Captain Hetu: Well, my roommate was a guy named Kemper K. Hyers, whom I still stay in touch with. I just talked to him a couple of weeks ago. Kemper and I were in intense competition for everything we did, liberty. We could walk in a bar and see the same gal, and we'd both be after her. You know, it was crazy. We were great pals and great competitors. He had the fourth division, and had the forward three 5-inch mounts, and I had the after. So we were always in competition for gunnery shoots and stuff, betting ice cream to the crews and all that stuff. We had worked out a code on the intercom so that he and I could talk to each other, and the gunnery officer was going crazy because he didn't know what we were saying.

Paul Stillwell: What kind of messages would you pass in this code?

Captain Hetu: Well, not terribly complimentary. [Laughter] When he would miss a sleeve or something, I would—God, this was a long time ago, forward one, after—gosh, I can't remember the call sign now.* But I would call him and give him a 743 or something, which was a code that we had worked out in the room so we knew. Not unlike the codes they had in Vietnam for the air people when they started taking them off the air for using obscenities. Well, we had pioneered this back in the '50s. [Laughter]

Paul Stillwell: How well received were Americans in some of those ports you went to, say, in the Med?

Captain Hetu: Oh, I don't remember us ever having any problems over there.

Paul Stillwell: Yankee dollars speaking very effectively.

Captain Hetu: Yes, in the '50s. And our ship was the prettiest ship, and the advantage of the flagship was you usually tied up. You didn't anchor out, seldom anchored out.

Paul Stillwell: Some of those countries had dabbled or been interested in Communism in the late '40s, and that was part of the reason for the Sixth Fleet.

Captain Hetu: That's right. We went to some extraordinarily interesting ports that other people didn't get to. We went to Split, Yugoslavia, and that was interesting. I have some pictures someplace. We went to Split, and I remember they had a bar there that they served beer in glass boots. Of course, if you drank it down, if you could chug-a-lug a boot, you got a free boot of beer. That was really what you needed after a chug-a-lug.

Paul Stillwell: You earned it, right?

Captain Hetu: You needed that real bad.
    I have a wonderful picture someplace in one of my boxes that they came right up and took pictures. They had a photographer that would come and take an old Speed

---

* For antiaircraft gunnery practice in that era it was customary for an airplane to tow a tubular canvas sleeve that served as the target.

Graphic camera and take your picture and then sell you prints. They took a picture of our table, and sitting behind us or two tables behind us, sort of in the background and people at both tables were covering their faces, which we always thought was kind of fun. I remember we had a briefing before we went into each port, and we used to get a little piece of paper that I helped write, I guess. Split was a very intrigue-ridden place in those days. Split was still part of Italy, not Yugoslavia. I forget. It was a free state, I think.

Paul Stillwell: I'm not sure.

Captain Hetu: I don't remember it as well as I should, either, but it was like a free-floating state. It was not yet assigned to either Italy or Yugoslavia.

Paul Stillwell: What were you warned against?

Captain Hetu: Just the fact that this was sort of a free area, and there were a lot of spies and people of intrigue and deserters from both sides. It was just, "Be careful, watch your 6:00 o'clock, and don't get involved with strangers." They sort of scared us a little bit.

Paul Stillwell: Did you have any intelligence-collecting role as you went to these places?

Captain Hetu: No. Maybe some of the senior people did; I suppose they did. I didn't know about it.

Paul Stillwell: How much awareness or contact did you have with Admiral Cassady as the fleet commander?[*]

Captain Hetu: Well, almost none. I made jaygee on the ship, so the vice admiral and I were not terribly close, except that it was my first real opportunity to do public affairs. It was public information in those days. They were looking for a public information officer for the ship when I came aboard, and I volunteered. It sounded like something I would

---

[*] Vice Admiral John H. Cassady, USN, commanded the Sixth Fleet from May 1952 to March 1954.

like to do, and so I became the public information officer, collateral duty as a young ensign.

Great job, because I got involved in all of the honors and ceremonies, and if we entertained people and we had a lot of dignitaries come to visit the ship. You know, famous sports people when we'd go into a port overseas and just interesting people, and I always got to take them around the ship and pose their pictures on the quarterdeck and stuff. So I had a lot of fun doing that.

Paul Stillwell: Any specific individuals you remember in that context?

Captain Hetu: Boy, the only person I can think of immediately is a guy that used to play for the Knickerbockers, basketball player and his wife, and she was gorgeous, and she was as tall as he was.* I can't remember what the heck his name was. It was long time. Other dignitaries when we would come in. Fechteler came aboard, I remember, once; he had been the Chief of Naval Operations and then left and took CinCSouth, sort of strange.†

Paul Stillwell: He got another billet because he hadn't reached the retirement age yet.

Captain Hetu: Is that right? I don't remember why, but it always seemed strange.

Paul Stillwell: Well, they just had a two-year tour as CNO, and it wasn't necessarily a terminal job.

Captain Hetu: Yes. I remember he came aboard, he was one.

---

* Two of the visitors to the <u>Salem</u> in Venice were Ernie Vanderweghe of the New York Knickerbockers and his wife. The latter, tall and thin like her husband, was the former Kay Hutchins, who had been Miss America in 1951.
† Admiral William M. Fechteler, USN, served as Chief of Naval Operations from 16 August 1951 to 17 August 1953. Fechteler served as Commander in Chief Allied Forces Southern Europe from August 1953 to July 1956.

Paul Stillwell: Was there any consciousness of a NATO role in this?*

Captain Hetu: Yes, yes, there was. We did NATO exercises, and I remember one of the many highlights of my tour on the Sixth Fleet, we went into Malta and got a briefing by Lord Mountbatten, him very self—I mean, the man.†

Paul Stillwell: Was he as charismatic as he's been advertised?

Captain Hetu: He was. He knocked our socks off. I'll never forget that. He gave the briefing. It was a NATO briefing, and the U.S. Navy briefers were all captains, as I remember, sort of ACOSs, assistant chief of staff for this and that. When it came time for the Brits to give their half, Lord Louie himself got up, not terribly—was he impressive or what. He looked like about eight feet tall and all his medals. My God, and he was pretty famous.

I remember, for some reason I was sitting very down front, all the officers from the ship and the staff. I guess it's because by then I was also acting as the assistant fleet public affairs officer, and so I guess I sat with the staff or something, I don't remember. But I was sitting close, and we were blown away by this guy. He gave the whole briefing—I mean everything—and once or twice called on one of his captains or aides to say, "What's the detail on that" or something, but always something innocuous. He knew all the numbers; he knew everything. He was just impressive, because I remember I was going back to the ship and saying, "My God, can you imagine what—how come our admirals don't do that?" Our admirals all sat up there and introduced the briefers and then sat down, and, boy, Mountbatten was really something.

Paul Stillwell: Probably didn't even use notes.

---

* NATO—North Atlantic Treaty Organization, which was established in 1949 as a means of coordinating defense against a potential attack from the Soviet Union.
† Admiral the Earl Mountbatten of Burma, RN, served as British Commander in Chief Mediterranean, 1952-54, and as Commander in Chief Allied Forces Mediterranean, 1953-54. The U.S. Sixth Fleet, however, was not under his command during the latter role.

Captain Hetu: No, I don't remember him even having a podium, just walked around on the stage.

Paul Stillwell: Did you have interaction with other foreign naval officers?

Captain Hetu: Oh, yes, lots. Well, lots, yes, with the Brits, Australians. I went aboard an Indian cruiser once. And, of course, they used to love to have the Americans come aboard, because then all the drinks were on the Queen. And the drinks flowed. As you well know, they serve booze in their wardrooms.

The Indian ship was probably the most interesting, because they had some Sikhs with the turbans and the whole thing. Then we found out these guys all talked with high British accents, and they had all been to the British Naval Academy and so forth, and they were great guys. We had a lot of fun, and had some British girls and American girls. Where they found them, darned if I know, but they had them there.

Paul Stillwell: Did they wear turbans as part of the uniform?

Captain Hetu: Some of them did, because they were Sikhs. Yes, and very dark skin, but very attractive and very smart guys; they were fun. The Australians were the crazy ones, and the Canadians were even worse than the Australians.

Paul Stillwell: I've heard that the Brits can get really wild at some of their parties: physical horseplay and what have you.

Captain Hetu: Oh, yes. Well, later in my career and I went to Australia with the CNO, and we went to dining-ins. The Australians got wild and crazy and the Canadians too.

Paul Stillwell: How much contact was there between the ship's wardroom officers and the staff officers?

Captain Hetu: A fair amount. We all ate in the wardroom, although they sort of had their own table and so forth. But we talked to them, and there were some great guys on the Sixth Fleet staff, as I can remember, who were nifty.

Paul Stillwell: Any specifically that you recall?

Captain Hetu: Yes. Herb Schwab was the name of the lawyer.[*] I just saw his obit not terribly long ago. He was, I think, then a commander. He was the fleet legal officer, funny guy. He used to emcee all the shows on the fantail and stuff, and was one of my heroes as a naval officer. He never took anything terribly serious.

Paul Stillwell: Which is what you'd been preaching since boot camp.

Captain Hetu: Yes. I mean, he was great, I really liked him. Herb Schwab, a neat guy.

Oh, I was telling you about the executive officer on the Salem, a guy named J. L. P. McCallum. I don't remember whether P. X. was in on this caper or not. Probably, so I probably shouldn't implicate him. But we came back one night flying a little low, and they used to leave the desserts out from dinner on the sideboard in the wardroom. So as you came back from liberty you could have a piece of pie, and unfortunately they had cherry pies and after a few bites it seemed appropriate to some of us that we might decorate the exec's cabin with the cherry pie, and we did, and almost all went to jail for that. We never got caught, but it was our cherry pie incident on the ship, not unlike The Caine Mutiny.[†]

Paul Stillwell: What do you mean, you almost went to jail? Did you get put in hack?

---

[*] Commander Herbert S. Schwab, USN.
[†] Lieutenant Commander Philip F. Queeg, USN, was the fictitious commanding officer of the destroyer-minesweeper USS Caine in Herman Wouk's classic naval novel of World War II, The Caine Mutiny, published by Doubleday & Company in 1951. Queeg was a mentally unstable martinet, so his name has become associated with overbearing, eccentric skippers. In one episode in the story, Queeg turned the ship upside down trying to learn what became of a missing quart of strawberries.

Captain Hetu: Oh, well, he started a full-scale investigation, NIS and the whole thing.* We never got caught, but he's still around, I think.

Paul Stillwell: I take it he wasn't in this room at the time?

Captain Hetu: Oh, no, no. No, certainly not.

Paul Stillwell: What a mess that must have been.

Captain Hetu: Yes, I guess it was. I mean, this is foolish for young naval officers, but we had had a few pops, and we had just had about enough of his foolishness. So we decided to let him know we thought about him. He had his pennant from the submarine and everything up on the bulkhead. The exec had an office off the wardroom, and then his stateroom was behind his office. We didn't do anything to his stateroom. It was locked.

Paul Stillwell: Were you starting to think in terms of a career when you were in that ship?

Captain Hetu: Well, I'll tell you a McCallum story later, because after I made captain I ran into him once and he almost fainted when he saw me as a captain. [Laughter] But literally I thought he was going to choke.

Oh, the public affairs. Yes, well, I had some great opportunities as the assistant PAO for the fleet. Charlie Rainey was the public affairs officer then.† He was delighted to get my help. As I learned later, you're always glad to get free help, and I was delighted to do it, because it was a step up for me, sort of.

I remember one of the great opportunities I had. There was a large earthquake in the Ionian Islands, probably 1953-54, and we were the first ship.‡ We were in that end of

---

* NIS—Naval Investigative Service.
† Lieutenant Commander Charles W. Rainey, USNR.
‡ From 11 to 15 August 1953 the Ionian Islands—Cephalonia, Ithaca, and Zante, off the west coast of Greece—were hit by earthquakes that killed 427 people.

the Med, and they sent us in there to do relief operations. The place was devastated; I mean, it was a bad earthquake. A lot of people dead. I remember the Marines went over—P. X. and Joe Taylor—and set up a tent city for them. Our cooks went over and set up chow. I mean, they had no power or nothing; the hospital had been leveled. The insane asylum on the island—these are all things we were told—had been leveled, and the people were wandering around.

So I went over as the public affairs officer. Charlie Rainey was in Paris or someplace on leave, and so I was it. And there was nobody. There were no other ships there and there was no press, so I wrote the first communiqués coming out of this terrible thing. As I recall, Commander Wilson was the exec then.* Our captain was plenty busy doing other things, and Wilson approved all the stuff that I was sending back to Chinfo—I think Chinfo—by flash message or immediate message.† I wrote all the first communiqués, and for the first 12-18 hours, everything in the press worldwide was coming out of the Salem, and I was writing it.

Paul Stillwell: So that was probably going on the wires like AP and UP?‡

Captain Hetu: Oh, yes. And I got a little carried away with my writing. I can remember one of quotes that Time magazine picked out of one of my communiqués. I'd written a passage that said something like, "The deathly silence—walking down the street in Argustolian, all one can hear is the deathly silence of the water lapping the shores and the crunch, crunch, crunch of the stretcher bearers' boots on the gravel roads." This was quoted in Time magazine.§

Paul Stillwell: That's pretty graphic.

---

* Wilson did not become executive officer until January 1954. Commander McCallum was still in the billet at the time of the earthquakes.
† Chinfo—Chief of the Office of Information, basically the Navy's public relations and media relations arm.
‡ AP—Associated Press; UP—United Press.
§ The article, "Greece: Rescue in the Dust," appeared in Time, 24 August 1953, page 23. The quote in the magazine, quite similar to the way Hetu recalled it in the interview, was as follows: "The silence is broken only by the cries of the injured, and the crunch beneath the shoes of the stretcher bearers."

Captain Hetu: Well, it got in Time magazine, and I don't think it quoted me by name. It said a Navy communiqué or something. For months after that, every time that I'd open the door and start into the wardroom, everybody would go, "Crunch, crunch, crunch" when I'd walk to my seat. [Laughter]

Paul Stillwell: Was there any basis for the rumor about the insane asylum?

Captain Hetu: I don't know, never dealt with that. I experienced my first earthquake tremor there, though. I mean, that's an eerie, strange feeling, like standing on Jello. You're scared. These were aftershocks, I guess, the night after this happened.

Paul Stillwell: Well, this has traditionally been the sort of ancillary role that the Navy's very good at.

Captain Hetu: Yes. Well, we, I think, made a lot of friends there. The ship stayed there for several days, maybe a week. I think we had a destroyer or two pull in the next day to help us out, to set up power supply and water and medical, of course.

Paul Stillwell: And obviously the ship's own communications were a tie to the world.

Captain Hetu: Yes, and we had a helicopter. So that was a great opportunity for me in the sense of public affairs.

Anyhow, we were homeported in Boston, and not a bad place to be either. Boston was a great homeport; I enjoyed Boston. I knew a little about it, because my mother was from there, and we used to go there every summer when I was a kid. So I knew a little bit about Boston, and I liked Boston. So it was a good place to be.

But I was the public information officer when we were in Boston, and the First Naval District was there, headquarters. Barney Solomon was the public information officer for the district, and because we were the newest and prettiest ship on the East

Coast, why, we did an awful lot of work with local Navy League and giving tours to the mayor's office and all kinds of stuff.[*]

Paul Stillwell: And they had Com 1 there in the Fargo Building.[†]

Captain Hetu: Yes, right, and we were right there. So I did a lot of work with the public information staff from Com 1.

Paul Stillwell: So you fell into it sort of gradually.

Captain Hetu: Yes, exactly. I would spend a fair amount of time over there, and every time they wanted to take somebody for a ride or take them on a tour, they'd always bring them over to the Salem, and we took good care of them. Didn't have baseball caps then; I forget what we gave out, something we gave them.

Paul Stillwell: Cigarette lighters were popular.

Captain Hetu: I think maybe we had lighters, but we always gave them a good show and it was a pretty ship.

I was coming up to the end of a two-year tour. They weren't quite sure what I was going to do, because I was on a total of three years' commissioned service, whether I'd stay on the ship for another year, which was fine with me, or go somewhere else.

Barney said to me, "You like public information."

I said, "Yes, it's great. I think I've kind of decided that's what I want to do when I get out of the Navy is to get into some PR or advertising or something. I enjoy doing advance writing and stuff."

He said, "Well, why don't you send in a letter, apply for duty in public information your last year?"

I said, "Well, . . .

---

[*] Lieutenant Commander Bernard S. Solomon, USNR.
[†] The headquarters of the Commandant of the First Naval District (Com 1) were in the Fargo Building, near the South Boston Annex of the Boston Naval Shipyard.

He said, "I'll help you write it. I've worked with you, and you've been the Sixth Fleet guy, and, God, you've got all kinds of good credentials for a young jaygee, and you worked for the district, blah, blah, blah."

Anyway, we wrote a letter, sent it through the channels, got a nice endorsement from the—I guess I got a nice endorsement. I think McCallum was still on board and didn't give me a very good endorsement, said he didn't think that a guy that was only in for three years should get taken off the ship and put in shore duty doing PR or something else; it was kind of snide: "This officer's done a great job, but we ought to keep him here." I thought McCallum really wanted to keep me on the ship, and he didn't want to see me go.

Anyhow, the next thing I know, I get a phone call and offered me a tour of duty in Chinfo, the home office. You know, it's just like I'm out in Timbuktu, and they said, "We want you back in the tower."

I said, "Wow, bingo, this is terrific."

But they said, "Yes, but you're going to have to extend a year. It's a two-year tour of duty. We can't bring you back here and do all this for one year."

So I said, "Yes, sure, you bet. If I'm going to do this on the outside, it's perfect, be a good segue, a tour under my belt." So I leapt at it, and I got married to my first wife. She was a stewardess for American Airlines, and so we got married and moved to Washington. A guy that had been on the ship with me had come to Washington as a communications officer, and he was getting ready to leave. I called him to say, "Where do you live in Washington?"

He said, "You live in my apartment. I'm leaving in a month." And they were not easy to find even then.

So he described it to me on the phone, and I said, "I'll take it." So we lived right over by the Iwo Jima monument, apartment buildings right up on the hill, on the other side of Route 50.* You could see the Pentagon from there.

---

* The Iwo Jima Memorial is on Marshall Drive, between Route 50 and Arlington National Cemetery, in Arlington, Virginia. The memorial was officially dedicated by President Dwight D. Eisenhower on 11 November 1954. This largest cast-bronze statue in the world features 32-foot-tall figures erecting a 60-foot-tall bronze flagpole.

Paul Stillwell: Was Chinfo then in the Pentagon?

Captain Hetu: Yes, yes. And, boy, so I came to Washington and off we started. You know, the best, niftiest thing about the Navy in those days, particularly in public affairs, I think—of course, I was lucky on a ship, I got the good jobs, I always thought, the OD job and so forth. If you really extended yourself and sort of volunteered for stuff, you could do anything you wanted. I mean, people were great. I mean, I volunteered for the public information job on the ship, terrific, fine. I edited the cruise books on the ship. That's my great P. X. Kelley story. Can I retrogress a little bit?

Paul Stillwell: Sure.

Captain Hetu: On one of the cruise books, when P. X. was on the ship, and P. X. was then writing a letter a week to get off there and go to Korea. We used to go on the beach and get drunk, and P.X. said, "You know, I'm never going to make captain, that goddamn Marine Corps. I should be in Korea, killing gooks. Here I am on the 02 level drinking beer with you, pantywaist sailors. I may as well get out of the Marine Corps, if you don't go to Korea, be a platoon leader, I'm dead. I'm not going to go anywhere."

Paul Stillwell: He could wind up dead another way if he did go to Korea.

Captain Hetu: Well, that was a Marine's dream, Valhalla. But, anyway, when I was doing the cruise book that year, we did the football picture, the group picture of the divisions and so forth. I asked each officer where they would like to have an informal shot taken: on the bridge, on their GQ station, you know, wherever they would like to be, sort of an inset in the book.

P.X. said, "You take my picture in the goddamn wardroom. All I do in this ship is sit in the wardroom and drink coffee," so we did. I have it someplace, but there's P. X. sitting on his GQ station—what he called it—in the wardroom, drinking a cup of coffee. Of course, I kept that cruise book, and the day that he made brigadier general I made a copy of that page and sent him a note, and I said, "Do you remember the first lieutenant on the <u>Salem</u> that wasn't going to make captain?" And said, "Congratulations, General." Then every time he would make another star, I would send him the same picture.

Paul Stillwell: Did he ever get to Korea?

Captain Hetu: No. No, he didn't.

Paul Stillwell: He showed his talents in other ways.

Captain Hetu: Yes. He never did get to Korea. Of course, he had tours in Vietnam and stuff, but he never got to Korea. He went with the British commandos and a bunch of other stuff, but I always thought that was funny that P. X.—but he persevered.

Paul Stillwell: Well, he had more of an outgoing personality than your stereotype Marine, who's all business.

Captain Hetu: Oh, yes. They loved him. I can remember on the <u>Salem</u>, the Marines on that ship worshiped him. Joe Taylor was a great Marine too. Joe didn't make general. I don't even know if he made colonel. He got into some strange intelligence stuff. I'm not so sure he wasn't working for the CIA at one point in his career.* I say that advisedly, because I've worked at the CIA. I'm not just saying it.

But, anyway, the point I was making was that in those days, and I suppose it's still true, I don't know, but if you volunteered for something and wanted to do something, they'd let you do it. I had a great time in the Navy, I mean, a wonderful time. Well, I had a great time for my whole career. As a young officer, that's probably one of the things that hooked me. I'd want to do something, they'd say, "Okay, go ahead and do it." I thought, "Where else could I do this?"

Paul Stillwell: The opportunity.

---

* CIA--Central Intelligence Agency.

Captain Hetu: So I went to Chinfo as a young jaygee, right off the ship. And I was thrown in with a lot of these old elephants, great guys. A lot of them are dead now, but some of them aren't. But, you know, Merle MacBain, who has since passed on, and Frank Lovelace.* The Chief of Information then was Whitey Taylor, who was quite a character himself.†

Paul Stillwell: Good old destroyer man.

Captain Hetu: Yes, wonderful guy, white hair. My dad met him and couldn't get over it. I took my dad in to meet him one time. I hadn't made lieutenant; I didn't make lieutenant until I got to Pearl Harbor. He was so gracious and so nice, but when we opened the door to his office we were wearing blues, and he had on red suspenders. He had his coat off, and my dad just about fell over. Here's this two-star admiral wearing those big red suspenders, and he was a big guy, white hair. My dad said, "My God, he looks like Santa Claus."

I said, "He does." He was a sweet man.

Paul Stillwell: Did he have a sense of humor?

Captain Hetu: Oh, God, Whitey Taylor, what a wonderful man he was. Yes. I remember the junior officers liked him, because he wasn't above us. He seemed, in my recollection, to have an appreciation for public information and didn't get into the knickers of the professionals. He let the pros do it.

Paul Stillwell: Well, that was sort of a fish-out-of-water arrangement with having a line officer manage it, because he didn't have the specialized knowledge that his subordinates did.

---

* Commander Merle MacBain, USN.
† Rear Admiral Edmund B. Taylor, USN, served as the Navy's Chief of Information from September 1955 to December 1957.

Captain Hetu: That's right. Yes. And he didn't know the nuances in how to deal with the press and the fact that that was so necessary. I hadn't been there terribly long; some of the other people were—I'm trying to think of some of the other great people that were there at that time.

Paul Stillwell: What was the typical background for a public information specialist in those days?

Captain Hetu: Well, I was not yet a specialist.

Paul Stillwell: Had the people you worked with in Chinfo come in from civilian newspaper careers?

Captain Hetu: Yes, a lot of them had. See, a lot of the original "40 Thieves" were working there then. I didn't even know who I was working with until later.

Paul Stillwell: You might explain that term.

Captain Hetu: The 40 Thieves. Well, those were the first people after World War II who, when the Navy decided to make public information a specialty, a separate designator, 1650, 1655, these were the first 40 people.[*] People now are not sure there were exactly 40, but I'm working on that in my other hat as the public affairs alumni association. We're trying to make sure we get the list of those people.

Anyway, they were called, predictably, the 40 Thieves, and these were the great pioneers in our business. A lot of them were characters, and a lot of them were very talented people. Pickett Lumpkin, who was my mentor, and Merle MacBain, who had been a publicist for the Barnum and Bailey Circus, and some of the newspaper people.[†]

---

[*] The designator for public affairs specialists of the regular Navy is 1650; for those officers with reserve commissions it is 1655.
[†] Commander Pickett Lumpkin, USN.

Very few academy people. I think then the only academy person was Dick McCool, who had won the Medal of Honor in World War II on an amphibious ship.*

Paul Stillwell: Yes, I think it was an amphib.

Captain Hetu: Small amphib, yes. He carried some people out of the bowels of the ship after they were sinking or something. Jim Shaw, who was the technical adviser on <u>The Caine Mutiny</u>, was working then.†

Paul Stillwell: He was a straight line officer.

Captain Hetu: Yes, he was, but he was there in Chinfo. I was meeting all these people, and I wasn't really sure who I was meeting. I worked in a section, when I first went there, with Bob Mereness and Bob Jones; they're both still around.‡ Bob Jones wasn't a specialist yet; he and I were selected—Lovelace, Jim Lovelace. These were lieutenant commanders and commanders. I was a jaygee, and so I was thrown into this. My boss then was a guy named Russ Bufkins, a commander, and Russ is still around.§ He retired as a commander. He was the youngest commander in the Navy or something; he made it at 27 and never got anywhere else. But Russ used to always say, "If you're going to stagnate, stagnate in the highest grade possible." [Laughter]

Paul Stillwell: Right. What was the role of Chinfo? How proactive was it?

Captain Hetu: Well, it was pretty active. As I recall, as a young officer, it was pretty highly respected. We did a lot of work those days with the reserves. We did a lot of press work. I got an extraordinarily good job as a jaygee. I hadn't been there terribly long

---

* Lieutenant Commander Richard M. McCool, Jr., USN, was a former line officer who by this time had been designated as a public information specialist. As a lieutenant he earned the Medal of Honor for his heroism on 11 June 1945, while in command of the LCS(L)-122 in the Okinawa campaign.
† Commander James C. Shaw, USN. He was technical adviser for the movie version of Wouk's novel.
‡ Lieutenant Commander Robert H. Mereness, USN. Lieutenant Commander Robert S. Jones, USN.
§ Commander Russell L. Bufkins, USNR.

when the head of the magazine and book branch, which was the branch that dealt with writers, authors, and publishers, and tried to sell magazines on stories.

Paul Stillwell: I think Bill Lederer had been in it.*

Captain Hetu: Bill Lederer had been, yes, whom I later worked for in Pearl Harbor. I went to work for a guy named Ellis when it began.† And some of the people in the magazine and book branch had gotten themselves into trouble about giving Collier's a six-week lead time on a picture of a missile. A classic story where Collier's says, "We won't come out until you release it, but we'll have it on the cover and ready to go the day you release it." Whoever it was, wasn't too bright. Of course, when that happened, the rest of the press corps went bananas and said, "You mean they've had it for six weeks, and you didn't give it to us until today?" You know, the classic. So he got fired.

I was working for Ellis, and then he left, and it was sort of a ploy to downgrade magazine and book, in a way, and they didn't have anybody that wanted it, as I recall. So they put me in charge of the magazine and book branch as a jaygee, and I had a jaygee assistant. Hessman, who's now the editor of the Navy League magazine, worked for me in the magazine and book branch as a jaygee.‡

I could do whatever I wanted to. I didn't know anything about magazine publishing or book publishing or anything of the sort. I was almost fresh from a ship. So I just started doing things.

Paul Stillwell: What did you do to educate yourself?

Captain Hetu: I went around to the other services and went down to DoD.§ Their magazine and book guy then was a guy named—ended up being the number-two in DoD in the public affairs shop. I'll think of it in a minute. Just went around and talked to them, and said, "Hey, I'm a new guy, and I don't know anything about this business.

---

* Commander William J. Lederer, Jr., USN.
† Lieutenant Commander Walter J. Ellis, USN.
‡ Lieutenant (junior grade) James D. Hessman, USN.
§ DoD—Department of Defense.

Help. Will you give me a couple hours of your time?" They were very generous and nice people, and I remember them well. A guy named Chestnut, Colonel Chestnut in the Army, who was a peach of a guy and took care of me, and a guy in the Air Force named—he was a very famous Air Force public affairs officer.

Paul Stillwell: Barney Oldfield?

Captain Hetu: No, I knew Barney. No, this was a guy who ended up working for Boeing after he retired. Old-timers' disease, I can see him. He died about two years ago. Anyway, they were very generous in helping me and sort of giving me the basic, "Here's how you treat magazine people, and here's how you don't."

Paul Stillwell: What were some of those lessons? How do you treat magazine people?

Captain Hetu: Well, just the fairness, things that I pretty much instinctively knew. That you don't give one guy a beat over the other guy. That if you offered them something—if you had a lot of the work done for them, you had a pretty good chance of placing. Magazine writers were busy people, and if you could offer them something that they could do easily and that was almost an exclusive, why, you could do pretty well.

I went to New York and just started hiking around. I was a young officer, and I found that the editors of these magazines were just great. I would call up and say, "I'm coming to New York. I don't have anything special, but I'd like to meet you and let you know who I am. I'm in Washington, I can help you." I went to New York a couple of times, spent a week each time, went around and talked to—you know, Popular Mechanics was a big magazine then, Saturday Evening Post, Collier's, and so forth.

Paul Stillwell: Any specific stories that you remember coming out of your efforts? Guided missiles were just coming in then; nuclear power was new.

Captain Hetu: Yes. I remember a guy with Missiles and Rockets magazine, Eric Burgost. He had a picture of one of our new Navy missiles he was going to run before anyone else. I was sent over as a jaygee to talk the great Eric Burgost out of running this story.

Paul Stillwell: What was your arguing point?

Captain Hetu: Well, I just said, you know, "You're just going to kill us and . . . "

Paul Stillwell: Because of classification?

Captain Hetu: Classification, yes, classified picture. I said, "We're working on getting it declassified, and I will be sure that you get the first picture that runs off the machine, but please don't use this one." I don't remember what it was; it showed an antenna or something that in those days was something terrible. He did; he backed down. He was a good guy, he said, "Okay. I don't want to make the Navy mad for the rest of my life for one picture. But you've got to take care of me."

I said, "I'll take care of you," and we did.

We started a newsletter for authors and publishers—story ideas. I went around and to all the Navy, like ONR and NRL and places like that and said, "I'm going to be starting a newsletter with story ideas. I'm going to send it around to New York and stuff. Send me your things."* BuShips, all those old places.† It was great. In fact, Murray Smith, who was my other jaygee, left the Navy and started a magazine doing this. He's now the publisher of a commercial pilot magazine or something like that. He parlayed this into his life's work.

Paul Stillwell: To what extent did the stories originate with you, and to what extent from outside?

Captain Hetu: Oh, probably 10% of what we did ended up in stories. Most of it was people coming to us with requests. Although I think it helped them to know that we were

---
* ONR—Office of Naval Research. NRL—Naval Research Laboratory.
† BuShips—Bureau of Ships.

sending out this stuff, that we were responsive, and that even though I was a—the nice thing was that whether I was a jaygee or a commander didn't seem to matter to most people; they didn't know the difference. I was the Navy book guy.

Paul Stillwell: They wanted the information.

Captain Hetu: Yes. It didn't seem to matter to them what my rank was, and that was good. So I learned an enormous amount there.

Paul Stillwell: Admiral Burke came in during that period.* Did that make any changes?

Captain Hetu: I don't remember any changes when I was there. I remember being there the day he was named and this incredible furor over all the people who had been jumped over to make CNO. There was talk of all kinds of crazy things that were going to happen. These guys were all going to resign. Of course, they didn't. Some did, I guess.

I never knew him well, because I left shortly thereafter. I don't think I ever met him. I did subsequently, probably about four years later. He was there for quite some time, six years, I guess.

Paul Stillwell: Right.

Captain Hetu: Do you want to jump ahead to those Burke stories?

Paul Stillwell: Sure.

Captain Hetu: I'll forget it otherwise. A couple jobs later I went to Pearl Harbor for two tours and then Hollywood, and then I was back in DoD. These were all short tours, working for Pickett Lumpkin. Pickett was the head of the Navy Press Desk and I was his assistant, and we used to meet almost every Friday afternoon. Lloyd Norman, who was

---

* Admiral Arleigh A. Burke, USN, served as Chief of Naval Operations from 17 August 1955 to 1 August 1961. His oral history is in the Naval Institute collection.

then the Pentagon correspondent for Newsweek, now dead, great guy, really, a real gentleman, a real pro. He used to come over on Friday afternoon, and Friday afternoon was "Periscope" day because in those days, and I guess it went on for some time, if a correspondent got an item in "Periscope," he got 100 bucks or something. You remember "Periscope" used to be little vignettes . . .

Paul Stillwell: They were supposedly things that you got here before you could get it anywhere else.

Captain Hetu: Yes, exactly. So we were sitting around one day, and it had been the week or month of the pop-up test, where they first shot missiles out of the water, the early Polaris testing, and shot a missile out of the water.* We were sitting there conjecturing what you might do with this technology, and so we were sitting there drawing pictures on paper and stuff. We came up with the idea, the three or us, that why couldn't you put these missiles in boat davits on ships? You could have them everywhere. You could have them in merchant ships and everything else, and you could have hundreds of these things all over the world. When the balloon went up, they'd just roll them off the side of the ship and right themselves and shoot—a great idea.

So he wrote this up: Navy planners were working on this idea. Well, I'll be damned if Monday morning the NIS didn't come down to our desk and wanted to know if anybody at the desk had talked to Lloyd Norman about this "Periscope" item on these pop-up things. Pickett said, "Yes, we did."

"Oh, yes? Come with me." Cuffs or whatever—not quite that bad, but marched us up to the CNO's office.

Paul Stillwell: What year would this have been, 1960 about?

Captain Hetu: It was '61, because I had just gotten back to DoD. I guess it was Burke.

---

* Polaris was the name for the U.S. Navy's first submarine-launched ballistic missile. The missile entered fleet service in 1960 in the nuclear-powered submarine George Washington (SSBN-598). She fired her missiles for the first time on 20 July 1960.

Paul Stillwell: Burke was still CNO then, yes.

Captain Hetu: Yes. We went into Burke's office, and I was just there, scared to death.

Paul Stillwell: A fly on the wall.

Captain Hetu: Scared out of my mind and said to Pickett, "Where'd you get the information about these pop-up missiles?"

I said, "We didn't get that information from anyplace, Admiral."

"Come on, you know, did somebody tell you about this? Did you read it in a message? Do you know that we're working on a top-secret plan to do this?" Ughhhh.

Oh, my God.

I said, "No, sir."

He said, "We were . . .

Paul Stillwell: Just having a bull session.

Captain Hetu: Really, and I remember, I was scared to death. I thought, "Oh, my God, I'm going to get drummed out of the service as a lieutenant." We convinced him, Pickett did, that we just pulled it out of our ear. I mean, really just was trying to think of some kind of a technology feature for the "Periscope." God, they interviewed Lloyd Norman, I mean the investigative service and the FBI and I don't know, everybody. And Lloyd told them the same thing: "They didn't give me anything."

"What'd they give you, a piece of paper, a message, what?"

"Nothing, we just sat and drew it on a yellow pad."

So, anyway, we escaped and probably should have been put into the technology branch or something. [Laughter]

Paul Stillwell: Well, I think there was a NATO plan to put them in merchant ships.

Captain Hetu: Yes, oh, yes. There was, I mean, it happened. We were just smarter than we needed to be, I guess.

Paul Stillwell: Did you run into Clay Blair at all when you were in that magazine and book branch?[*]

Captain Hetu: Yes, I did.

Paul Stillwell: He had been a thorn in the Navy's side on the Rickover promotion.[†]

Captain Hetu: Yes.

Paul Stillwell: What do you recall of him?

Captain Hetu: That was over my head. I was a little too junior to get into that mess. My recollection is that Bill Lederer was somehow in that mix. I'm not sure.

Paul Stillwell: I'm not sure. I know that he had some dealings with Slade Cutter.[‡]

Captain Hetu: Oh, yes, Slade Cutter, yes. Well, to back up, I left Chinfo in 1956. I had served my time in Chinfo, and after I was there a year, I had to decide whether I was going to just do my two years and move on or what I wanted to do. I applied for a 1650. They had not chosen anybody since the 40 thieves. They were going to do another selection, and I got all sorts of varying advice on how to do this.

I was an 1105, a reserve line officer, and I was applying for 1650; I wanted to go to regular. I said, "If I'm going to stay, I'm going to just do it."

---

[*] Clay D. Blair, Jr., an enlisted submariner during World War II, later became a correspondent for Time and Life magazines and still later editor of The Saturday Evening Post. He wrote many books, including Silent Victory: The U.S. Submarine War Against Japan (Philadelphia: J. B. Lippincott Company, 1975).
[†] Hyman G. Rickover was considered the father of the nuclear Navy. He ran the U.S. Navy's nuclear-power program for many years, from 1948 until he eventually left active duty in 1982 with the rank of four-star admiral on the retired list.
[‡] See the Naval Institute oral history of Captain Slade D. Cutter, USN (Ret.) for an account of his dealings with Blair in connection with the submarine Nautilus (SSN-571).

They said, "Well, I'm not sure you can go from reserve line to regular. Probably have to go to a 1655 and then later be selected for regular Navy. You've got to do it in two jumps; you can't do it in one jump."

I said, "No, no. I can't live with that sword hanging over my head for the next two or three years. If I'm going to stay, I'm going to stay, and if they don't want me as a regular public affairs officer, then I'm out of here." Not a threat, but just that was my personal preference. And so I did. I applied for regular Navy and change of designator and got it. I'm trying to remember whether I was designated before I left Chinfo or not. We were selected, but I don't know if we actually got the blessing. Because then they offered me a job in Pearl Harbor. I was married and had a baby and one on the way, and Pearl Harbor sounded awfully good. So I accepted that and I accepted the regular commission, and off we went to CinCPacFlt, Pearl Harbor.* Another great adventure, another great time in my life.

Paul Stillwell: Was it customary then that you would just go directly into that designator without having some education in journalism?

Captain Hetu: Yes. Happily, social science was one of the undergraduate degrees that they considered to be qualifying.

Paul Stillwell: So your on-the-job training was really the background you brought to it.

Captain Hetu: Yes, the Sixth Fleet, and then the Chinfo. I'd had two tours essentially, one and a half; one was collateral duty. I was fairly junior; I was still a jaygee, so I guess they felt I had some sort of future, so I was picked.

Paul Stillwell: You mentioned the magazine work. What about the book side of it? Did you get involved with any books?

---

* CinCPacFlt—Commander in Chief Pacific Fleet.

Captain Hetu: Oh, yes, I sure did. I think I have some of them down there. I worked with John Toland and Ships in the Sky; he wrote a book on dirigibles.* I should have pulled those out; I have them here someplace. I have several books with my name in them, thank-you notes for help. Yes, I worked on several books, authors.

Paul Stillwell: Walter Lord was putting together Day of Infamy.†

Captain Hetu: I worked on that. I have a mention in that book. I got involved with a Navy doctor, Dooley, and I was involved when Burke wrote the foreword, as I recall, for his book.‡

Paul Stillwell: Dooley died young, as I remember.§

Captain Hetu: Well, Dooley came back with his corpsman, and I had a hand in arranging their tour—Dooley was writing the book. He was a doctor in Vietnam early on that did this sort of people-to-people work and had this group of hospital corpsmen; they set up these medical facilities.

He turned out to be a little different than he portrayed himself. He was, first of all, gay, and that was a little different in those days than it is now. They found out that he and his sailors were running more than a dispensary, and it was very embarrassing for the Navy. I mean, I remember getting involved in that, and, of course, the CNO had written the foreword to his book and endorsed him and they had given him a medal and taken him around Washington as a hero, and so forth. And I'd helped arrange this book tour. Well, we didn't know.

Paul Stillwell: So how was it handled when that became apparent?

---

* John Toland, Ships in the Sky: the Story of the Great Dirigibles (New York: Holt 1957).
† Walter Lord, Day of Infamy (New York: Holt, 1957). This is an account of the 1941 Japanese attack on Pearl Harbor, told mostly through the stories of individuals involved.
‡ Thomas A. Dooley III, USNR, Deliver us from Evil: the Story of Viet Nam's Flight to Freedom (New York: Farrar, Straus and Cudahy, 1956). The book was a bestseller.
§ Dooley died of cancer in 1961 at the age of 34.

Captain Hetu: Very discreetly.

Paul Stillwell: I'll bet.

Captain Hetu: Yes. I remember the day that I was told. I don't think we used the term "gay" then.

Paul Stillwell: "Homosexual" was term of choice.

Captain Hetu: Yes. He was quietly mustered out of the Navy, given an opportunity to resign, and he did, without too much noise. I think he made a few parting shots and sort of intimated that the Navy was not doing right by him or something. That happened a couple of times. I think the lawyers called him up and said, "You better back off. You're lucky." Because in those days that was an offense you went to jail for.

Paul Stillwell: Yes. Well, was his people-to-people work legitimate?

Captain Hetu: Yes, it was, the best we knew. Of course, the book—I don't think I have a copy of it—was all self-aggrandizement and so forth, and he was mentioned for the Medal of Honor and all kinds of stuff. I don't remember, but he did get a fairly high decoration. Congress passed resolutions. I mean, we had to do that as quietly as possible, just move him aside very softly.

Paul Stillwell: Walter Lord's book was one of the first detailed accounts of the human side of the attack on Pearl Harbor.

Captain Hetu: Yes. When we turn this off, I do have some of those books, I think, down there someplace. I do have some of those books that I helped on that they wrote nice little comments on.

Paul Stillwell: Did you work any with James Michener? He came out with The Bridges of Toko-Ri.*

Captain Hetu: No, I didn't know him. Knew who he was, met him later in my career, but I didn't really work with him then. The guy who wrote The Caine Mutiny . . .

Paul Stillwell: Wouk.

Captain Hetu: Yes, Herman Wouk was an interesting guy.

Paul Stillwell: In what ways?

Captain Hetu: I didn't meet him till later. I didn't know him when I was in the branch. I met him when I was working for John Warner as the Secretary.† We were up at the Naval War College once when he was speaking. He gave the first distinguished lecture series that they established or something.

I think Stan Turner was there then, and, of course, Stan had worked for Chafee, and that's how I met Stan Turner.‡ In fact, first time we were together he was the aide, and Chafee was the Secretary. Then Stan went up and was the head of the war college, and Wouk was giving the first—I really have to reconstruct that, because I remember that Wouk and Warner and I and Stan were in the room afterwards. Wouk gave a wonderful talk about his background. His parents, I think, were from Germany and Jewish and so forth. He was a very dynamic speaker, bring tears to your eyes, and then have that opportunity to sit with him after that for two or three hours in a room over scotch and hear his stories. That was one of the great times in my life.

---

* James A. Michener, The Bridges of Toko-Ri (New York: Random House, 1953). This is a novel about aircraft carrier operations during the Korean War.
† John W. Warner served as Secretary of the Navy from 4 May 1972 to 9 April 1974.
‡ Vice Admiral Stansfield Turner, USN, served as president of the Naval War College from 30 June 1972 to 9 August 1974. As a captain, he had been executive assistant to John H. Chafee, who served as Secretary of the Navy from 31 January 1969 to 4 May 1972.

Paul Stillwell: Well, could there have been a tie-in there with Spruance, because he had been president of the war college?* I think they may have been honoring him.

Captain Hetu: Yes, I think it was the Spruance series or the distinguished lecture series, yes. This is a while back. Yes, I think you're quite right, Spruance.

Paul Stillwell: I would think, as a jaygee, there was an enormous satisfaction in seeing your work directly appear in things that went out to the public.

Captain Hetu: Oh, yes, and that started me off. I've always felt that if you're a good public affairs officer or information officer, you're not seen. You're quoted occasionally when you talk to the press, but I think part of the joy of doing this job, even since I got out of the Navy, is seeing something that you've done blossom and take root, and not see your name attached to it. If that's what you're want, you're in the wrong business.

Paul Stillwell: That was intriguing to me sometimes in a public relations-type job: seeing my words appear under somebody else's by-line.

Captain Hetu: Yes, just seeing them was enough. That's all I cared about.

[Interruption for break]

Captain Hetu: Where were we?

Paul Stillwell: Well, I think you had just finished up in Washington, and you want to put in a little insert here to tell about your father's further career.

Captain Hetu: Oh, my dad, yes. After the war, World War II, he came back to Sharon, Pennsylvania, and got an offer from the local newspaper, the Sharon Herald, to become

---

* Admiral Raymond A. Spruance, USN, served as president of the Naval War College from 1 March 1946 to 1 July 1948.

their business manager, really vice president and treasurer. So he got out of the public accounting business and went into the newspaper business—not on the editorial side, on the business side—and spent the rest of his time there, from '45 to when he retired at 65 years old, which was about 20 years later, I guess.

It was a nifty little paper. I worked there. I worked in the areas during my summers in college. The first two summers I worked at the steel mill, one summer on a hot strip mill and the one summer in the newspaper. And my dad started me at the bottom in the newspaper. I worked in the janitorial department, really, pushing a broom and working with some wonderful guys who I still remember fondly. We were the repair crew and cleanup crew, and that was great.

But, anyhow, they had a radio station, and they had a job printing plant. Job printing plant being menus and stuff like that.

Paul Stillwell: Business cards?

Captain Hetu: Yes. And they had a metal decorating company that made plates. Their big customer was Westinghouse, which had a big plant in Sharon, and they made all the transformers for Westinghouse worldwide, big plant. It's closed now. Anyhow, he did well. He developed a metal decorating company and the job printing plant. He was a businessman, not an editorial type.

It was an employee-owned paper. There were no unions, and everybody was eligible to have stock in the paper, and I think Daddy put a fair amount of his earnings into stock. The last thing he did before he left the paper, before he retired, everybody supported this, they sold the paper to Ottoway Papers, which runs The Wall Street Journal, among others. Ottoway gave them a nice Dow Jones stock in exchange for their Sharon Herald, and he made a fair amount of money on that.

Paul Stillwell: I can imagine he had a very positive reaction when you opted to go regular Navy.

Captain Hetu: Well, yes, he did. He loved it. In fact, he did one of the only dumb things that I know my dad ever did in his life, particularly for a man who was an accountant, a numbers man. He resigned his commission in the reserves in 1952 or '53, because I remember I was on the <u>Salem</u> in the Mediterranean when I got this letter from my dad saying he was resigning. He was tired of going to the reserve meetings, and he was up to his armpits in his new newspaper duties, and he just couldn't go anymore. He was a captain, and he said, "I'm going to reserve meetings in Pittsburgh and watching old movies about the 5-inch/38 gun breech. This is madness. I'm driving to Pittsburgh in snow and rain and everything else to see training movies that are 15 years, 20 years old."

If I had known then what I know now about that—I mean, he was three years short of retirement as a captain. He wouldn't have got it until he was 62, but, my God, he lived to be almost 90. You know, 28 years of retirement that he blew and medical and everything else. The one thing in his life he never thought through or just didn't know the details or something—dumb. I think of the money he poured down the drain, but that was my dad; he was focused. He was loyal to what he was doing now, and he didn't want a free ride.

I remember talking him about the retirement. He said, "No, I didn't earn it. That's not fair."

I said, "Hey, sure, it's fair. It's the system; that's the rules. I mean, don't be holier than the Pope here, kid." But he resigned. That always broke my heart about that, and I think he was sorry later on that he didn't have that captain retired behind his name.

Paul Stillwell: We all do dumb things along the way.

Captain Hetu: Yes, yes. I mean, he still was very successful for a guy who never finished high school. I mean, he did pretty well. He did very well.

Paul Stillwell: Well, please, you were on the verge of going to Hawaii.

Captain Hetu: On the verge of Hawaii. So, anyway, I went regular Navy. I was selected for lieutenant before I went to Hawaii, and I guess they gave us a bad time. They said we had all made it in record time; making lieutenant in four years was unheard of or something. Some of these old guys, it had been taking them eight years to make lieutenant.

Anyway, I went to Hawaii with my wife and relatively new child; Mike was about a year old. Peggy was my then wife; we were subsequently divorced in 1981. We decided that we wanted to go by ship, and it took us some dealing to do. I remember this so well. They wanted to send us by airplane; I think the old Mars or something flew out of San Francisco then, 1956.

We really wanted to go by boat. I had been regaling Peggy with stories about my time at sea and how wonderful it was and so forth. So we made a special effort to go by ship and finally won. They didn't want to send her by ship, because she was about seven months pregnant. We went on the USS Breckinridge, which was a Navy MSTS ship.[*] I have to remember—it was not a USNS; it was a USS.

Paul Stillwell: But operated by the Military Sea Transportation Service.

Captain Hetu: Yes, but they had Navy crew on it, because I remember they wanted me to stand deck watches.

Paul Stillwell: Did you?

Captain Hetu: No. And we had to dress every day for the wardroom and put on our khakis and ties and the whole number. I mean, it was hardly a fun cruise. It was dreadful.

Paul Stillwell: You got what you asked for.

Captain Hetu: I sure did. I learned another object lesson. Boy. We were on the USS Breckenridge, one deck down, and we were in a room half the size of this, which doesn't tell you much on tape, but it couldn't have been much more than 8 by 8 or 10 by 10, with

---

[*] USS General J. C. Breckinridge (AP-176).

two bunks, upper/lower bunk and my wife seven months pregnant, and we had a baby. So they gave us a crib, and when we set the crib up, we couldn't get out the door. It was really something.

And sailors going by the room with lines over their shoulders. Oh, my God, this was just an operational ship. They did have families, and I forget how long it took us to go to Hawaii, three or four days, I guess. They said they wanted me to stand deck watches, and I finally convinced the exec or the operations officer, whoever it was, that I was a limited duty, 1650.[*] I was no longer an 1105, and so that I couldn't really stand deck watches unless they wanted me to go to jail if I hit something. So I got out of that. I did have to do some kind of deck inspection watch a couple nights, walking around to make sure the ship wasn't taking on water or something.

Paul Stillwell: That was your penance.

Captain Hetu: My penance. It was hot as hell and no air-conditioning on this ship. We had a porthole, thank God, and I can remember getting dressed for dinner in my khaki shirt, and by the time I would get it buttoned and the tie, my collar would be wet. It was nuts; we had to wear coats, and it was crazy. It was just one of these dumb Navy things: "These are the rules and, my God, that's the way it's going to be. All you people getting a free ride, you're going to have to wear the same uniforms as the officers working the ship." Okay.

So, anyhow, we got to Hawaii, and we were met at the dock by Pickett Lumpkin. Pickett's one of the 40 Thieves. Pickett Lumpkin was one of the greatest guys we've ever had in this business. He was a sweet, smart, nice man and taught me an enormous amount about public affairs.

Paul Stillwell: Was he a commander?

Captain Hetu: Pickett was then a commander. When I got there, CinCPac/CinCPacFlt was Admiral Stump, Felix B. Stump, a gaunt, tall, interesting guy who scared the hell out

---

[*] A public affairs specialist is a restricted line officer, not eligible for command at sea.

of everybody, and particularly junior officers.* He was an interesting man. Anyway, he had both hats in those days. Bill Lederer was there, and Bill was a captain. Bill worked the CinCPac side of the house, and Pickett was really the deputy, but he worked the CinCPacFlt account. So I really worked for Pickett, although for the first several months in the job, Bill Lederer had an office in our radio studio. We did a weekly radio show out of there, "Across the Blue Pacific," great show.

Paul Stillwell: What did it comprise?

Captain Hetu: Well, I used to help write the scripts and stuff and produce the shows.

Paul Stillwell: What this the Armed Forces Radio Network?

Captain Hetu: Yes. And we used to send it direct to stations. We had a sort of an interesting distribution. We had a lot of stations in the States that we just mailed it to every week. We had reel tapes, I guess, then, no cassettes.

Paul Stillwell: So you must have had some means for mass-producing them.

Captain Hetu: Yes. We did them one at a time, as I recall. It was a long process; get a JOSN in there running off tapes.†

But we had a lot of people who came to Honolulu, a lot of movie stars and things. They were on vacation, and so we had a deal with the visitors' bureau and they would keep track of these. When they would come there, we'd leave a note in their room or call them and tell them we were from the Navy, and we produced this 15-minute radio show every week and would they come and take a lead role in one of our radio shows. And they did.

---

* Admiral Felix B. Stump, USN, served as Commander in Chief Pacific and Commander in Chief U.S. Pacific Fleet, 10 July 1953-14 January 1958. After he was relieved as CinCPacFlt on 14 January, he remained in the joint billet as CinCPac until 31 July of that year.
† JOSN—journalist seaman, an enlisted man in training for the journalist rating.

Paul Stillwell: Any you remember specifically?

Captain Hetu: Oh, yes. Robert Mitchum came and did one.[*] Danny Kaye—trying to think of some of the others. Sports figures, I mean, anybody with a name, and I wish I had a list of those because we had quite a lineup. It was great fun. We'd write these stories, always about the Navy. These were my first production days, where you'd sit around brainstorming story ideas and rescues and missions, and we just made them up. We all took part in the show; we were different characters every week. It was fun, and the wives would come in and take parts and stuff. "Across the Blue Pacific." It had music and my first time ever. We had a little radio studio, and half of the radio studio was an office. I shared the office for several weeks with Bill Lederer.

Paul Stillwell: He's an interesting man. Please tell me your recollections of him.

Captain Hetu: Oh, he was, yes, a real character. I haven't seen him for several years. The last time I saw him he hadn't changed a bit. We used to go to his house, and he'd have junior officers over and take us over there, and we'd drink a lot of scotch and sit around and talk about the world and why we needed a Navy and didn't need a Navy. Bill then was writing The Ugly American with Burdick, and he had this affectation of stuttering that none of us were quite sure was real.[†]

Paul Stillwell: I think it was.

Captain Hetu: But even with the two of us in the office, he stuttered, so I thought, "If he's putting it on, he's playing to a small audience for me." I read the book as it came out of the typewriter, and he used to kid me a lot about going to a Jesuit college, John Carroll in Cleveland. He used to say, "Okay, Hetu, read this and see if it Thomistic philosophy, if this makes any damn sense to you."

---

[*] Mitchum was a movie star who in the 1980s portrayed Navy Captain Pug Henry in the television miniseries "Winds of War" and "War and Remembrance."
[†] William J. Lederer and Eugene Burdick, The Ugly American (New York: Norton, 1958).

Paul Stillwell: It's interesting that he really introduced that term to the lexicon, "the ugly American," but now . . .

Captain Hetu: Yes, but they got it backwards.

Paul Stillwell: Yes, right. The ugly American was a good person in the book.

Captain Hetu: Yes, he was the hero; that's right. It broke his heart. The Ugly American was always considered the bad guy, and he wasn't at all.

Paul Stillwell: What was he like to work with?

Captain Hetu: Well, he was wonderful. He liked to do iconoclastic things, if you had ideas. Bill was a fun guy to work for, although he was CinCPac, and so I didn't work—some directly for him, but not a lot. While we were there, they split the command, and Stump went up to be CinCPac, and Admiral Curts took over as CinCPacFlt. He got his fourth star. He wasn't CinCPacFlt Fleet very long, though.* Then he retired, and Hopwood came.† What I did have to do with Lederer, he was great, he was so much fun. Had a wonderful wife whom he divorced. We were never quite sure; she probably divorced him.

Paul Stillwell: Well, he was unusual in the public affairs business in being a Naval Academy graduate, and he had line background.

Captain Hetu: That's right, and he had written All the Ship's at Sea, and that was his first big book.‡ He was always working on books, which always upset the rest of the staff people that he was working on this book during the daylight hours. I suppose now they'd fire you for something like that. It was a little different then. But Bill was always

---

* Admiral Maurice E. Curts, USN, served as Commander in Chief Pacific Fleet, 14 January 1958 to 1 February 1958.
† Admiral Herbert G. Hopwood, USN, served as Commander in Chief Pacific Fleet, 1 February 1958 to 30 August 1960.
‡ William J. Lederer, All the Ship's at Sea (New York, Sloane, 1950).

working for the Navy 24 hours a day, so it was pretty hard to say, "You can't work during the eight hours from 8:00 to 4:00.

I remember one of the great—I guess it became sort of a standard speech. He was always speaking, because he was famous even then because of his books, <u>All the Ship's at Sea</u> and stuff. Gave a speech at the officers' club, Pearl Harbor officers' wives, whatever it was. Big turnout, and I went with him.

He was great for that. I loved him for that. He would take us junior officers. I have a picture somewhere. He pinned on my lieutenant bars when I made lieutenant, shoulder boards. He would take you along. If he was going someplace for a meeting, he'd say, "Come on, come on with me. See how the big guys do it." It was great. I learned that lesson from him, and I did it all my career, to take junior officers with you and make sure they got involved and you didn't shut them out and have closed-door meetings and stuff. That's something I really did learn from both him and Pickett Lumpkin, was involve people, let them know at a young age to see what goes on. Bill was good at that.

He gave this one speech for the officers' wives' club, and he started off by saying, "You may have noticed that in the ladies' room one of the booths wasn't working. It was locked shut." I don't know if they remembered, but they said, "Oh, yes." And he said, "That was me." He said, "I was standing on the seat." This was pretty racy. [Laughter] He said, "Let me tell you about the conversations I heard." And he was identifying these ladies by the color of their shoes, and, of course, it's easy to do, white shoes.

Paul Stillwell: This was all a put-on.

Captain Hetu: Oh, yes, sure. This was all this thing he had written, but it was all stuff that probably they had said. [Laughter] And I remember he just brought the place down. I thought that was one of the funniest speeches I've ever heard. White shoes comes in and says, "Who the hell is Lederer, anyway? Why have we got this guy? He stutters; you can't understand him." And he went through this whole thing, and he had the place in his hand, and it was so funny. He was a funny guy. I got to do a lot of stuff out at Pearl Harbor because of him and Pickett.

Paul Stillwell: What qualities do you remember in Lumpkin?

Captain Hetu: Boy, write a book about Pickett. Pickett was the consummate leader in including you in everything and teaching; he was a great teacher.

Paul Stillwell: What were some of the lessons?

Captain Hetu: Well, I did Pickett's eulogy at his funeral. Ed Castillo and I did a Huntley/Brinkley, not at his funeral, but we did a ceremony for him at the Navy Yard.* We did a lot of Pickett Lumpkinisms, some of his sayings. But Pickett just taught me so much about how to deal with the press and to be patient. Patience, patience, I'm not very patient, not one of my great attributes. I want to get things done.

I remember there was a guy at the Honolulu Star-Advertiser named Bucky Buckwalter, who was a sort of a pain the Navy's side out there. Bucky would come for an interview with the admiral with—of course, nobody wore shirts and ties out there. He'd come with probably what would be old pants, an Aloha shirt, and open-toed sandals, needed a shave. This used to drive me up a tree. I'd say, "You know, he's coming to talk to a four-star admiral. I mean, this guy comes dressed like a bum and he wants all this stuff."

I'd be grousing, and Pickett would take me aside and say, "Hey, do you think you're ever going to change this guy?"

I said, "No, I don't think so."

He said, "Then relax. You're driving yourself crazy trying to change something that you're never going to change. Bucky Buckwalter is the front page of the Honolulu Advertiser, and that's how you've got to think of him. You've got to play him like a violin." That was one of Pickett's sayings, "Play him like a violin. Write the music and play him like a violin. You know what he likes. He likes you to kiss his behind, he likes you to do this, do that. Do it, and you'll see the next day that you've ended up winning; he hasn't. You'll see all of the stuff you want in the story will be in the story."

---

* Captain Edmund L. Castillo, USN (Ret.), a public affairs specialist.

Paul Stillwell: And the admiral will be happy.

Captain Hetu: "And the admiral will be happy, and I will be happy. We'll all be happy. Go play tennis, and Bucky will be harassing somebody else." So Pickett was wonderful. And Pickett gave you opportunities to do things.

They came out from 20th Century Fox to do movies. The Enemy Below was the first film, I guess, that I worked on, which was a great story.* It was a good film, I think, about an American destroyer skipper played by Bob Mitchum and a German submarine commander played by Kurt Jürgens, and it was this cat-and-mouse game. It's quite a good book, and they were very true to the book. We gave them cooperation. I wasn't a submariner or a destroyer sailor but I was sort of the technical facilitator, I wasn't really the adviser. We had a destroyer officer and a submarine officer work out the torpedo problems and stuff. But I worked on the film, and the director of that film was Dick Powell. Remember the song-and-dance man?

Paul Stillwell: Right.

Captain Hetu: The producer was Frank McCarthy from 20th Century Fox; he later produced The Longest Day. And Dick Powell was a prince of a guy. He was a very nice man and a good director, knew what he was doing, and I spent a lot of time with Dick Powell. He went to dinner with us and he used to sing in the car in the back seat, and he was really a fun guy.

I remember one of the stories. We were having dinner down at the Hawaiian Village, which was then not a high-rise. It was a village, but it was a very famous Hawaiian restaurant. And what's his name sang there.

Paul Stillwell: Don Ho?

Captain Hetu: No, before Ho. The guy that died servicing Mrs. Kaiser, his boss.

---
* The film was released in 1957.

Paul Stillwell: I hadn't heard that one.

Captain Hetu: Oh, yes. Oh, gosh, he was very famous in Hawaii in those days. I'll think of it, but anyway we had a table with him, and we were all in civilian clothes and Dick Powell and Pickett and his wife and I don't remember who all, but Dick Powell, of course, and people knew who he was. He was a fairly famous movie actor, and we'd all had a few pops and went in the men's room. A guy who was just sort of drunk staggered in next to me and said to me, "Isn't that Dick Powell you're with?"

I said, "Yes, yes, it is, but I was sort of surprised you don't recognize me." [Laughter]

He sort of looked at me with one eye, and he said, "Who the hell are you?"

I said, "Kirk Douglas."

He said, "You're not Kirk Douglas." [Laughter]

I said, "Yes, I am." [Laughter] I said, "I had my hair cut for"—I then had a crew cut. I said, "I had to get my hair cut. We're making a Navy movie out here. I'm making a movie with Dick Powell."

"You're not Kirk—you're Kirk Douglas?"

I said, "Yes."

"You don't look like Kirk Douglas."

I said, "Well, we all look different off the screen."

"No kidding, you're really Kirk Douglas?" [Laughter]

So he walked out, and I had told Dick Powell about this, and he laughed. So we walked out of the restaurant, and the guy was standing there with a bunch of three or four, I guess, tourists, and he said, "There he is. There's Kirk Douglas." [Laughter]

The people then said, "You're crazy, that doesn't even look like Kirk Douglas." Dick Powell thought that was hilarious, he laughed. He was a good guy.

But Pickett would assign you jobs like this. He was only a commander; he might have jumped on that himself. It was a pretty good job. I mean, it was fun, but I was a lieutenant. Then, as a result of that, the same unit production manager, a guy named

Stacy, was sent out to scout the islands for South Pacific.* Twentieth Century Fox also made South Pacific.

So Pickett assigned me to him to help him look for locations both on Oahu and on Kauai for South Pacific. Then when they sent the production out, he assigned me as the technical adviser for the movie. There wasn't very much technical advice to give, a lot of support we gave them: Marine stuff and ships. That was one of the highlights of my life.

Paul Stillwell: Please tell me some of the things involved in that.

Captain Hetu: Oh, it was so much fun. The director was the guy who did the Broadway show, Joshua Logan. Leon Shamroy was the cameraman, who was a very famous cameraman in Hollywood in those days. Logan was the producer and director of the stage production of South Pacific. First movie he ever made, and he drove them crazy. I went over on Kauai and was the full-time adviser on the movie for several weeks and had my own Jeep. I drove around the island in my command Jeep. I was a lieutenant, had extraordinary fun, learned a lot about movie making.

Because it was the first movie that had ever been shot in Todd-AO, which was 70-millimeter film, big film, expensive film. Even then it was, I forget how much a foot, $38.00 a foot or something like that, going through the camera.

Paul Stillwell: Wow.

Captain Hetu: And this guy had never directed a film, so I learned so much about the rank structure in Hollywood. Wow. I mean, the producer and the director and who's in charge, and nobody cuts the camera except the director—nobody. He used to get mad at scenes, and he'd do things like walking off the set into the water and take a swim, and the camera was rolling.

Paul Stillwell: Because he hadn't cut it.

---

* South Pacific was a musical released in 1958. It was based on James Michener's novel Tales of the South Pacific.

Captain Hetu: He hadn't cut it. And Stacy, I remember, was going crazy—the unit production manager. He was in charge of the money, and he was watching this money going through the camera rolling. They worked that out eventually, and then he let the assistant director do some of the cutting.

We had a second unit there that did all the nifty aerial scenes and all that, a guy named Ray Kellogg. I worked closely with Ray; Ray was an old Hollywood hand. He was sort of a grumpy old guy, but he really knew his stuff. We did an interesting thing. We got some old Grumman airplanes and painted them up, flew them off Kauai. We went to an old airstrip. These were the days when you could kind of do crazy things. They had their pilots; they weren't our pilots. But I remember some of the wild things they did. They put a camera right on the centerline and laid down and had the planes take off over them, things like that. Interesting group.

I remember once when they were shooting, I guess, it was the Bloody Mary scene or the nurse's speech on Kauai. At this time of year they were starting to lose the sun earlier in the day. I learned some lessons, that when the director speaks, he's God.

He said one day, "How can we get more light? We need another half hour, or we're never going to make this."

One guy said, "Well, I don't know. We could move this out to the point."

"Oh, we can't do that. We've got all the sets up here and stuff. We've got this hill behind."

I said, laughingly, jokingly, "Well, you could cut down the trees."

"Great idea," he says. I thought he was kidding, and I was the only one that wasn't starting up the hill with a saw in my hand. [Laughter] They went up and cut down the trees on the top of the hill. Gave them an extra ten minutes of light or something. Josh Logan didn't know anything about making movies.

Paul Stillwell: In fact, I think he did Mister Roberts.

Captain Hetu: Yes, but he did the stage of that. I got to know all these stars and they were great fun.

Paul Stillwell: Well, tell me about those.

Captain Hetu: There were only two hotels on Kauai at that date, and one was a pretty nice place. They had double-duplex cottages. I had half of a duplex where I stayed, and the other side was Mitzi Gaynor and her husband, Jack Bean. Rossano Brazzi was Italian, but he played the French plantation owner, and his wife was there. Little fat Italian woman, and he was this great macho-looking guy, and he had this sort of dumpy Italian wife. We all had our own little pools outside. And I remember him drying her off and taking care of her. Women were going crazy for this guy.

John Kerr played the young Marine lieutenant. He had played in <u>Tea and Sympathy</u>, one of the very first movies ever about gay people. So nobody was sure about him, except his wife had just had twins and he used to laugh about it and say, "I'm not homosexual." I got to know all these people, sit down and talk with them, you know, Juanita Hall was Bloody Mary, and France Nuyen was Liat. Ray Walston who played "Our Favorite Martian," or whatever it was, he was Billis. These were great people; they were fun people. They did an awful lot for the sailors, really good to the sailors.

Paul Stillwell: What role did the sailors have in this?

Captain Hetu: Well, we had a lot of background scenes, where they had operations going on in Kauai, and they'd bring the ships around and put them off the beach for a day or two, so they could shoot these scenes with the ships in the background. And we'd bring sailors and take them to dinner.

Leon Shamroy, this tough, crusty old photographer—photographer means he's in charge of all the photography. It doesn't mean he runs the cameras. I got very fond of this guy. He was an older guy. He had a son who was a paraplegic, had broken his neck in a diving accident and he had a great love for these young sailors, I mean, in the best sense of the word. Every night he would take about a dozen of them to dinner, get a big table in this Kauai Inn, which was <u>the</u> place on the island, spend a couple hundred bucks on dinners for sailors, loved it. Nice guy, there were a lot of good people; they were fun people to be around.

One of the locations we went to—remember the scene in the movie--did you see South Pacific?

Paul Stillwell: I don't remember it, no.

Captain Hetu: Well, one scene is a point of land where de Becque and Nellie Forbush, the nurse played by Mitzi Gaynor—this was a plantation that we spotted when we went over months ahead, when we had gone looking for locations. It was an interesting old plantation, sort of overgrown, and we were told about it by we went to the local, I forget, chamber of commerce or whatever they had there. Kauai was nothing then, not a tourist place like it is now. In fact, they built a big hotel on the scene of where South Pacific was shot.

Went to this old plantation house; it was a neat location on the side of the island, on the water, rolling hills of sugar cane. And the woman who lived there—her husband had died some time before and she was a very spooky lady, sort of spaced out. She was a Hale, a white person, I remember had white hair. She invited us to come over for lunch one day, and we went to lunch, Eric, Stacy, and I. He was the production manager, one of the camera people, and me, I think, four of us or five of us drove over to her place.

She has us for lunch, and there was an empty seat at the table, which was set for her husband. The maid there said that she kept a seat at the table for him at all times, sort of spooky-wooky. He was buried out on the plantation someplace, and she had an old car in her garage, which was an old, old touring car with a top that went down. It hadn't been run for 15 years—on blocks, mint condition, but it wouldn't run.

Later, when we started shooting the film there, the mechanics were there. Movies, certainly on location, bring everybody along; they can fix anything. They fixed this car for her, and she let us drive it around. I have some pictures again somewhere of us driving around in this big wonderful open touring car. They got it running like a top; it was in beautiful condition. We drove all around the island in this touring car with the top down, two seats. Anyway, a lot fun things that went on in these movies.

Paul Stillwell: And you were getting paid for all this too.

Captain Hetu: I was getting paid. Wonderful time, yes, great fun.

Paul Stillwell: Anything else to wrap up that tour of duty? Anything about Admiral Stump specifically?

Captain Hetu: No. I stayed in Pearl Harbor for another tour; we can do that next time.

Paul Stillwell: Okay.

Captain Hetu: But I went from CinCPacFlt to the service force and got my own command as a lieutenant. Yes, Stump just about drove his aide, Beetle . . .

Paul Stillwell: Beetle Forbes.*

Captain Hetu: . . . Forbes. I knew Beetle. In fact, Beetle took my house. In Hawaii I moved out of quarters after a while and found a nifty house up in Halava Heights right near Camp Smith.

Paul Stillwell: Forbes is the classic worrier.

Captain Hetu: The classic worrier. My recollection is Pickett and I used to play tennis a lot in Pearl Harbor, and Beetle used to play tennis with Admiral Stump. Admiral Stump used to play tennis in this long white duck, you know, a la Bobby Riggs. He didn't wear shorts; he wore long white pants and a tennis sweater and very often had a cigarette in his hand while he was playing tennis. I think Pickett and I almost died one day, because

---

* Lieutenant Commander Bernard B. Forbes, USN. The oral history of Forbes, who retired as a vice admiral, is in the Naval Institute collection.

Beetle was playing with him. I remember the admiral sort of stopped and said, "Beetle, if you're going to play tennis with me, hit the ball to me." [Laughter]

We just about collapsed, said, "Admiral that's not the way to—it's not the idea."

But Beetle said, "Yes, sir," and he hit the ball to him. Oh, God.

Paul Stillwell: Forbes told me that the admiral had a trophy wife who had little or nothing to do with the Navy.

Captain Hetu: Oh, yes, Vampira.

Paul Stillwell: I hadn't heard that name.

Captain Hetu: Oh, yes, I had forgotten about her. Yes, she was a very exotic, long black hair. Yes, she was the mystery lady. Yes, that's right, I had forgotten about her. Because I had to go one day to Admiral Stump's house to show Mrs. Stump something. I think it had to do with South Pacific. I think they were entertaining the cast and crew or something, and we had a group of SecNav guests or something. I had to go over and brief her on who the people were and what the hierarchy was, who was senior and the director and the producer, and I had to go over to Mrs. Stump, yes. That's right, I had forgotten about her.

I went over there scared to death, young lieutenant, and she went into those big quarters in Makalapa there. It was a lovely place, and I just went by myself. Walked up there from the headquarters; it wasn't very far up the road. She came out with this cigarette. She was a long, thin, I guess, pretty—I don't remember—and I had to brief her. And she was very nice. I had regaled her with stories of Mrs. Stump. Nobody had ever been alone with Mrs. Stump before. She was a little frightening, yes.

Paul Stillwell: Well, that's an interesting note to end on for today.

Captain Hetu: Okay.

Interview Number 2 with Captain Herbert E. Hetu, U.S. Navy (Retired)
Place: Captain Hetu's home, Alexandria, Virginia
Date: Friday, 17 May 1996
Interviewer: Paul Stillwell

Paul Stillwell: When we left off last time, Captain, you had just finished up your first tour out in Hawaii with the fleet staff. And then in the summer of 1958 you moved over to ComServPac staff.* How did that change come about?

Captain Hetu: I had had about a year and a half at CinCPacFlt, and ServPac was literally across the street, out the back door of the fleet headquarters and down the street a half a block into ServPac headquarters. And that job came open; I can't think it right off who the guy was I relieved.

Paul Stillwell: Was this a case of being a bigger fish in a smaller pond?

Captain Hetu: Yes. ServPac was a two-star command, the Service Force, Pacific Fleet, and I was at the Pacific Fleet headquarters, which obviously was the sort of home office for the Pacific. Oh, it was a great opportunity and the Navy liked the idea, because they didn't have to move somebody. All I had to do was literally go across the street. In fact, I had a couple journalists carry my desk over, and I had my own command. I was a lieutenant, and it was a great opportunity for me and I loved service force ships.

Paul Stillwell: What about them appealed to you?

Captain Hetu: I think because of my grandfather; that's the only thing I can think of. You know, I loved being on his freighter when he was the chief engineer. And I just loved these cargo ships and oilers and fleet tugs. I used to ride them all the time. I had

---

* ComServPac—Commander Service Force Pacific Fleet, the logistical support arm of the fleet.

an opportunity to go out and spend overnight on the ships, and they were wonderful ships. They were comfortable, and, to me, had a great lure.

Paul Stillwell: I would think that your perception was not the common one, because the combatants usually have the more glamour.

Captain Hetu: Oh, sure. Oh, yes, they did, of course. But the beans, bullets and black oil, you know, which was our slogan, really appealed to me. I just loved it.

Paul Stillwell: And absolutely necessary for the combatants.

Captain Hetu: Oh, couldn't do it without. And I got to be friends with a lot of the skippers, not surprisingly because I just loved publicizing these ships. And they liked publicity, positive publicity.

Paul Stillwell: Well, it really is an unsung job in many cases, so anything would be a real step up from what they were used to.

Captain Hetu: True. Well, I got a couple of stories in <u>Navy Times</u> and in the local papers and was somewhat, I hesitate to use the word hero, but, yes. We were competing with the Fleet Marine Force; we were competing with the Pacific Fleet and the submarines. You know, Pearl Harbor, all the commands are there. So if you got something in the paper about your little part of the world, it was always fun. It was a great challenge.

Paul Stillwell: What specific stories do you remember?

Captain Hetu: Geez, I remember taking a picture of the <u>Genesee</u>, which was an AOG, a small oiler. They were wonderful little ships. The captain was a guy named Chet Chertavian.* He and I had been friends before, and we became much better friends

---
* Lieutenant Armen Chertavian, USN.

afterwards. In fact, we lived near each other here in Washington after we got back, quite by accident. I took a picture of the ship mirrored in a tuba being played by a Navy band and, for some reason, this caught the fancy of the photo editor, I think it was the Honolulu Star-Bulletin, and they ran it on the front page. And, wow, you know, it was so much fun for me because, you know, to get something on the front page of the Star-Bulletin, which was The Washington Post of Honolulu in those days. Everybody read it.

Paul Stillwell: Were you more likely to get feature-story type inserts?

Captain Hetu: Yes. Oh, yes, you had to be very innovative. I remember we also took a picture—I don't know if I took it or a photographer, that's not important. But for Halloween I had gone to sea aboard one of these ATRs, the rescue ships, the diving ships, and I was struck by the way they stored the diving helmets. They stored them in a room with light bulbs inside of them to keep them from drying out, or from getting mold. And it was a wonderful picture, and I said, boy, jack-o-lanterns.

And so we took this picture of three or four or these old diving helmets. And that made the front page of the paper on Halloween. Obviously we released in on Halloween with that in mind. But, anyway, things like that, it was fun. It was a great fun job, innovative ways to get publicity for our ships.

It taught me a lot about bureaucracy. There was really no public affairs office there, and I had to actually literally build one in one of the old out buildings. I mean, I didn't build it myself, but I caused it to be built and built up a staff and started a magazine for the service force. We used to justify columns of type then by hand; we didn't have the machines we do now. We didn't have a printing press; we justified it by hand. The kids that worked for me thought I was crazy, I guess.

Paul Stillwell: This is making the right side flush.

Captain Hetu: The right column flush, yes, so it would look professional and not like it came out of a typewriter. It took a couple extra hours every month, but it looked better. Whether anybody noticed but me, I don't know.

Paul Stillwell: Did you do stories on individuals as well?

Captain Hetu: Yes, we did feature stories on the missions of each of the ships and we did stories on individual sailors and COs, more sailors than COs.[*] We had a lot of up-and-coming officers on the big oilers then. We had the big ones, the new ones, AO-148.[†] Oh, gosh, what were the names of the two big oilers that had just come in the fleet? Now, this is 1958.

Paul Stillwell: These are probably aviators being groomed for carrier commands.

Captain Hetu: Exactly right. Yes, big ships, learning their ship-handling skills. I know Chick Clarey was captain of one our oilers, and Clarey later became the VCNO.[‡]

Paul Stillwell: Right, he was not an aviator.

Captain Hetu: Not an aviator, no; he was a submariner. But we had people like that, and I'm trying to remember some of the others that came along that I met. Of course, I was a lieutenant, so we weren't exactly pals, but they knew me because I was the public affairs officer.

Paul Stillwell: And thus in a position to help them.

Captain Hetu: Yes.

Paul Stillwell: Well, it was probably an education for you in the logistics side of the Navy.

---

[*] COs—commanding officers.
[†] The Navy commissioned six large fleet oilers of the Neosho (AO-143) class between 1954 and 1956. The two in the Pacific Fleet were the Hassayampa (AO-145) and the Ponchatoula (AO-148).
[‡] In 1958 Captain Bernard A. Clarey, USN, commanded the Hassayampa. As a four-star admiral, he served as Vice Chief of Naval Operations, 1968-70, and as Commander in Chief Pacific Fleet, 1970-73.

Captain Hetu: Yes, it really was wonderful. I enjoyed it, and I learned a lot about bureaucracy.

Paul Stillwell: What were some of the lessons you learned?

Captain Hetu: How to set up your own command and how to get your—well, you know, a lot of this was due to Pickett Lumpkin's tutoring and fine Italian hand, as we used to say about Pickett. For instance, I think I reported to the assistant chief of staff for personnel, which made no sense. What Pickett taught me early on was you've got to report to the boss. You've got to report to the admiral; you can't be going through some guy that doesn't know what you're supposed to be doing.

So I started a campaign as a lieutenant to get my number changed to a 00 number, instead of whatever my staff number was, so that I would be in a box off the admiral's box. That took some doing, with the chief of staff and all this kind of business. What you learned as a public affairs officer, and this carried on throughout your career, was that you deal with very senior people from your very earliest days.

When I was a jaygee in the Pentagon, I was dealing with admirals and Lord knows on the ship. Before I went Chinfo as a jaygee, I saw the admiral only coming up and down the gangway when I had the deck watch. We didn't even live on the same level of the ship with an admiral.

Paul Stillwell: But the wise admiral would do well to cultivate you as well, because you can help him in an area he's not that familiar with.

Captain Hetu: Yes, that's true. And that got, of course, easier and better as you go along. But as a young lieutenant, I worked for an admiral there: Robert Lord Campbell, I remember, a good guy.[*] Nice fellow, was sort of imposing.

Paul Stillwell: What do you remember about his personality?

---

[*] Rear Admiral Robert L. Campbell, USN, served as Commander Service Force Pacific Fleet from May 1958 to February 1961.

Captain Hetu: He was sort of an imperial guy; he was a good-looking admiral, a big guy. But that was the interesting part. I got to know him and he wasn't like that at all. I mean, he was . . .

Paul Stillwell: That was his public persona?

Captain Hetu: Yes, that was his up-front persona, but when I started going on trips with him and sit down in the office going over his monthly column for the newsletter and things like that, he turned out to be really quite a charming man, and with a great appreciation, it turned out, for what I was doing, and he was interesting. I got so I could kind of giggle with him a little bit, you know, not in public, and I wouldn't be so silly as to try and fool around with him, joke with him, in front of other senior officers, but he was good. I could giggle with him a little bit in the office, and he had a good sense of humor, and he thought I did, so we got along really well. This was my sort of first exposure working directly for an admiral—that when the button on my desk rang, he wanted me, not somebody else. [Laughter]

Paul Stillwell: Did you have opportunities to say tactfully, "Maybe you should work on that public persona"?

Captain Hetu: Well, he didn't have very many speaking opportunities. He was a fairly junior person in the scheme of things in Honolulu, so there wasn't a lot of opportunity to do public appearances and that sort of thing. Although, I did, on occasion, get some reporters out to talk to him about the ships. I also became a believer early in those days of getting media out on the ships.

Our ships went out back and forth a lot, in and out of port on short trips, so I was able to get media out on the ships. I don't know if I was the first. I think maybe I was, I don't know, to get the SecNav guest cruise people that came to Honolulu often to take a day on an oiler. At first, they thought, well, that might be a wasted day, going out on an oiler and they did go out on a carrier, but they enjoyed it, they loved it. They were big ships, and we would always do a replenishment, of course, didn't just go out and steam around. We always combined it with a replenishment, and the admiral would go. Obviously, he liked to go out with these big wheels, so-called, from the States.

So I had a good time. I guess this was the first time I started into crisis management. We had a fire in one of our ships, killed a couple people, which was a big story out there; it was peacetime.

Paul Stillwell: Which one was that?

Captain Hetu: Gosh, I can't think of it.

Paul Stillwell: Was that an exception, to deal with a hard-news-type situation?

Captain Hetu: Yes, yes, at a very young age. Of course, CinCPacFlt would get into it; I wouldn't do it to their exclusion. But I learned early on get the facts out, get the people on board the ship, let the people stand up and talk about it. And it fared me well in later days when I handled some major, major crises. So it was a good, wonderful learning experience, a good way to get started and upward and onward.

Paul Stillwell: Well, and the other part of that is that if the media perceive you to be open and cooperative, they are less likely to be critical.

Captain Hetu: Absolutely. Absolutely. Yes, I learned that at a very young age.

Paul Stillwell: Was there any sense of what you were doing was briefing ships on the way to Seventh Fleet on what they would need to do out there in terms of public affairs?

Captain Hetu: Not in those days. No, this was '58; it was a ways before Vietnam—saw our people on the way to the Seventh Fleet. The Seventh Fleet was sort of an entity onto itself out there. Although, obviously, our people did rotate in and out of the Seventh

Fleet, but I don't remember having any interface with the Seventh Fleet. CinCPacFlt would do that.

I had, as I said, my own command. I had ended up with two or three journalists working for me. I had one first class who ended up years later working for me in the Secretary of the Navy's office. So you make lasting contacts. Also, I remember I first ran into a guy named Toby Marquez, and Toby was a JOSA, I think, then.[*] He was one of the first Filipinos to come into the Navy and not go into the steward training. I kept running into Toby along the way for many years. In fact, stood up for him for his citizenship years later in Puerto Rico.

Paul Stillwell: He became a talented photojournalist.

Captain Hetu: Yes, and retired as a commander. Really a wonderful success story and a terribly talented guy. I still know him. He lives here in Washington.

Paul Stillwell: Well, what can you say about the role of the enlisted journalist vis-à-vis the public affairs officer?

Captain Hetu: Those were the relatively early days of journalists. I ran into a lot of really talented, good, solid people. I'm sure are still around, but they were people who were generally excellent writers. The ones that I worked with, certainly in the early days out there, Chief Joe Harrington, who turned out to be an author and a writer. Tokulsky— I can remember a lot of these guys.

Paul Stillwell: Harrington, I guess, coauthored a couple of books about World War II.[†]

---

[*] JOSA—journalist seaman apprentice. Octavio J. Marquez later became a commissioned officer public affairs specialist and also wrote articles for the U.S. Naval Institute Proceedings.

[†] Zenji Orita, with Joseph D. Harrington, I-Boat Captain (Canoga Park, California: Major Books, 1976). Pat Frank and Joseph D. Harrington, Rendezvous at Midway: U.S.S. Yorktown and the Japanese Carrier Fleet (New York: John Day Company, 1967). Joseph D. Harrington, Yankee Samurai: the Secret Role of Nisei in America's Pacific Victory (Detroit: Pettigrew Enterprises, 1979).

Captain Hetu: Yes. Generally the journalists that I can remember from those days were sort of iconoclasts. They were sort of outgoing, talented guys.

Paul Stillwell: How would you explain that?

Captain Hetu: I don't know whether it's because the Navy thought that's what they ought to be, or whether that's the kind of people they were. I'm not sure. But most of them, although some weren't—I can't say that. They just all were very interesting, nice people. I mean, I liked the journalists. We got along well and I never had the feeling so much with journalists of the enlisted-officer chasm between us. We were in the same business. And public affairs then, I suppose still is, was a lonely job in one sense. For instance, at ServPac, where I was the public affairs officer and the only people around me that knew what I was talking about generally were the journalists, and we sort of had our own little fraternity. So we were pretty close, and I still maintain contact with all these people many years later, the journalists. Yes, good people.

Paul Stillwell: How much autonomy did you have in that office?

Captain Hetu: Really, quite a bit because, as I say, I was off in my own corner. And once I got so that I could report directly to the admiral—and that's vital if you're going to be successful at all—people let me alone a lot.

Paul Stillwell: But you were less likely to get rudder orders than, say, the ops officer.

Captain Hetu: Yes, that's right. These were the days, remember—I keep saying that; maybe I'll edit that out a lot, but when a public affairs officer or a public information officer, as we were known then, walked into the op center people would cover up classified messages and say, "Oh, oh, here he comes."
    I'd say, "Come on, guys, I'm an American."

Paul Stillwell: We're all on the same team.

Captain Hetu: You know, look at my collar, I'm a naval officer. What do you think I'm going to do, sell the secrets to the Honolulu Star-Bulletin? Because we were thought of by a lot of the operations people as "them," i.e., part of the media, you know, that we were on the other side.

Paul Stillwell: Was there any perception on the part of some of these other ratings that journalists aren't real sailors?

Captain Hetu: I wondered about that, sort of like yeomen and hospital corpsmen.

Paul Stillwell: And supply types.

Captain Hetu: Yes, and storekeepers. I never got that impression, ever. I think journalists were pretty well respected because of what they did. Even way back on the Salem I had a journalist, JOSN, working for me on the newspaper we put every day on the Salem. I didn't mention that before, but that was one of the interesting feats. We put it out overnight from dispatches we got in. But, no, journalists were generally respected.

Paul Stillwell: Would it be fair to say that the journalists, as a group, were better educated than their counterparts in deck and engineering?

Captain Hetu: Oh, yes, I think so, or educated in a different way. I mean, generally a lot of them had college training. A lot of the journalists that I met along the way were only in for a temporary stay, particularly during the draft years. They wanted to be in the Navy instead of the Army, and had college educations and were bright kids who went back out and did all sorts of interesting things. Better educated—that doesn't necessarily mean they were better people, but they were . . .

Paul Stillwell: Well, it was a different field, certainly, because, say, a boatswain's mate gets a lot of hands-on training, which is very useful.

Captain Hetu: Yes. Well, you know, we had probably more in common, I suppose. We were both specialists in a sense, being in public information. We were sort of a breed unto ourselves as well, so the journalists were in the same sort of kettle of fish. So we had a camaraderie, I suppose, that you don't necessarily have. I suppose in aviation you might have something like that, where the pilots and the crew members are much in the same sort of business. Medical Corps—I was a hospital corpsman, and hospital corpsmen and nurses and doctors were—not so much doctors, but I remember as an enlisted corpsman, we were very close with the nurses, in the best sense, because we did all their work for one thing.

Paul Stillwell: Well, another thing is that the journalists used more journalistic-type prose, as opposed to the stilted prose that the Navy has seemed wedded to for so long.

Captain Hetu: Yes. Yes. Yes. Well, as I say, when the frustrations came and bubbled out and you had to talk to somebody, you talked to your journalists. I remember at ServPac, I had a chief of staff who was a guy that read everything with a pencil in his hand. He was the kind of guy who would change your adjectives in a memorandum. I'd send him a memorandum about something, okay, to the chief of staff, wanting him to do something or go my way or whatever, and I'd get it back, and it would be edited. And I'd say, "For God's sake, this is madness. I wrote it to you. Why are you sending it back edited. I didn't mean aqua, I meant green."

Paul Stillwell: Who was he?

Captain Hetu: I think his name was Steere; that seems appropriate.[*] I think that was his name.

Paul Stillwell: Well, there was a Dick Steere who had been a fencer at the Naval Academy, I think, in the early '30s.

---

[*] Captain Richard C. Steere, USN

Captain Hetu: Richard, yes. Okay, I think that's the guy. Nice enough guy, but he was just nitpicker, perfect chief of staff.

Paul Stillwell: He once showed me a bronze medal, I think he got it at the 1932 Olympics.

Captain Hetu: Would he have been a captain in '57, '58?

Paul Stillwell: Yes.

Captain Hetu: That would about right, 30 years, I suppose. You know, I think that was the guy. With apologies, I didn't know he could fence, or I wouldn't have been so smart with him.

Paul Stillwell: How much of your work was in the print media, as opposed to electronic, in that era?

Captain Hetu: Oh, electronic was almost nonexistent. I mean, we did that radio show across the street at CinCPacFlt, but as far as making news, TV kind of wasn't around. Well, it was, but not very prominent, and it was all film in those days, of course. I don't even remember us ever doing a news release on film. You just didn't do it. Occasionally you would get a cameraman that would want to aboard the ships and film things. But that just wasn't part of our worry in those days, films. Newsreel was the big thing, you know.

Paul Stillwell: And the newsreels probably weren't too likely to be interested in service force ships.

Captain Hetu: No, not unless we got in trouble, and they didn't very often—a collision occasionally, small collisions or something. But a good training ground. I enjoyed it. I went away from there happy, learned a lot.

Paul Stillwell: And then you went back to Hollywood. Was this in any way a result of your work on the movies earlier?

Captain Hetu: I think that helped. I don't think I got orders, but I was told that I was going to the journalist school and be an instructor and I'm afraid Great Lakes didn't appeal to me. My recollection of Great Lakes was from boot camp and corps school, and all I could remember was that it was cold, and it was a long way from anywhere. I guess my feelings of having gone to corps school there gave me my impression of service schools, rightly or wrongly.

So when they said I was going to be an instructor at the journalist school, I conjured up—the immediate picture in my mind was standing inside. I thought, "Well, at least I'll be able to stand inside and drink coffee in the morning when they have to muster in the cold and rain like I used to." Really, my instant thought in my head was standing inside a dark building on a dark morning drinking coffee, and I thought, "Is that what I really want to do for two years?" You know, that was the wrong impression, but I petitioned, asked for Pickett's help.

Paul Stillwell: Who did the detailing?

Captain Hetu: I don't remember who it was in those days, whether Chinfo--I guess Chinfo. I was a 1650 by then, and I was a lieutenant. I don't recall who the detailer was.

Paul Stillwell: But, I mean, Chinfo would make recommendations to BuPers for orders?

Captain Hetu: Oh, yes, yes, yes. That was pretty well driven by Chinfo. They were the ones that moved us around. There weren't that many of us then, I don't believe. So, anyway, I made a plea to go anywhere else. Hollywood was not something I was after. I didn't even realize it was a billet. I wanted to go somewhere more operational or, I don't know, wanted to stay in the Navy. Anyway, my orders were changed, and they sent me to Hollywood, which was a whole different world.

Paul Stillwell: Well, please tell me about it.

Captain Hetu: A whole different world, boy, oh, boy. One of the great fun jobs—well, they were all fun. I don't know how I can rank one above the other. First thing we had to do was find a house to live in. I had three children at that stage, and Peggy was not yet pregnant, but soon to become pregnant again. Peggy, being my first wife. We found a house we lived at in Monterey Park. The office was in Hollywood on the corner of Sunset and Gower, which is a block over from Sunset and Vine.

We were across the street from Columbia Studios. Upstairs was an old shoe store, and we had the balcony. Down below us was the Air Force and I guess part of the Army, because we could look over and see who they were talking to down there. The Air Force was down there. All good people, and upstairs, I think, a couple floors up was the Army public affairs office, run by a guy named Chestnut, and Colonel Hess was the Air Force guy then. He was the sort of famous Air Force pilot who got religion in Korea and, I don't remember his whole story, but he was sort of a persona unto himself.

Paul Stillwell: Didn't Rock Hudson play him in some kind of movie?*

Captain Hetu: Yes. It was something where he got religion in one of his missions over Korea and then—he bombed an orphanage or something by mistake and then went back and built orphanages. Dean Hess, I think was his name. A nice guy, interesting guy.

Chestnut, the colonel upstairs—I shouldn't go into all this trivia, I guess, was the guy who had been the head of the Army magazine and book branch when I had been in the Navy and he's the one that really helped me a lot back in the Pentagon. I got back to California, and there he was, running the Army office upstairs. I liked him a lot; he was really a nice, terrific guy.

---

* Actor Rock Hudson portrayed Colonel Dean Hess in the 1957 movie Battle Hymn. It was the story of a World War II pilot who became a minister to atone for having bombed a German orphanage in World War II. He returned to the service for the Korean War and aided a Korean orphanage. The movie was based on Hess's book Battle Hymn, published in 1957 by McGraw-Hill.

We were called the Navy Unit Armed Forces Information Office Hollywood. We were really assigned to the naval district in San Diego, but we were in independent duty in Hollywood. My boss was Junior Coghlan who had been one of the original little rascals in Hollywood.* He was a child actor, and he became a naval aviator and never went beyond lieutenant commander, but Frank was a nice, gentle soul. He's still alive. I saw Frank at our public affairs reunion last year. I guess Frank's got to be 80, at least. In fact, he just wrote a book called They Still Call me Junior. That was his nickname, Junior Coghlan. Anyway, he was a fun guy to be around.

Well, I worked for Joe Williams too. Joe Williams was there when I first got there, and then Joe left and Junior Coghlan took over for Joe.† Joe Williams was the OinC when I went there.‡ My first experience with driving freeways, and this was 1959, and I lived pretty far away. We were on the other side, where we could find a house that could take three and a half kids on a lieutenant's salary in Los Angeles.

In any case, to get away from all that. The fun of the job was that the Navy uniform in Hollywood was then—this was before Vietnam got going, and when you went around Hollywood in the Navy uniform, you were highly respected. People really looked at it with pleasure. So I learned very early on that you could go around studios and sell stories, just knock on the door, and we did. I mean, literally knock on the door, or just call and say, "I'm the Navy officer, I'd like to come over and see your production head, or whoever it is."

And they'd say, "Okay, come on over."

Paul Stillwell: What were some of the stories you remember?

Captain Hetu: Well, we went to some of the most unusual shows and sold stories. Well, I did a "Perry Mason," for instance.§ You remember the "Perry Mason" series?

---

* Lieutenant Commander Francis E. Coghlan, Jr., USNR. He was born 15 March 1916 and appeared in dozens of movies from the 1920s to the 1940s. In the 1950s he was adviser on two television series, "Navy Log" and "Victory at Sea."
† Lieutenant Commander Joseph N. Williams, USN.
‡ OinC—officer in charge.
§ The "Perry Mason" series ran on CBS from 1957 to 1966; Raymond Burr played the title character, a defense lawyer with a talent for defending accused murders.

Paul Stillwell: Yes.

Captain Hetu: We went over there and sat down, and they said, "Well, what do you think we can do?"

And we'd sit down with the story people and say, "Well, we've got things to offer you. We can take you down to Long Beach. We have a submarine down there, and we have ships and good location stuff, which is only 30 minutes away." That was always a grabber because they were always looking for cheap locations and something different. Yes, we did the "Case of the Slandered Submarine."

Paul Stillwell: Do you remember any of the details of the plot?

Captain Hetu: Oh, yes. The skipper of the submarine is murdered, which the Navy sort of hiccupped when I sent this script in. [Laughter] But it turned out that, of course, he was the good guy, and his brother-in-law was a contractor and, I guess it was the brother-in-law that turned out to be the bad guy who actually had killed the skipper. They killed him by putting poison in the ventilating system or something.

But, of course, the highlight of the Perry Mason shows were always the trial, not so much the crime. So they had a court-martial, and that was where we came in, not only getting them down to Long Beach to get the background and so forth, but we helped them with the court-martial to make sure it was legal, that it was accurate and got a legal officer up from the naval district in San Diego to help us out, because, you know, you could have a civilian defense attorney and so forth. And I was on the court-martial. Clark Gammell was the other lieutenant in the office, and there were three of us among the six people on the court, so we got our faces in the show.[*] I have a picture of that somewhere.

Paul Stillwell: Did you wear you own uniforms?

---

[*] Lieutenant Clark M. Gammell, USN, was a public affairs specialist.

Captain Hetu: Oh, yes. And the guy that was the director for this particular segment was a guy named Art Marks, who had been a Navy journalist. I didn't know him in the Navy, but he became aware very quickly that Clark and I were public information officers, and so he started giving us a bad time, in very good—you know, we had a lot of fun with him. I used to tell Art, "You're never going to catch the nose pick." I said, "I'm going to get one in in one scene, and you'll never catch me until you're ready to put it on the air."

And we had a lot of fun. He used to catch me doing things. I remember I sat at the end of the table, so I got a lot of, at least, profile and trying to look like I was interested, I kept tapping a pencil on the table. And Art, I remember, one day cut it and said, "Herb, for God's sake, will you stop tapping that pencil. The only thing I can see through the viewfinder is that pencil going up and down. I can't see Perry Mason or anybody else." Anyway, we had a good time, the show turned out well, and the Navy was pleased.

We went to a show called "The Real McCoys," I don't know if you remember that; it's an old show with Walter Brennan and Dick Crenna, and we went there. The same way, we walked in and said, "We're from the Navy." Now, how would you take a hillbilly show and do a good Navy show, I mean, something that would put the Navy in a good light? That, after all, was our objective. Well, we sat down with the writers, and we came up with a story. The show was about Grandpa and Dick Crenna, who played the grandson, sitting the cabin or wherever they were, and Crenna said, "Look at this." He said, "There's a story in the paper here that says that there's a USS <u>McCoy</u>, and they're going to scrap it. It's an old ship."

And Grandpa said, "My God, that's named after my grandfather from the Civil War McCoys. They're going to what? They're going to scrap it?"

"Yes, they're going to cut it up and throw it away."

"Well, let's get in our car and get up there. Where are they going to do this, Long Beach? Let's get going." So the family hikes up to Long Beach, and the story is that they decide they're going to stop the Navy from cutting the ship up. Grandpa gets on the ship with a fire hose and won't let the workmen on and the things that go on. So how do you get out of this? How do you make the Navy come out of this looking good?

After all this comic relief, the last sequence of shots showed the commissioning of a new destroyer, and we got the bunting on the set and so forth. And the daughter-in-law played by—she's still around, I can't remember her name. She and Walter Brennan didn't speak to each other. Things you learn: they didn't like each other at all. Anyway, she's the sponsor for the new USS McCoy. So the big, beautiful ship goes down the waves, and Grandpa and everybody is waving their hats. Says a couple nice things about how great the Navy is, dah, dah, dah, dah. That's the end of the story.

But it was fun. It was probably a little frivolous, I suppose. Some people would think it was a waste of time, but the McCoys then had a good big audience; they were one of the top shows. We said something about the Navy to those people and that's what we were trying to do.

Oh, we worked with a lot of the typical shows. "McHale's Navy" was on then, which got informal cooperation. The Navy wasn't all that excited by McHale's scripts sometimes, because they always made fun of the captain and so forth. And we always thought they were hilarious. "McHale's Navy" probably did more for Navy recruiting than anything before Top Gun.[*]

They had another show called "Hennessey" then, which was about a Navy doctor. Jackie Cooper was the doctor, and we had very informal cooperation with them. I used to go over on the sets, because I had been a corpsman—this is then my medical background—but just to help them make sure the uniforms were correct. And we let the people from the show go down to Long Beach—I guess it was two days every year, and they would just shoot everything in sight, for stock footage. You know, ships, anything, cars going by with Navy on them, anything they could, so they'd build up a film library for the year and then go back to the studio and use all the stuff for the year.

Paul Stillwell: Cooper was a Naval reservist.

Captain Hetu: Navy reserve, yes. Nice guy, very good guy, and he was really helpful when we wanted things done. I did--I was only there about a year, I guess. But every year they had a big Navy Relief show/day down at the Navy base in San Diego to raise

---

[*] Top Gun was a 1986 film in which Tom Cruise portrayed a Navy fighter pilot.

money for Navy Relief. We always loaded up a planeload of stars and took them down. Jackie Cooper always went and Glenn Ford. You know, Glenn Ford was a reserve captain. And we would get a bunch of starlets. Angie Dickinson went the year I was there. In fact, I took Angie; I was her escort, and she didn't like to fly. She and her mother didn't like to fly at all, and we were going to drive them down, and then at the last minute they decided to fly. We got a reserve airplane to fly us down and took all the stars that we had that year.

We got a stuntman; I don't remember his name. We took him just as sort of a nice, good guy, and somebody, I guess it was Glenn Ford, or somebody that maybe suggested that we take this guy, and he had a shtick. Of course, when the plane would arrive the admiral would come, and all the people would meet the plane and so forth. This guy stepped off in a Navy uniform; I think he wore an admiral's uniform or something. He waved to the crowd and fell down the steps. You know, did a pratfall. [Laughter]

Paul Stillwell: Just rolled down.

Captain Hetu: And rolled down the steps. And, of course, nobody knew this was going to happen, and it really was hilarious and probably gave everybody a heart attack. And the admiral said, "Oh, my God, my career. You know, here I've got this star walking out of this plane and falls down the steps."

Paul Stillwell: Did you work on any feature films?

Captain Hetu: Yes, I worked on Wackiest Ship in the Army.* Remember with Jack Lemmon and Ricky Nelson. There was a bar around the corner from our office where we went fairly often in the evening after work, an attitude-adjustment hour, and a lot of secondary stars went in there. A lot of fun guys. Frank Gerstall, who is somebody you probably never heard of, but you'd know him if you saw him. He worked in a lot of gangster movies and he always had white, close-cropped hair. He used to call me

---

* Wackiest Ship in the Army was released in 1960.

"Hehetu" because when he came in the office to see me, my desk plate said, H.E. H-E-T-U, so he called me "Hehetu."

And Frank was there, and I remember Peter Lorre used to come in, people like that. I mean, they were just great fun, and I got to go over there. Anyway, after one of the shoots on Wackiest Ship we had drinks and dinner with Jack Lemmon and his wife, Felicia Farr, because I remember it was summertime, hot. I was in khakis and, I guess Joe Williams, maybe, was the other part of the foursome. We were there, and Felicia was about ten months pregnant—very large, very pretty, but very pregnant. I had ordered a Manhattan straight up. You know, it was the end of day. Man, I was looking forward to this Manhattan. She reached over to say something to me and knocked the Manhattan over right into my lap, I mean, you know—

Paul Stillwell: There was a lot of it.

Captain Hetu: A lot of Manhattan and right into my khakis, and it ran right down the front of my coat into my, you know, groin, and I tried not to jump up because here's this poor woman. She was embarrassed to death, and she was about two tons large. Anyway, I don't know why that's an interesting story, but I remember I just tried to stand up very carefully and wipe all this sticky goo and get the cherries out of my crotch and not embarrass this woman. [Laughter]

Paul Stillwell: What do you remember about Lemmon and his personality?

Captain Hetu: Oh, he was a delightful guy, very, very nice fellow. And, you know, most of them were when you met them close up. I don't remember running into anybody that wasn't nice. And they treated us well because we were in the Navy. It was a good time to be in the Navy. People liked you if you were in the Navy.

On the "Real McCoys" show, the grandson was Dick Crenna, and Crenna's gone on to be a fairly substantial star, but he started off in the early days on "Our Miss Brooks" as Walter, one of the students. And Dick was a good, super nice guy in those days. He taught me to drink Black Russians.

Paul Stillwell: He was later the skipper in The Sand Pebbles, which is a great Navy movie.*

Captain Hetu: That's right, exactly right.

Paul Stillwell: And Jack Lemmon had played Ensign Pulver in Mister Roberts, which is also a classic.†

Captain Hetu: Oh, boy, my favorite show, yes. I can't remember any other features in those days. I was only there about a year, but I got an awful lot done in a year, it seems like, met a lot of people.

Paul Stillwell: Were there any situations in which outsiders were proposing the ideas and the Navy had to vet them in terms of accuracy or content and tone?

Captain Hetu: Yes, yes. Wackiest Ship in the Army was not our idea; that was something that came out of a book, I think. And that was a tough one to get cooperation, because if you remember story, it was an old sort of schooner, sailing ship that they took over and made into sort of a coastal raider or something. It was kind of a semi-comedy about this ship. The Navy wasn't all that excited about it, but the Navy came out of it okay. The people looked good, and Ricky Nelson was hot then; he was the Tom Cruise of 1960. And Lemmon was a solid character. I mean, they didn't do anything to make the Navy look terribly foolish.

---

* The Sand Pebbles was a popular 1966 motion picture starring Steve McQueen, Candice Bergen, Richard Attenborough, and Richard Crenna. It was based on Richard McKenna's novel of the same name, published in 1962 by Harper & Row. McKenna served in the U.S. Asiatic Fleet shortly before World War II, including two years on board the gunboat USS Luzon (PR-7).
† Mister Roberts was a book of fictional stories written by Thomas Heggen on the basis of his World War II experiences as a Naval Reserve officer. Published in 1946, it depicted life on board an imaginary cargo ship in which the officers and crew flouted rules and regulations. It was later made into a successful stage play and movie, both starring Henry Fonda. Lemmon was in the movie version.

Paul Stillwell: Well, sometimes you hear about these cases that in return for cooperation from the Navy, then the producer tones down the script or whatever it is.

Captain Hetu: Oh, yes. They had to in many cases, yes. I later worked on <u>In Harm's Way</u> with Otto Preminger, got to know Otto fairly well.* Well, in many instances, like <u>In Harm's Way</u>, they had to have the Navy's cooperation, or they almost couldn't make the film. Now, they do them without the Navy, I think and they're able to do all sorts of things with animation and video animation and so forth. In those days they couldn't do that and make it look real; they had to go to sea.

Paul Stillwell: Well, one question about an earlier tour, what was your family life like in Hawaii? I can imagine that would have been quite enjoyable.

Captain Hetu: Yes. Oh, yes. Family life in Hawaii was terrific. We lived in Navy housing when we first went there, NHA-1, where a bunch of us lived. I mean, a bunch of PAOs lived there. Ken Wade lived up the street from us.† Ken just died here about a year ago. But we got out of Navy housing. I guess we lived there maybe a year and then found a house. They let you get civilian housing if you could and gave you an allowance. Some places where they have Navy housing allowance, they'd let you live elsewhere, but you'd lose your housing allowance.‡

We found a really nifty house up in Halawa Heights, which was right below Camp Smith, the Fleet Marine Force headquarters.§ In fact, their fence was my backyard fence, and we had an absolutely glorious view. From our living room and little dining room we could see literally from Diamond Head all the way to a panoramic view below us of Pearl Harbor, Ford Island, and it was just beautiful. Not a big house, but terrific. The kids loved it. I can remember cutting the grass there, and it took me forever, because

---

* <u>In Harm's Way</u>, released in 1965, was a sprawling fictional epic about the Navy in World War II. It starred John Wayne, Kirk Douglas, and Patricia Neal, among others.
† Lieutenant Commander Kenneth W. Wade, USN.
‡ Presumably what Captain Hetu meant here was that Navy families could get a housing allowance only if no Navy housing was available for them.
§ Camp H. M. Smith, home of the headquarters of the Commander in Chief, U. S. Pacific Command and the Commanding General of Marine Forces Pacific, is located on Oahu's Halawa Heights, at an elevation of about 600 feet above Pearl Harbor, near the community of Aiea.

every time I'd get to end of a swath, I'd stand there and look at the view, and I can still remember it. We had pikake trees in our front yard, and we had banana trees, and mango trees, fruit-bearing trees. Oh, it was great.

We lived next door to a Japanese fisherman, Jimmy Omani, and Jimmy's mother, who lived with them, did not speak English, Ba-Ban. Boy, you brought back a lot of memories there. Jimmy had fought with the Army in Italy; he was one of the Nisei people—great, wonderful family, really.* We got very close with them. In fact, with all our neighbors, we got very close up there. They were really nice people. We were the only Navy people in the area, and Jimmy used to take me out occasionally on his fishing—he had two fishing boats, one on each side of the island. They weren't covered boats, but they were big flat boats. And he was a trap fisherman, built these big chicken wire traps and he had a trap line. I'd go out and help him reel them up by hand, ratchet up the traps and empty them into a big—the center of his boat was a big cooling vat.

A great guy. We worked a lot together, did a lot of things together. He taught me how to build the traps, and I remember we built a great big sandbox. He had little kids and we had little kids and built a big sandbox. His Grandma used to baby-sit our kids; his mother from Japan, and she didn't speak English, but our kids just loved her to death, she was so sweet. Taught us how to cook rice the right way. Yes, Jimmy used to bring over Longustos to us when he'd have them left over and a very pleasant time.

Paul Stillwell: What were some of the family activities together there?

Captain Hetu: A lot of beach. We never got island fever. We heard a lot of people talk, "Oh, boy, you're here a year, and you're going to think you're in a prison, you know, that you're on the island." We never got that feeling, there was so much to do. We drove around a lot, and we saw every inch of the island. We had a old red Ford station wagon and loaded the kids up, and you could drive anywhere—this was 1956, 1957. I guess they thought it was crowded then, but this was a long time ago. There were no high rises on Waikiki. The only high rise was the Royal Hawaiian. That was the biggest hotel

---

* The Nisei were sons and daughters of Japanese immigrants. They were American citizens by virtue of being born in the United States, and in many instances their parents had become naturalized.

The Hawaiian Village was a village—I mean, huts, nice huts, but huts nonetheless. They didn't have a high rise. We drove all over the island and saw things, and we spent a lot of time on Sunday down at the beach, loved the beach. Our kids liked the beach, plenty of beaches there, pretty beaches.

Paul Stillwell: Last year I watched <u>From Here to Eternity</u> for the first time in many years, and I was struck by how bare Waikiki Beach was.*

Captain Hetu: Yes, I saw that. I watched that again, I don't know if that's the same time, but it was just on about two weeks ago, on Sunday afternoon or something.

Paul Stillwell: Well, I saw it last year, and you saw the Royal Hawaiian and the Moana and maybe one other and that's it.

Captain Hetu: That was it. That's what it was. Driving was Kamehameha Boulevard, and there were no freeways or anything. That was as close to a freeway as you could get. Well, I loved Hawaii. I would have loved to have lived there. I almost got out of the Navy there. Pan American sort of offered me a job. They were going to set up a station on either Guam or Wake, and they wanted a PR person to go out there, why, I don't know, but I guess to handle the passengers on layovers and stuff. I knew a guy from Pan Am, I can't remember his name now, but he made a run at me, and I thought about it but not very long.

I had three kids, I was then a lieutenant, and I had a lot of time invested. It was tempting, but not real tempting. A good place to be, a lot of camaraderie with the rest of PAOs, because it was one of the few times in my life that I was anyplace except Chinfo where we had a lot of public affairs officers, Navy, so we had sort of a nice group. Pickett Lumpkin and Ken Wade and Dick Phillips.† Dick Phillips, I guess, was the guy I

---

* <u>From Here to Eternity</u> was an Oscar-winning movie released in 1953, starring Burt Lancaster, Deborah Kerr, Frank Sinatra, Montgomery Clift, Donna Reed, and Ernest Borgnine. Based on a novel by James Jones, it depicted social situations of Army personnel based in Hawaii in late 1941.
† Lieutenant Commander Richard B. Phillips, USN.

relieved at ServPac. We did a lot of stuff together, parties—it was a fun time. Pickett and I played tennis, a lot of tennis.

Paul Stillwell: Any specifics on Ken Wade. I know he had a role in preparing Admiral Raborn to testify on the Polaris hearings.[*]

Captain Hetu: Ken was probably my other mentor. I liked Ken very much, and we became even closer friends after retirement, and I did his ceremony, his ...

Paul Stillwell: Funeral?

Captain Hetu: Yes. Well, he didn't have a funeral, but we had a—Ken donated his body to the Armed Forces Medical College. We did a memorial for him at the Navy Memorial, and I was sort of the master of ceremonies. I did his wife the year before. I said, "I'm getting a bad reputation here."

People say, "Hey, you do great funerals.

I said, "No thanks. I'd rather not." I did Pickett's too.

Paul Stillwell: What were some of the things you learned from Ken Wade?

Captain Hetu: Oh, Ken was a gentleman. Ken was a very smart guy. I learned some of the same things from him that I learned from Pickett, and that was just relax and do things well, and right will come out in the end. Ken was a hard-working guy, never complained about anything. I don't believe I ever saw him get mad—probably did, but I can't remember him being mad. Maybe frustrated.

He's the one that got me selected to be the CNO's public affairs officer. That's another story, I guess, down the line here. Then I can tell you story about Puerto Rico and him. I got selected for commander, which was unheard of in Puerto Rico; nobody

---

[*] Rear Admiral William F. Raborn, Jr., USN, was director of the Special Projects Office, which developed the Polaris submarine-launched ballistic missile system. He held the post from 1955 to 1962, being promoted to vice admiral in 1960. His Polaris oral history is in the Naval Institute collection.

got promoted in Puerto Rico, let alone early. But that's another story I can tell you when I get to Puerto Rico.

Paul Stillwell: Well, in my brief dealings with him, he struck me as a really straight shooter.*

Captain Hetu: Oh, Ken, yes. The press loved Ken; they respected him. That's why I think he was one of the reasons, in addition to his competence, that he was so successful at the Polaris program. He spent a lot of years there, you know, right from inception of the Polaris to getting it on the submarines. He was highly regarded in our specialty for that reason. I think the Navy, too, but Raborn got the Navy's plaudits for that and Ken got certainly our plaudits in the public affairs business. He did a marvelous job. Not an easy job. That was a tough sell, until it worked, and then everybody—you know, they say success has many fathers.

Paul Stillwell: Right.

Captain Hetu: But it wasn't always so. A good fellow, Ken.

Paul Stillwell: Anything else you mention about the Hollywood tour before you move on to Washington?

Captain Hetu: No, I could probably think of other things. It sort of stands out in my memory as one of the more surreal years of my life because it was all make-believe. That's what Hollywood is, it's all make-believe. And that was what the fun was about going around with these people. They are people who deal in fantasy, and I learned pretty early on that you could go into these people and say, "I'm an idea man."

And they'd say, "Terrific. We don't have to pay you. We'll listen to you for an hour and see if you've got anything to sell. At this price we can afford to listen to you."

---

* In 1970, when Wade was a captain, he served as Deputy Chief of Information in the Pentagon. He was quite helpful to the interviewer, then doing research for a master's degree in journalism.

And you could sell people. I learned, I guess, through my earlier experiences with South Pacific and Enemy Below that nothing was impossible to these people. You could come up with an outlandish idea or something, and they'd make it happen. I guess this was my first real exposure or appreciation for brainstorming. I mean, you could just sit down and talk about anything a la the "Real McCoys" and so forth. And they'd say, "Hey, great, we can do that. We'll do it." What fun.

Paul Stillwell: Masters of illusion.

Captain Hetu: But what fun for a public affairs guy to just go and sell ideas. It was terrific. I loved it.

Paul Stillwell: You had a receptive audience.

Captain Hetu: Yes, yes, and nobody ever turned you away. They'd always hear what you had to say. I'll probably think of ten other things we did after you leave.

Paul Stillwell: Well, make a note, please, and we can talk about those the next time. So then in 1961 you went to DoD in Washington. What was your role there?

Captain Hetu: I was the assistant on the Navy press desk. Pickett Lumpkin was the Navy press officer. Pickett was still the commander, and they had a billet open up, and I guess he requested me, because I had only been in Hollywood just about a year, 13 months, much to my wife's chagrin. In fact, we'd just had our fourth baby in Hollywood. Actually the baby was born at St. Luke's Hospital in Pasadena, probably one of the first people to use non-military medicine.

So when I came home and said "We're going to Washington," which was about as far as you could go in the other direction, why—well, she was terrific.

I should tell you, I don't know that it's of interest for this. But Jack MacKercher was a contemporary Navy man.[*] Jack and I were in the same year group, and we had

---

[*] Lieutenant John C. MacKercher, USN, a public affairs specialist.

been friends throughout our Navy career. Jack was later Moorer's public affairs officer, when he was CNO and Chairman.* Anyhow, Jack and I were then lieutenants, and we got orders at the same time to go east. Jack was at the Com 11, the 11th Naval District, and he got orders to go to ServLant. And so we decided to drive across country together, in one of the famous trips in public information lore, which I can't go into great detail about.

Paul Stillwell: Well, give me a few hints, please.

Captain Hetu: Well, his family was going to Michigan, where he, his wife and his folks were from, and he had five kids. I'm trying to remember, we had kids about the same age. He had four boys and one girl; I had four girls and one boy. We always talked about a Chinese arrangement someday, marry them all off and have one big wedding, didn't happen.

Anyway, Jack and I were leaving at the same time, and so one of my favorite stories about Jack, and I hope that I won't offend him, but, I mean, I tell this story any time we have a few pops and some of the boys together. I went down to San Diego. As it turned out, I moved out of the house. We stayed and put my wife, who had just had a baby in October, and this was December, on a plane with the other three kids. This was our fourth child. We drove to San Diego and spent New Year's Eve with MacKercher. MacKercher's family had driven off to Michigan, and so Jack and I were then going to leave, the day after the first or second of January and start our own trek from there to the East Coast in my station wagon.

And New Year's Eve together with Jack MacKercher at the Old Mexican Village, which is kind of a fear, and we had quite an evening. But, anyway, the next day, I think, it was a holiday, of course, and then we were supposed to leave the next day. I was staying in a BOQ, and Jack came back and said, "Well, I'm not going."†

---

* Admiral Thomas H. Moorer, USN, served as Chief of Naval Operations from 1 August 1967 to 1 July 1970. He was later Chairman of the Joint Chiefs of Staff from 3 July 1970 to 30 June 1974. His oral history is in the Naval Institute collection.
† BOQ—bachelor officers' quarters.

I said, "What? What do you mean, you're not going. I've been sitting here for three days, I could have been in Ohio by now."

He said, "No. You know these people, they won't pass my quarters. They said that the oven's dirty and some other stuff." And, of course, he had four active boys and he said they—oh, I know what it was. It was a broken door; that was it. This was the broken-door story. There was a hole in the bedroom door, and he maintained that the wind blew the door against the wall or something. They wouldn't buy that, and they were going to make him pay for the door. He wouldn't pay for the door, and he was going to resign his commission. Jack was a very principled guy, and you didn't step on Jack's honor for anything. And he went all the way to admiral, to the commandant, and this took about three days. I'm sitting there biting my nails saying, "Geez, I'm on leave here, pal, you know, travel time."

So Jack persisted, and they finally let him off about the door, said, okay, they would buy the door story. But then the captain who was the chief of staff for engineering, the big public works guy, inspected Jack's quarters and found everything else imaginable wrong, everything. I mean, he went through it with a fine-tooth comb and just stuck it to him something awful.

Paul Stillwell: Worse than the cost of a door, I presume.

Captain Hetu: Oh, the door, yes. God, he and I could have gone and hung a door for a lot less. I kept saying that, "Let's just buy him a door I'll pay half of the damn door, and let's get out of town. Let's get out of Dodge."

"No, sir, by God." Anyway they stuck him real good. I don't know, they just found everything wrong. The stove was dirty, the refrigerator needed cleaning. The bathroom was—I don't remember, he had a list of 25 things, and they really stuck it to Jack for a couple hundred dollars worth of repairs, and the door would have cost him, I don't know, $28.50 or something. But he kept his honor and off we went across country.

We had a lot of fun. We had no reservations anywhere. We just drove until we got tired and pulled into a motel. We had a bar in the back of the station wagon and opened up the back and opened up the trunk and we had a bar ready made to take into the room so we didn't have to spend money in the bar, although we usually did, but at least we got started. We had a hell of a time going across country. He was a nifty guy; he still is a nifty guy. He lives in Florida. Anyway, that's not a very interesting story, but it was fun.

Paul Stillwell: Well, you went into DoD then after having been in Navy environments. How was the office structured in the Pentagon?

Captain Hetu: We were in the Defense information division or section, which was Hershel—I'll think of his name, who headed it up, a civilian headed it up. Arthur Sylvester was the Assistant Secretary.

Paul Stillwell: The man who defended the right to lie in the public interest.

Captain Hetu: I was there the day he said that. And they had Army, Air Force, Navy press desks. We were right across the hall from—pretty much the same location where they are now, although it's a lot different, it's refined, they've built it up, it's quite nice. This looked like a newspaper city room. We had a desk around which we had a journalist. Pickett sat on one side, I sat on the other, and a secretary and a journalist--great, big—and took press queries and just dealt on a day-to-day basis with all the press people across the hall in the pressroom. Great job. It was a fascinating job. Always busy, always doing something, putting out blue-top releases.

The Kennedy Administration was in, and, at least to my knowledge, the Kennedy Administration people were the first ones that when any contracts were let, they wanted to see them first.[*] The White House would call the congressman to tell them that there was a contract in his district, and I remember this caused a great hullabaloo down in the engine room where we were saying, my "God, these people are putting it out before the release time." We used to put them out at a certain time of the day so they wouldn't affect the stock market and all that stuff. They didn't worry about such things.

---

[*] John F. Kennedy served as President of the United States from 20 January 1960 until he was assassinated on 22 November 1963.

Paul Stillwell: Politics reigned supreme.

Captain Hetu: Absolutely, it was an interesting time.

Paul Stillwell: Any impressions of Sylvester that you have?

Captain Hetu: Yes. I have a lot. One of the most interesting things I did when I was there was I was there during the Cuba Crisis—"Cuber Crisis," as we called it.[*] I was head of the Cuban press desk for—we had a 24-hour press desk and I had the watch from—they were odd hours.

[Interruption]

Paul Stillwell: Well, back to Sylvester, what kind of person was he?

Captain Hetu: Well, the Sylvester thing--interesting thing happened when I was on the press desk. The Cuba crisis came up—bingo, you know, overnight literally when Kennedy announced the embargo and so forth.[†]

Paul Stillwell: Well, according to this you were in Chinfo by that time.

Captain Hetu: Yes, I was upstairs in the audio-visual branch and Pickett brought me back down to take over this Cuba crisis desk, they called it.

Paul Stillwell: So you went back to OSD?[‡]

---

[*] With his Boston accent, Kennedy pronounced "Cuba" as if it had an R at the end.
[†] The Cuban Missile Crisis was triggered in mid-October 1962, when a U.S. reconnaissance plane photographed a Soviet nuclear missile site in Cuba and the presence of Soviet bombers. On 22 October President John F. Kennedy went on national television to announce a naval quarantine of Cuba, to be implemented on 24 October. On 28 October Premier Nikita Khrushchev of the Soviet Union notified President Kennedy that he was ordering the withdrawal of Soviet bombers and missiles from Cuba.
[‡] OSD—Office of the Secretary of Defense.

Captain Hetu: Just walked down one floor, just to be in charge of one of the three watches on the Cuba crisis desk temporarily. In other words, until the crisis was over and I'd go back upstairs, which I did.

So I had the afternoon watch, I had the 10:00 or 6:00 or something. We were oddly configured so that we would cover the two press briefings or something. I don't remember why, but it was an odd time. Good for me, because come in at 10:00 and leave at 6:00 and beat the traffic and be there for the most interesting part of the day.

The big problem then was censorship—early on, as soon as this all started—about what the press could print and couldn't print, what it could tell and couldn't tell. We really weren't ready for this, and so they decided to come up with sort of ten rules of engagement that DoD would come out with, which would be voluntary rules for the press to follow. And so a bunch of us sort of sat down and wrote up these rules. I'm sure Pickett was part of this.

Then we sent them down to the front office with a recommendation that these were the ten things we thought we probably ought to do. And I never heard about them again. I mean, they just sort of went into the great beyond. The next thing we knew, somebody called me over to the wire machine and said, "Look at AP." I went over and looked at AP, and here were our ten rules coming out of the wire. Sylvester had promulgated them; he just gave him out to his friends and so forth. We didn't really have a press briefing or anything, which really caught us flat-footed because the phone started to ring.

People in Florida, "I just saw this or saw that, can I print it, can I . . . ?" And we were trying to make a judgment with no training, I mean—

Paul Stillwell: No preparation.

Captain Hetu: No briefing. They didn't sit us all down in the room and say, "Now, here's the ten things and let's go over, spend an hour running over these, make sure everybody here knows what we're talking about and here's the kind of things you may get"—you know, a dry run. Never had a dry run; the phones just starting ringing. So for hours, we just sort of sat there, and I was, I guess, still a lieutenant making all these judgment calls on just what I thought. because the news guys didn't want to wait for, say, "I'll call you back."

"Hey, these are voluntary, I'm calling, asking you on a voluntary basis what should I do. You know, I'm not going to wait for you to call me back. I've got a deadline to go to. As far as I'm concerned, making the phone call, I've satisfied my obligation. If you don't want to tell me, good-bye."

Paul Stillwell: What was the thrust of these rules?

Captain Hetu: Oh, if they saw troop movements or ship movements, if they saw airplanes, missiles, being carried on carriers and along the roads, things of that nature, that they shouldn't report those. We didn't want to let the Cubans or the Russians know what we were up to and so forth, pretty nuts-and-boltsy things. I've probably got them someplace. I have a Cuba Missile Crisis folder in one of these boxes.

Paul Stillwell: You were asking the media to do this in the national interest.

Captain Hetu: Yes. We couldn't impose national or any sort of formal review. We didn't have the authority to do that; we couldn't do that.

Paul Stillwell: Would there be any sanctions for not following the voluntary rules?

Captain Hetu: No. Wouldn't talk to them or something, but we didn't have any sanctions, no. And it worked quite well after the first day, I must say. My recollection is the press bent over backwards not to go around the rules, but they were grateful to have these sort of general rules to follow. And calls sort of petered out, really, after the first day or first two days. They just sort of went away.

Paul Stillwell: How much awareness did you have of events before the public became aware of them?

Captain Hetu: Not much or very reactive. As I said, I was there the day Sylvester defended the government's right to lie.

Paul Stillwell: What was the context for that?

Captain Hetu: I remember he was standing on one of the desks. He used to come down and do a briefing every day. Arthur unfortunately will probably be remembered for that, and yet he was really a nice man, and he was respected by the press. He was one of them; I mean, he was a newspaperman by trade. He was standing on the desk, and I don't remember what the exact issue was, it was something that was sort of a no-comment kind of thing and they were trying to back him into the corner about, "Well, you've got to be lying to say you don't know this because we know you know and dah, dah, dah, dah." He finally said something, and I don't remember the exact quote, but something that in the time of crisis in the interests of national security it's perfectly all right for the government to lie.

Paul Stillwell: Was it something he sort of blurted out in frustration?

Captain Hetu: Yes. Oh, yes, he didn't come down to announce that policy. [Laughter] Yes, he got backed into a corner. You know, it's hard to make a judgment on that. I mean, nobody lies. You know, I've spent years at the CIA and so forth, and as a press person you don't lie.

Paul Stillwell: Well, there are certainly cover stories.

Captain Hetu: Or you just say, "I can't comment on that, and the reason I can't is because of national security." Sometimes that's kind of bad because that tells them what they want to know, but by refusing to confirm something you confirm it, so that's very hard sometimes. But lying—bad choice of words. I think what he really meant was that you don't always have to put out all the information. He didn't mean you don't tell the truth. He meant that there are occasions where you know something is happening because you're in the military, but you can't put it out because it's classified, you know, or an unfair advantage to the enemy, etc., etc., but that doesn't mean you lie about it. I'm sure that's what he meant, but that isn't what he said. Unfortunately it's what you say and not what you mean. That's why you have to be careful in this business.

Paul Stillwell: Well, that policy of neither confirm nor deny on the presence of nuclear weapons served the Navy well for a long period of time.

Captain Hetu: If you stick with it, if you never get away from that story. Yes, that's right, exactly right. After the Navy, I was at the CIA for four years as the public affairs director out there, and, of course, we had the same policy on identifying people, because we would just say, oh, "We can't confirm or deny." We never do, whether a person is really working for the CIA, because you could--if you said, yes, no, yes, no, I can't tell about that one, they could go through the phone book looking for it, if they had enough patience they could find out who all your people were.

So if you get a cover story like that and stick with it, you're okay. Once you start to go off the track, you get in trouble. It's a slippery slope.

Paul Stillwell: For example, if there's ten ships, and you say there are no nuclear weapons on nine, then the tenth one is probably it.

Captain Hetu: Yes, mostly, yes. That doesn't work.

Paul Stillwell: What is your memory of individual events and highlights of the Cuban Missile Crisis, viewed from your perspective?

Captain Hetu: Well, the Navy was sort of in the forefront, so we felt proud of that fact, that he had used a naval embargo, the classic use of sea power in a modern confrontational problem. That the President, who was, of course, Navy, chose to use that. There were a number of things, I suppose, he could have done, but he chose naval power to do it. So we were pleased, and we did a lot to try and spotlight that, "This is a classic use of the Navy. That's why we're in business and it's working."

Paul Stillwell: Well, it was essentially a blockade that, for political reasons, was not labeled a blockade.

Captain Hetu: Yes, that's right. There was no blockade, embargo.

Paul Stillwell: Quarantine.

Captain Hetu: Quarantine, quarantine, yes. There were two planes that went down to cover the ship bringing the missiles out. I think Dave Cooney was on one plane, and I was on the other one.[*] We took motion picture and still photographers and print media to overfly the Marucla, which was the Russian ship bringing the missiles out.[†]

Paul Stillwell: That the Joseph P. Kennedy went alongside.

Captain Hetu: That's right, and you remember the pictures. We were flying in P-3s that were not operational yet. They were Navy planes, but they were just coming on line, and they were the first two P-3s in service.[‡] And so we flew in these wonderful airplanes. God, they were brand new. They were beautiful airplanes and I remember that White, a photographer from Life magazine was on our plane. And these pilots were just showing off to beat the band, because they had all these media guys captive on this plane, to not only see the Russians but also to show them what this airplane could do.

We came in and overflew—the destroyer was behind, and we had radioed to the destroyer and told them we were coming and we wanted them to take the missile covers

---

[*] Lieutenant Commander David M. Cooney, USN. As a rear admiral, Cooney later served as the Navy's Chief of Information from February 1975 to August 1980.
[†] On 26 October 1962 the destroyers Joseph P. Kennedy, Jr. (DD-850) and John R. Pierce (DD-753) halted and boarded the Soviet-chartered, Lebanese-flag freighter Marucla. After the Americans inspected her cargo, she was permitted to continue to Havana, Cuba.
[‡] The Lockheed P-3 Orion (originally P3V) is a high-performance land-based patrol plane. It first entered operational squadrons in August 1962. The P-3C is 116 feet, 10 inches long; wingspan of 99 feet, 8 inches; gross weight of 135,000 pounds, and top speed of 473 miles per hour.

off the missiles. They had put canvas and wood covers or something over the missiles on the ship. They said, "Oh, my God, we just inspected them. They just put them back on; it took a long time to get them covered. They're not going to be happy."

Well, "They lost, too bad. You know, we've got to show the world that this really happened and you can't see them under the covers. I mean, we've got to see those missiles on the ship because . . . "

Paul Stillwell: This is your communicating with the Joseph P. Kennedy?

Captain Hetu: Yes, yes. I'm paraphrasing, but this is pretty much what was said, "Too bad, go up and tell them." Kennedy didn't mind; hell, they thought it was great. So they steamed up alongside the Marucla and told them to take the covers off again. There was a lot of waving of fists, and I don't know what was said.

Paul Stillwell: Anything more about that episode to convey?

Captain Hetu: No, except that I was up in the cockpit, I remember, and this guy from Life magazine sat in the copilot's seat and turned the seat around. Those seats had swivels, and it was a big cockpit on those planes. You could stand in them, and he turned all the way around and faced the side window of the cockpit and put his feet up on either side of the window and asked the pilot to do an almost 75-degree turn around the ship so he could shoot straight down. And the pilot did; he loved it.

Those planes were so maneuverable; you know, they were the ASW planes.[*] He put down his flaps, put down his wheels. He had those four big, powerful engines, and he did it. We just slowed down and flew around that ship and I thought, "Oh, my God, we're going to go in. How am I going to explain this—if I survive?"

But he did it, and then on the way home, the skipper said to me—I guess I was flying with the CO of this experimental squadron, and he said, "Okay, if we put on a little show for these guys?"

---

[*] ASW—antisubmarine warfare.

I said, "Hey, you're the pilot. You're in charge, pal. Whatever you want to do is okay with me." So he put on a nifty little flying show for them, and it was really fun. He told the Kennedy what he was going to do and we flew out, I don't know, 20 miles or something, and then he went down on the deck, looked like we were about to touch the top of the water. We weren't more than 50 feet off the water, and just put these things into the stops and we were flying, really moving. I don't know how fast those things could go.

We got, it seemed like, right up on top of those ships, and he gave it the old pull back the yoke and we just took off right over the Marucla. It looked like we were going to touch the tops of their masts. Obviously, we were a lot higher than that, I'm not a pilot so my judgment was—I got a pucker. Boy, do those planes fly. He gave them a show, all right, and they really saw what the P-3 could do. That was the first time that I know of that any media had ever flown in a P-3. So we got a doubly whammy out of that one.

Paul Stillwell: And it's interesting, the P-3 is still around more than three decades later.

Captain Hetu: Still around. It's a good airplane. Anyhow, that's the end of my Cuba story.

Paul Stillwell: Did you share the collective sense of relief that the rest of the country had with the resolution of the crisis?

Captain Hetu: Oh, yes. And probably a lot of pride. I suppose Americans had pride in what happened, the fact that we won, and Kennedy had the courage to face these people down. We in the Navy were doubly proud, because it was pretty much a Navy operation. Remember the first planes that went over Navy photo planes that got the pictures of the missiles. Yes, interesting time.

Paul Stillwell: What was disturbing was to read in 1992, on the 30th anniversary, that the Cubans had contingency plans to launch tactical nuclear weapons against the United States if Cuba was invaded.

Captain Hetu: Yes. Oh, boy, you don't know how close you come, do you?

Paul Stillwell: You're right. Well, a year earlier was the fiasco at the Bay of Pigs.* What are your recollections of that?

Captain Hetu: Not much. Sort of a feeling of incredulity that this was allowed to happen, that we were so ill prepared. I was in the Navy, of course, and not CIA, but just the fact that it was so poorly planned. I remember some folks saying, "Why in the hell didn't we let those guys go in there and go 100 yards inland and plant a flag and declare the revolutionary government or the democratic government of Cuba and then back them up?" Because I think the feeling we had, and I guess the whole country, was that we really dumped on those guys, put them in there and then turned our back on them. And if you had enough courage to do it, we should have followed up.

Paul Stillwell: Well, probably there was an unrealistic expectation also about the popular uprising that was supposed to result.

Captain Hetu: Yes, they went during siesta hour or something, because nobody rose up to help them. And we sure didn't; we let them just get beat up on the beaches, terrible feeling. That was kind of an opposite feeling of the blockade working—embargo—terrible feeling, yes.

Paul Stillwell: What was the turf division between OSD and Navy Office of Information?

Captain Hetu: Well, I was there with Pickett, who was sort of a person that ran things unto himself, and I'm sure I said before the lesson I learned from Pickett. Pickett always

---

* In mid-April 1961 a force of 1,400 Cuban exiles, secretly trained by U.S. personnel in Guatemala, landed in the Bay of Pigs, on the southwestern coast of Cuba, in an attempt to overthrow Fidel Castro, that nation's Communist dictator. The invasion attempt was a disaster. President John Kennedy decided that U.S. naval intervention would worsen the situation, so ships and aircraft offshore were prohibited from taking part.

learned to work within the system and turned the system around to his benefit. He didn't curse the darkness; he lit a candle.

Paul Stillwell: What would be an example of that?

Captain Hetu: Well, you know, Pickett was highly respected by the news media down there. And Pickett could do things for the Navy in the newsroom that the Navy couldn't do it for itself. I mean, he could background people and brief them, which he did all the time. And Pickett never forgot that he was a naval officer. I mean, none of us did, but there was no purple suit in Pickett.[*] But Pickett used the fact that he was down in DoD, and he was ten feet away from the newsroom across the hall, to the great benefit of the Navy. Some people didn't take advantage of that, and Pickett did. Pickett stayed in very close touch with his friends up in the Navy Department, didn't get sucked into the DoD milieu. He never forgot that he was a naval officer and stayed in very close touch with Jim Jenkins up in the Secretary's office and the people up in CNO and Chinfo.[†] He made daily walk-arounds up to Chinfo, let them know. I think, over the years, that wasn't always the case. Some people in DoD forgot their beginnings, worried too much about the DoD position on things.

Paul Stillwell: Well, you need to strike an appropriate balance between parochialism and the joint interests.

Captain Hetu: Yes, yes. And Pickett was smart enough to know when he had to get something cleared down below. The people down there and the front office liked him and respected him. He was great; he was the perfect man for that job.

Paul Stillwell: Any specific stories that you remember, this approach of his?

---

[*] "Purple" is a slang term to describe joint-service staffs, purple supposedly being the color that would emerge from blending the uniforms of the various services.
[†] Commander James E. Jenkins, USN, was the public affairs officer on the personal staff of the Secretary of the Navy.

Captain Hetu: God, every day. I'm trying to think of what some of the issues were going on then that he was—well, I wish I could remember specifics. I may when I review this.

Paul Stillwell: Would it be a case of making sure that the Navy got mentioned in a particular joint story?

Captain Hetu: Yes, yes. But, see, Pickett wouldn't be a guy that would go down and fight and pound on desks to get a line or two in the story about the Navy. Some people might do that, and that's one way to do it. Pickett would go across the hall and sort of corral people like Charlie Cordry from United Press, and Steve Garwin from INS was there then, Lloyd Norman of <u>Newsweek,</u> a lot of the old pros, Jack Raymond from <u>The New York Times</u>.[*] They were really a group of good people.

Paul Stillwell: So it was a smooth, low-key approach.

Captain Hetu: Yes, and people listened. The press knew Pickett told the truth, and they knew what was happening to them, in a sense, but they knew also that he was telling the truth. Pickett would go across and hold his own little backgrounder in the corner over there. People spent a lot of time at our desk just shooting the breeze with Pickett. Pickett was a wonderful guy to background stories, and we always had a newsman or two at our desks. Sometimes you couldn't get your work done, but that was—

Paul Stillwell: Well, that was your job.

Captain Hetu: Yes, that was our work. Yes, that's what I'm saying.

Paul Stillwell: Well, did they get the sense that he told them as much as he possibly could on a given subject?

---

[*] International News Service (INS) had by then merged with the United Press to form United Press International.

Captain Hetu: Absolutely. Yes. They didn't have to go up to the Navy, they knew Pickett was across the hall, and Pickett would give it to them.

Paul Stillwell: To what extent did things that originated in Chinfo have to be cleared by DoD?

Captain Hetu: Yes, that was just the beginning of the DoD clearance, or at least in my recollection, when they really started. All the releases had to come through DoD and all the blue toppers and stuff.* But Pickett would say, "Don't play the games, do all that stuff. I'll get it cleared for you. We'll walk it through the system, but you know, So-and-So ought to go up and talk to admiral what's his name or Captain Doodah up there about this. And I'll make sure that you get a request for that from whoever's writing the story, and I'll get them up there. We'll get the good background."

Because DoD—that's why we were there. We'd let DoD know, "Yes, So-and-So wants to talk to Admiral So-and-So."

"Okay."

Pickett played by the rules but he used to say, "You play them like a violin." That's what Pickett said. "Yes, let DoD write the music, and then you play it on your violin." He taught me a lot. A lot of that washed off on me. The fact that I was respected, I think, by the press and so forth all started in my early days with Pickett. They knew that I was a Pickett-trained man and was a straight shooter, and it paid off.

Paul Stillwell: Well, we've heard of guilt by association. This was apparently the opposite, plaudits by association. [Laughter]

Captain Hetu: Yes. I'm proud to be a Pickett-trained man, I'll tell you that. He should have been the first Chinfo; he wasn't.† Didn't make admiral but he should have.

---

* In that era Department of Defense news releases were put out on paper that had a blue letterhead band across the top.
† Rear Admiral William Thompson, USN, served as the Navy's Chief of Information from July 1971 to February 1975. He was the first public affairs specialist to hold the billet. Until then the post was filled by rear admirals who were unrestricted line officers from the warfare specialties.

Everybody would agree with that, everybody that knew him.

Paul Stillwell: What were your impressions of the impact that McNamara and the "Whiz Kids" had on DoD in that era?

Captain Hetu: My recollection about McNamara, the Whiz Kids, and the Kennedy team was that these were people who were awful smart.* I mean, I thought they were pretty bright, from my vantage point as a lieutenant, but they were so smart that they could not conceive of being wrong. And that's where you can go off the track. They were arrogant. You know, it's like these press releases notifying Congress before we put them out on the wire and stuff. They didn't care, they just said, "That's what we're going to do. That's the way it is." They were very arrogant. I thought McNamara was brilliant. I went to the briefing that he gave the first time they started the budget process, one of the five-year plans.

Paul Stillwell: PPBS, Planning, Programming and Budgeting System.†

Captain Hetu: Yes, the zero planning or something, it took everybody to zero and we sort of started over, in a sense. I went to the budget briefing that McNamara himself gave, the first one, when they had that new budget process. He was smart, he was very glib and very articulate. I later didn't respect him very much because of what he did to Admiral Anderson and some other things, but he was smart.‡ They came out with the five-year budget plan which was supposed to be some sort of congressional overlap. Interesting man.

---

* Robert S. McNamara served as Secretary of Defense from 21 January 1961 to 29 February 1968. "Whiz Kids" was the nickname for the group of young civilian officials whom McNamara appointed to key positions in the Department of Defense hierarchy.
† PPBS—Planning, Programming and Budgeting System, which was started in January 1961 by Secretary of Defense Robert S. McNamara. For details, see Gordon G. Riggle, "Looking to the Long Run," U.S. Naval Institute Proceedings, September 1980, pages 60-65.
‡ The Chief of Naval Operations, Admiral George W. Anderson, Jr., USN, disagreed openly with Secretary of Defense Robert McNamara about disposition of U.S. ships during the Cuban Missile Crisis. For that reason and others, Anderson's tenure as CNO was cut short after one two-year term. For Anderson's side of the story, see his Naval Institute oral history.

Paul Stillwell: What do you remember from your time specifically in the Navy's Office of Information, the audio-visual branch?

Captain Hetu: Oh, I went from DoD up to the audio-visual. I had, I think, five officers. I was finally made lieutenant commander, I guess, while I was there in the audio-visual branch and had a bunch of lieutenants working for me. Bob Sims was one, who later because Assistant Secretary of Defense (Public Affairs).[*] Bob made captain and then went to the White House and then back to DoD. I can remember the names of the people, but they're not very important probably to this.

I had a guy—he was a navigator pilot—that ran my newsreel desk. We had newsreels then. His name was Bob Stadelhofer.[†] This makes no sense, this story. But I remember we were all in a big room, and I sat in the corner, lieutenant commander, and I was the branch chief. Bob sat in one of the forward desks in the middle of the room. I can remember him explaining to people who he called, trying to spell his name. Stadelhofer, you know, "S-T-A," and he'd go through this. And I had a lot of empathy for him because my name is short, but I was in trouble with my name too. People can never seem to get those four letters in the right order.

So Stadelhofer would go through this terrible thing, and he got orders to go to a squadron. The guy that took over from him was a guy named Arnie Schifferdecker.[‡] [Laughter] And this was just comic relief all day long, because Schifferdecker would be talking to this people and say, "I relieved Stadelhofer, and my name is Schifferdecker." Oh, God, we all started laughing, kept us all laughing all day long.

Well, Arnie got orders, and they wanted to give me a guy named George Kolbenschlag.[§] I said, "I don't think so. We'll never get anything done in this office. Schifferdecker and Stadelhofer and Kolbenschlag—it sounds like a German law firm."

Paul Stillwell: Were you finding that as the '60s progressed that there was more call for audio-visual material?

---

[*] Lieutenant Robert L. Sims, USN.
[†] Lieutenant Commander Robert R. Stadelhofer, USN, a naval aviator.
[‡] Lieutenant (junior grade) Arnold P. Schifferdecker, USNR.
[§] Lieutenant (junior grade) George R. Kolbenschlag, USNR.

Captain Hetu: Yes, it was starting to come alive. One of the things that we did was interfaced a lot with the office in Hollywood, because I'd been there, and I knew the capabilities out there. It was really the time when we first started to do industry-sponsored public service films. I think the first one we did was a film with Grumman called Goblin on the Doorstep, which was a film about ASW. It was a nightmare because with Sylvester's new rules on cooperation, we first went crazy trying to just get them to let a Navy contracting company produce a movie for the Navy, which the Navy was then going to use.

Well, we wanted to send it out as a public service film for TV and for anybody else who wanted to use it. It was a love story for the Navy's antisubmarine warfare people, and coincidentally for Grumman airplanes, which makes sense.* So we had a terrible time, I remember, with that film. That was one of the first films through the system and we showed that film to an auditorium full of Navy admirals, and it got a life of its own. I can't forget that film. They were so afraid that it was going to look like the Navy was endorsing Grumman products over other people, and I used to say, "Well, we are. We buy them. We're buying hundreds of them. I mean, isn't that an endorsement? What the hell are you talking about?"

But, anyhow, we went through that, and a guy named Milligan, Dick Milligan was the film guy from—I'll tell you a funny story about Hardy Glenn and me.† I haven't mentioned his name, I guess, but Hardy was one of my great pals, and Hardy died 20 years ago, at a very young age. Just retired and he died about a year later, terrible. Neat guy, swell. Talk to anybody in public affairs of my vintage, and they all remember Hardy. Hardy was a swell guy and fun to be with and smart.

I'm trying to remember the story; he and Bill Mack had to take a polygraph about something. Hardy almost resigned over that. I may think of that later. I can't remember the issue, something about a leak, and DoD made Bill Mack take a polygraph, which I

---

* Grumman S2F Tracker propeller-driven, carrier-based antisubmarine planes first entered fleet squadrons in early 1954. In 1962 the Tracker was redesignated S-2.
† Commander Hardy Glenn, USN.

thought was just dreadful.* Couldn't take an admiral's word, why you might as well hang it up and go away.

Anyway, it's a quick story. Dick Milligan came down. Hardy was the OI-200, which was head of the media division or whatever, and I was head of the audio-visual branch under Hardy. I think Hardy was commander, and I was a lieutenant commander. Dick Milligan came down to have a Grumman contract signed, and he was one of our pals we had done this film with. Dick came in the office, and all he had was the contract, and he had to have it signed by somebody. So he said, "Come on, I'll take you guys over to Trader Vic's and we'll have a drink. It's my wedding anniversary."

It was now about 6:00 o'clock, and we said, "Well, okay. We'll go over there with you."

So we went over to Trader Vic's, and the evening got going. We ran into some other people, and we were having drinks, and it got to be about 10:30. Dick said, "Oh, my God. I've got to take the last shuttle back to New York." So we had run into these other folks, and we all decided to drive over to the airport, and Dick got in one car. In fact, these were all New Zealand ladies who were in town for something or other. So we all drove over to the airport, and they had the old Connies, Constellations. When we got there, we couldn't find Dick anywhere. And you didn't need tickets then; you walked aboard and bought them on the plane.

It was 11:00 o'clock, and so we said, "My God, where's Milligan?" We said, "Well, we brought him here. Did he go make a phone call or something?" We looked all over and couldn't find him. "He's probably on the plane." So Hardy and I ran and got on the plane to go look for him. The plane was virtually empty; I think it was 11:00 o'clock or 10:00, whenever the last shuttle was in that time. So, anyway, we found Milligan sitting up front in the plane half asleep, and we started giving him a bad time and giggling and laughing. We didn't hear the doors close or the engines start. The first thing you know, Hardy, Hetu, and Milligan were on their way to New York, which was an interesting time. [Laughter]

---

* Rear Admiral William P. Mack, USN, served as the Navy's Chief of Information from August 1963 to April 1966.

Paul Stillwell: How did you explain something like that to your wife?

Captain Hetu: Very carefully. [Laughter] Oh, God, it was terrible, we had to call home and say we got on this plane; I guess we told the truth. I don't know what else there was to do, because we had called and said downtown, we were going to dinner with Milligan. And our wives were long suffering and knew that Milligan was an old pal and so forth. Then we had to sit around out there and wait for the first flight in the morning, which was 6:00 or something coming back. It also cost us a couple hundred dollars, which neither of us could very well afford.

Paul Stillwell: You mentioned Admiral Mack. What are your impressions from working with him?

Captain Hetu: Oh, boy, one of the great people in the Navy. He was a real gentleman. Yes, we all just loved Bill Mack, because he had a great sense of humor, and he also was smart. And I guess we liked him because he listened to us and seemed to comprehend what public affairs was all about.

Paul Stillwell: Well, I think he had had some experience in civilian newspapers so he probably knew.

Captain Hetu: You know, he's a writer now.[*] I've been getting his books, I love his books.

Paul Stillwell: Yes. Well, he probably knew more about your business than the average line officer.

Captain Hetu: I think he did, and he was smart and he was well respected around the Pentagon as an operator. I guess my first recollection of Bill Mack is 5,000 medals on his chest. I'd never seen that many medals on anybody.

---

[*] After he retired from active duty in the 1970s as a vice admiral, Mack wrote numerous naval novels.

Paul Stillwell: Well, he is politically astute without coming across as a politician.

Captain Hetu: Yes. A brilliant guy and he had all the right jobs and he had been, I guess, the legislative guy before or after Chinfo.

Paul Stillwell: I'm not sure.

Captain Hetu: I can't remember. I know he got screwed out of his fourth star, which was dreadful. I was in the Secretary's office when that happened.

Paul Stillwell: Well, maybe you can put your version of that on the record at this point, since we're talking about him.

Captain Hetu: Yes. Well, my understanding is, he had been selected for four stars and was going to go to CinCSouth. He was the Naval Academy, superintendent, wasn't he?

Paul Stillwell: I think he was put at the Naval Academy as a stash until CinCSouth opened up.[*]

Captain Hetu: Yes. I remember he was at the Naval Academy. I didn't remember whether he was actually there, whether he was going to study or something. Yes, I think you're right. They were just getting ready to give him his fourth star, and Means Johnston got it instead.[†] And his wife was the niece of Stennis or something.[‡] I'm trying to remember what the connection was.

---

[*] Vice Admiral William P. Mack, USN, served as Superintendent of the Naval Academy from 16 June 1972 to August 1975. His oral history is in the Naval Institute collection.
[†] Admiral Means Johnston, Jr., USN, served as Commander in Chief Allied Forces Southern Europe from November 1973 to September 1975.
[‡] John C. Stennis (1901-1995) was a Democrat from Mississippi. He was in the U.S. Senate from 1947 to 1989, including service as chairman of the Armed Services Committee. The aircraft carrier John C. Stennis (CVN-74) is named in his honor.

Paul Stillwell: I thought it was Johnston's father was Stennis's law partner. There may be some other connection.

Captain Hetu: I thought his wife somehow was a family member, could have been both. But it was very political, in any case. As I remember, the pressure was put on Warner to rescind it, not to send it forward, and that Bill would get the next one, whenever that was. I guess Warner said okay and went and told Bud Zumwalt. Zumwalt went apoplectic and just couldn't believe it. As I recall, Zumwalt got in the car and was driven to the Naval Academy to tell Bill Mack himself that the thing had fallen through. I mean, he would not even pick up the phone. As I recall, Bill Mack had been senior to Zumwalt before.

Paul Stillwell: Oh, he was six classes senior to him.[*]

Captain Hetu: Yes, several. They knew each other and I think Zumwalt was a great fan, like we all were, of Bill Mack, and it broke his heart, broke all our hearts, broke mine. And then he retired. He didn't wait around for the next one. I think he just said, to hell with them, I guess.

Paul Stillwell: Well, the Naval Academy wound up being his terminal assignment, which was not the intention.

Captain Hetu: Yes. Then he retired and left.

Paul Stillwell: Well, in the audio-visual branch, to what extent were your activities driven by the growing influence of television news? The networks expanded from 15 minutes to 30 a night, for example.

Captain Hetu: Yes, just getting started, yes. We didn't have a lot of film to give away, although one of the things I did have my television officer do, was we started to go over to the Navy photo center at Anacostia, which is not there anymore. I think they've now

---

[*] Mack was in the Naval Academy class of 1937; Zumwalt was in the class of 1943.

got a defense film center someplace in Los Angeles. Anyhow to start building up stock footage. I hadn't even thought of that until you asked me, but I spent a lot of time in those days at the Naval Photo Center helping networks and people find stock footage.[*]

The photo center, to my recollection, loved it. I mean, they finally sort of came into their own. They had been doing mostly training films and things. All of a sudden, they had all these people from CBS and the networks and so forth coming over there to start building stock footage libraries; they didn't have anything. So we spent an awful of time on that. I'm pausing because I'm trying to remember the fellow that ran the film repository at the Naval Photo Center. It was old guy who had been there for 100 years. I can see him, and I'll probably pull his name out of my head one of these days, in the middle of the night sometime. He smoked cigarettes, I remember, all the time.

But here was a little guy—you know, here's your country bumpkin librarian sort of, and all of a sudden he was a star. Everybody in the world wanted to know who this guy was. He was, as it turned out, a very positive guy. I mean, he didn't run the other way. He was delighted by the fact that somebody finally was going to use the stuff that he had been squirreling away for years and years. And he had a wonderful system, as I remember, could find anything. Greg Kennedy.

Paul Stillwell: Very good.

Captain Hetu: Now, isn't that funny? I mean, I remember him so well, and he could find you a piece of film on anything. Of course, the film was starting to deteriorate then, and we didn't have tape yet. Greg also had a program going, I remember, of copying old film onto new film before the nitrate all fell off and went away. God knows what happened to all that stuff. I guess it's still around somewhere.

Paul Stillwell: Well, this is sort of analogous to when you were in Hollywood. You've got a product and there's a consumer out there. You just need to match up.

---

[*] The Naval Photographic Center was then in Anacostia, part of Washington, D.C.

Captain Hetu: Yes, yes. We did a lot of fulfilling requests for stock footage, a lot of that, because the networks just didn't have their libraries built up yet. And a lot of even places in New York that sold other kinds of stock footage of buses and airplanes and anything else, had very little military film. So we were very busy doing that, fulfilling requests.

Paul Stillwell: Well, and even if those places in New York did have it, yours was a lot cheaper.

Captain Hetu: Yes, it was like free. I think they did pay a processing charge, but it was virtually nothing. It's in the public domain so, yes, free.

Paul Stillwell: Was there anything on the audio side? Did you work with radio?

Captain Hetu: Some radio. I don't remember doing a lot of radio stuff, to tell you the truth. Did some stuff with "Monitor," I remember. I had a radio officer, but I don't remember very much of what he did. I don't think we did a hell of a lot. Most of my interest was in the film business. We had an officer that worked with commercial films, we had a newsreel person, and we were heavy into the film side of things.

Paul Stillwell: That was really at the tail end of the newsreel era, I think.

Captain Hetu: That's right. We were still doing it, but it was mostly starting to switch over to television, television news, yes. Worked with people like Ike Kleinerman, from NBC. One of the things I did—my God, I had forgotten about this—was to get the Navy rights for "Victory at Sea." You know, the Navy didn't own "Victory at Sea."

Paul Stillwell: That was NBC's product.

Captain Hetu: I sort of stumbled over that. I remember I wanted to use something, and they said, "Sorry, so sorry, all that stuff belongs to NBC."

I said, "That's crazy. You've got to be kidding. You mean we can't use our own stuff, you know." It's like, I guess, the same as the day I found out the Navy didn't own "Anchors Aweigh." I don't think they still do, I don't know. We have to pay somebody every time you play "Anchors Aweigh."

Paul Stillwell: I didn't know that either.

Captain Hetu: Yes, we don't own "Anchors Aweigh." Let's get a new one here. But, anyway, I negotiated an agreement with NBC that we could use the footage and use the series on ships and all that sort of thing. We couldn't even show it to our own people.

Paul Stillwell: Well, it was a staple in Naval Reserve training centers for years. I know that from personal experience.

Captain Hetu: Yes, that was a wonderful series. I think the thing was negotiated at a time when nobody really thought it through, and then when I went back to them, I was only a lieutenant commander, but I got to know these people pretty well. They all sort of said, "Yes, that is kind of foolish. We're not getting any residuals out of this or anything, and the Navy sure as hell ought to have use of that."

It was about that time that I did my shtick with In Harm's Way—an interesting story in itself.

Paul Stillwell: Well, please tell me that one.

Captain Hetu: Bill Mack was then the Chief of Information, and Sylvester was still down below. Otto Preminger came in and wanted help in shooting this film and was pulling all sorts of political cards and everything else, and Sylvester wasn't bending very much.

Paul Stillwell: Why not?

Captain Hetu: Well, this was a story that's not particularly good for the Navy. All the ships and stuff you want and materials and Marines and things, and they just didn't want to do it. So they came to an agreement finally, after months of negotiating, that Preminger would submit a detailed list of everything he needed. I mean, everything, like 100 bayonets and 20 canteens and so on. And so they were just beside themselves, I mean, they wanted the cooperation but--and Bill Mack wanted to do the film. It turned out that they were willing to change a lot of the—I don't know if you remember, but Kirk Douglas was a drunk and reprobate in this film and gets a nurse impregnated and stuff. So they toned that down a little bit, and John Wayne was the hero.

Paul Stillwell: He played himself.

Captain Hetu: Yes, John Wayne was John Wayne, in his Navy costume. So they sent me to Hollywood—at no expense to the government, as they called it—to work with Preminger to put together his requests for cooperation. He didn't have it yet. DoD said fine, if the Navy wanted to send me, but that he'd have to pay my salary during that time. Bill Mack was all for it, so they sent me to California, and I spent, gosh, about three or four weeks there working with the assistant director but working with Preminger and going through the script page by page, figuring out how many of this he'd need, how many of that he'd need, and we did a big matrix of materials by day and stuff and X's and all kinds of stuff, really something.

Preminger could be a charming person. He was also a tyrant, but not to me. He needed me badly. I remember the day I walked into Preminger's office, and he said, "Commander, it's so nice to have you here. How are your accommodations?"

Well, I had a suite of rooms in the Hollywood Beverly Hills Hotel, I think it was, beautiful big suite. I had one of Preminger's white Oldsmobile convertibles at my disposal. He and Poopsie, his wife, had matching Oldsmobile convertibles, which they got new ones every year, because he used Oldsmobiles in his pictures.

So I had my own convertible, and it was in the garage down below, and they'd fill it up with gas every night when I brought it in, all this kind of stuff. And I had free range of the expense account in the hotel, all this stuff. So Preminger talked to me a little bit about what I was going to do and turned me over to the assistant director and anything you need, you know, dah, dah, dah. When I was about ready to leave the room, he said, "You can't charge everything in the hotel. Take this for a little spending money." The guy put this roll of bills in my hand, and I said, "Well, thank you very much, I don't think I need it."

"Well, don't worry about. Don't worry." So I went back to the hotel, and I took this roll of bills out. I got, as I recall, it was like $1,000 in $100.00 bills or $50.00 bills.

Well, I was a lieutenant commander now, five kids, $1,000 spending money. I said, "Geez, you know, I can't keep this money."

So I started a little notebook, and I did spend some of it, not very much. I went to dinner with some folks that I knew in California, and when I did, I'd take a bottle of wine or take a bunch of flowers and bottle of wine or something. And I did go out to dinner a couple of nights. I didn't want to eat in the hotel every night. So I probably spent about $200.00 maybe, in three weeks. Didn't have to spend it on a car, and I was taken to dinner a lot.

So, anyway, a long story short, the last day we got all this done and submitted it. DoD and liked it and so forth. He didn't have his cooperation yet, but they had accepted this as okay. So the last day I go back to see Preminger. In the meantime, I had seen him a fair number of times. In fact, he took me out to dinner one night with one of the co-stars from the film. That's another old story. And I gave him back the money. I had it in an envelope, and I had kept a log of everything I spent. I put it on his desk, and I said, "Oh, by the way, here's the change from the money you gave me."

He said, "What, what?"

I said, "Thank you very much and dah, dah, dah," and left the room.

This assistant director was driving me to the airport, and he said, "What the hell did you do?"

I said, "I gave him back the money. I only spent about $200.00."

He said, "He didn't expect to get that back."

I said, "I know, but I can't do that. That's not legal; I mean, that's not right. I don't know if it's legal, but it's not ethical and I can't do that."

And I was thinking to myself, "All I need is for him to get turned down for cooperation." I can see this letter coming in saying, "Well, I gave your guy 1,000 bucks." That wasn't the reason I gave it back, not the primary reason. But I guess I stunned him when I gave the money. A thousand bucks to them was nothing. It was a lot to me, I could have used the $800.00 change.

Paul Stillwell: Well, what proportion of all his requests did he wind up getting?

Captain Hetu: I guess virtually everything, as I recall. I didn't work on the movie after that. I mean, the motion picture went off in another direction and I think by the time the thing really got started I had orders to Boston University, and I was out of there. I guess he got virtually everything he wanted.

Paul Stillwell: Well, for example, he got the use of a cruiser, the St. Paul.

Captain Hetu: Yes. He did well. I mean, he owed me a lot.

Paul Stillwell: Which he tried to pay you for. [Laughter]

Captain Hetu: Yes, 800 bucks.

Paul Stillwell: Any other examples of his personality?

Captain Hetu: I say he was a tyrant. He had everybody scared absolutely to death, and he was a God, I mean, working around that studio. They gave me a nice office all to myself and a secretary and so forth. I was in the executive suite down the hall from Otto's office. I mean, they were all scared to death of him. I remember, I thought, "Boy, if you think the Navy is tough with admirals, you ought to be around Hollywood." I told you that earlier with South Pacific, the director/producer on the film is God. He is God, and Otto was a tough guy.

He called me one day and said, "Would you like to go to dinner tonight?"

I said, "Yes, sounds great.

He said, "Okay, we'll pick you up at whatever time, 7:00 o'clock, 8:00 o'clock at your hotel." So picked us up in a limousine, so he and Poopsie, who was a very nice lady, he called her Poopsie. They had twin daughters, I think, little ones. So Poopsie and Otto and I stopped by, and we picked up Barbara Bouchet, who was one of the upcoming stars of the film who never amounted to anything after <u>In Harm's Way</u>. She's the gal that played—I only remember that she was in a yellow convertible with Kirk Douglas in the beginning of the film. She was a beautiful girl, blonde hair and typical starlet.

So he picked up Barbara for the foursome, and Barbara came out wearing a dress that was cut down to her kneecaps. I don't remember where we had dinner, I can't remember dinner very well—trying to keep my eyes above the table, above Barbara's shoulders. After dinner we went to a place called the Whiskey-a-Go-Go, which was then the hottest place in Hollywood. I mean, it was <u>the</u> place to go and lines outside.

Of course, we pulled up in a limo in the back of the Go-Go and knocked on the door. The door opened, "Ah, Mr. Preminger, your table's ready," and we went in. Of course, the place was jam packed, about 10:00 o'clock at night. And Otto had one of the two booths sitting up, as I recall, sort of like thrones. In the other booth were Lana Turner and some of her cohorts, and, of course, she gushed all over Preminger.

I was thinking, you know, "I'm basking—this light is sort of shining on me, too, and everybody's saying, 'Who's that guy with Preminger? He must be somebody.'"

We were having drinks then, I guess; dinner was over. He said to Barbara, "Barbara, why don't you dance with the commander?"

And I was saying, "Blah, blah."

She said, "Oh, I'd be delighted, Mr. Preminger. Commander, shall we dance?"

I said, "Okay with me."

So we got out on the jammed dance floor, and I was thinking to myself, "The only bad part about something like this, you never see anybody you know."

I went in the men's room, and guys were saying to me, "Isn't that Barbara Bouchet with you and Preminger."

I go, "Yes it is."

"Are you going to be in her next picture?"

"Hey, I don't know. I'm just a tourist here. I don't know what's going on."

Well, make a long story short, I was dancing with Barbara on the floor and doing these wild gyrations, and I danced by a guy that I know who I had worked with quite a bit at CBS. He was a researcher, and I spent a lot of time with him on various projects. I danced by him, and he looked at me and did a triple take: "What are you doing here?"

I said, "Oh, you know, I'm just vacationing, you know."

"Isn't that Preminger you're with?"

I said, "Yes." I said, "John, I'm so glad you're here. Nobody would ever believe this if it wasn't . . ."

[Interruption for change of tape]

Paul Stillwell: Well, one of the things I remember from that era was a movie that showed Kennedy visiting the fleet in 1963.

Captain Hetu: I was there.

Paul Stillwell: Well, do you want to talk about that one?

Captain Hetu: Hardy Glenn and I escorted the press on that. That was when the President visited the First Fleet. I was on his last visit, too, when he went out on the <u>Observation Island</u> on the East Coast to see the Polaris shot.

Paul Stillwell: Well, if you could describe both of those, please. I had the oral history of Admiral Keith, who was First Fleet commander then, and he talked about the care with which they prepared the thing, to show off the new NTDS and the missiles and so forth.[*]

---

[*] Vice Admiral Robert T. S. Keith, USN, served as Commander First Fleet from 5 May 1962 to 11 December 1963. His oral history is in the Naval Institute collection. NTDS—Naval Tactical Data System, an electronic system that tracked radar contacts automatically, whereas previous practice had involved manual tracking. NTDS first entered the fleet in 1961.

Captain Hetu: Yes. I remember that. We went out on a rehearsal, of course. Hardy Glenn and I were sent from Washington to be the escorts, and Buzz Lloyd, good old Buzz was at the naval district then.[*]

Paul Stillwell: Well, you must have had a Navy film crew along for this.

Captain Hetu: Yes, but we were more press people. They had a combat camera team and all that stuff. A lot of those people were covering, but we were really press escorts, to make sure the press got aboard and everything was handled correctly with the press.

Paul Stillwell: What's involved when the President's in on one of these press pools or gatherings?

Captain Hetu: Well, of course, the White House press office handles everything, and they tell you what to do and that's pretty much where we just segued into their master plan and because we were naval officers handled and escorted the press and stuff. Made sure they got aboard all right and got their credentials, and we went out and got the briefing with the Secret Service and all that. But we were sort of minor players in a sense of just being escorts.

Well, my job, I guess it was the First Fleet visit that my job. The President was up on the flying bridge, and for the show he came down, and they had a big set of seats on the flight deck.

Paul Stillwell: This was the Kitty Hawk?[†]

Captain Hetu: Yes. And my job was to take the press up three at a time, photographers up to the bridge, photograph the President sitting in his chair. I don't remember if he had a hat on or not, watching the flight ops and then I'd take the three back down, and bring

---

[*] Captain Frederic M. Lloyd III, USN.
[†] President Kennedy visited the carriers Kitty Hawk (CVA-63) and Oriskany (CVA-34) on 6 June 1963.

three up. So that was exhilarating for me to be as close as I am to you to Kennedy, who I thought was really an incredible guy.

He went to Point Mugu, I think, after the show. You know, Kennedy had extraordinary charisma, at least to me; I mean, he lit up a room. I've been around several presidents, and I just never had that same feeling that he got. He was magic to me; he just had that electricity around him, an aura.

Paul Stillwell: How did the sailors respond?

Captain Hetu: Oh, loved them, boy, yes. You know, the PT boat hero and all this. He was an interesting—you know, he was aloof but not aloof. It was kind of a strange thing with me. I guess this was very personal—you know, when I shook his hand I was speechless. I mean, really, I was just in awe, I just couldn't believe I was really shaking John Kennedy's hand. I mean, he was that imposing.

Well, that being over, I'm trying to remember then the Polaris thing was really a couple of weeks before he was shot.

Paul Stillwell: Right, and Admiral Galantin was his host.[*]

Captain Hetu: Yes, yes, that's right. And we were on the Observation Island out of Canaveral.[†] And you know how it is, you do one of these and you're an expert, you do two, you're indispensable. So by then Hardy and I had done a couple of these, or at least one, and so we were sent out on the Observation Island to perform the same sort of escort duty with the press. We took some press and the Secret Service out the night before, and then the President flew out to the ship, because we were off the coast to do an actual shot from a submarine.

I remember the night before, and I've thought about this many times since. There were a bunch of Secret Service guys on board who went out with us the night before,

---
[*] Rear Admiral Ignatius J. Galantin, USN, served as director of the Special Projects Office from 26 February 1962 to 16 February 1965.
[†] President Kennedy visited the test ship Observation Island (EAG-154) on 16 November 1963 to watch the USS Andrew Jackson (SSBN-619) conduct a submerged firing of a Polaris A-2 missile. Kennedy was killed six days later.

shooting the breeze and drinking coffee in the wardroom after the movie. And they were interesting guys. These were White House guys and Presidential security, and they were interesting to talk to. They were saying what a nice respite this was for them, coming aboard a ship where virtually everybody was pretty well cleared and particularly a ship that was a technical ship like this. They realized there could be nuts on board, but this was very unlikely, so that it gave them a little down time.

Then we started talking about assassinations, or, "How do you guys do this, and how do you know that somebody's not going to jump out of the crowd and stuff."

I remember vividly this guy saying, "You know, our greatest fear is if somebody really wants to kill the President and doesn't care about his own safety, he could it any time. We can't stop something like that. We're in a deterrence, and we would take the bullet if we had to, but, you know." And I remember not too long thereafter, hearing that the President had been shot. I was in the steam room at the athletic club. Strange place, but, anyway, I remember somebody coming in and saying, "Kennedy has been shot in Dallas." And it popped into my mind about talking with these guys. I didn't know who shot him then, I thought, well, somebody didn't care. Terrible story.

Paul Stillwell: Last year I visited Dealey Plaza for the first time.[*] I had had this mental picture for years from the films and the still photos. And seeing it in person struck me how much more compact it was than my mental image, that it was not a very long shot from that book depository window.

Captain Hetu: No. That's true. Yes, I just went there not terribly long ago, probably four or five years ago, for the first time, had the same feeling. Yes, the film and everything it seemed it was like a great huge distance. It wasn't at all. It was like right up there.

Anyway, an interesting thing we get to do in this business is escort the President. I escorted the press for Nixon in Vietnam.

---

[*] Kennedy was shot in Dealey Plaza in Dallas on 22 November 1963.

Paul Stillwell: Did you have any contact with Captain Shepherd, Kennedy's naval aide?*

Captain Hetu: No. Tazewell Shepherd, no. I met, I think, but no, I didn't have anything to do with him. He never made admiral, that guy.

Paul Stillwell: I think you're right.

Captain Hetu: That's kind of strange.

Paul Stillwell: The film that the combat camera people shot and then put together for a movie for in-house Navy distribution—would you have had a role in that?

Captain Hetu: Not really, no.

Paul Stillwell: Did that fall under education and training?

Captain Hetu: Yes, BuPers or somebody would handle it.† We didn't get involved in internal information films. I remember that the combat camera people did a film of Kennedy's funeral. It was one of the best I've ever seen. It was one of the most poignant films of that time. It's got to be still around; I would hope so. No narration, all done with wild natural sound, from the time the caisson left the White House and all the way down, across the bridge up to the thing. And you'd think that'd be an awful long thing. It's edited, of course; you don't see it every step of the way, all just natural sound of the horses' hoofs and the drumbeats and things. Oh, powerful film and beautifully photographed.

Paul Stillwell: Inherent drama to it.

---

* Captain Tazewell T. Shepherd, Jr., USN, served as naval aide to the President from January 1961 to November 1963.
† BuPers—Bureau of Naval Personnel.

Captain Hetu: Yes, I'm trying to remember the name of the Navy lieutenant, photo officer that did that film. I have a recollection of the casket coming on the caisson down the driveway of the White House, framed in these trees with fall foliage on them. They got an extraordinary shot, I mean; it's just a grabber.

Paul Stillwell: There's a real art to that.

Captain Hetu: Oh, boy, yes. I don't know whatever happened to that film. I suppose it's laying over there on a shelf someplace. It shouldn't be; it was a beautiful film. But there was so much shot that day that nobody needed it, I'm sure, or wanted it.

Paul Stillwell: Was it in color?

Captain Hetu: Yes.

Paul Stillwell: Well, that was an exception, because the TV stuff was still black and white during that period.

Captain Hetu: That's right. Yes, this was a color film, it was a beautiful film, probably a 10- or 12-minute film, not very long.

Paul Stillwell: Well, anything else from the Chinfo period before you go to Boston?

Captain Hetu: Oh, boy, audio-visual. Well, Harry Padgett relieved me.[*] Harry and I had been friends and contemporaries, and we're still powerful friends, really love each other. He's a great friend of mine, a great pal. Harry was coming from Boston University, and I got orders to go to Boston University. And I should—no, I won't tell you that. There's a Cooney story here, but I probably shouldn't say it. I don't want to take any shots at people.

---

[*] Lieutenant Commander Harry E. Padgett, USN.

I was the primary for Boston University, and I got a secondary for the war college. I guess, in case I didn't get into BU, I'd go to the war college, or something, I don't know. I decided I wanted to go to BU. I thought a master's degree in public relations would be more useful to me there than the war college. I could always go to the war college.

Anyhow, Harry was coming from BU, and I was going to BU and Harry was going to relieve me in the audio-visual branch, and I was sort of relieving in a sense at BU. So I worked out an unusual relieving syllabus. I got us both TAD orders to New York for a week, and I said, "I'll take you around for a week and introduce you to all the TV and radio people in New York, and you can tell me about Boston University. No sense of you coming down and sitting in my office in the Pentagon. I can't tell you much there. We can go to New York. And, of course, we can do a little partying in the meantime."*

If you ever talk to Harry, I think he will admit this was one of our more unique turnover sessions, because I had engineered so that we were taken care of for breakfast, lunch, and dinner. And thereafter all the days we were there, and we had a great time, and we learned a lot. We did go around and met all the studio people and all of the network people that, by then, I had known pretty well and did our turnover in New York. It was great fun.

Harry helped me find a house in Boston, although I didn't take his house. I bought and found another house out in Framingham, which was a fair distance out of Boston. But to find a house that you could house a bunch of kids in was—I had five then.

I went to Boston under a program to get a master's degree in public relations, Navy sponsored obviously. A good year, a great year; I enjoyed it very much. It was sort of a sabbatical in the sense that you could go off and think about things, and it was kind of very interesting to me to know that so many people were worrying in an academic way about public relations. I mean, I hadn't been around this side of the place, so it made you sort of feel that you were in a profession that was recognized. People had written a lot of books about it, and there were people spending their lives teaching people about it.

---

* TAD—temporary additional duty.

Paul Stillwell: Your approach had been completely pragmatic up to that point.

Captain Hetu: Yes, exactly. I had never had any formal real training. On-the-job training from the get-go, and now starting to take courses like PR-101, I mean, literally, public relations principles and practice, although we were in the graduate school; we weren't in the undergraduate school.

Paul Stillwell: Don't public affairs officers now get that kind of training earlier in their careers?

Captain Hetu: Yes, I think they do.

Paul Stillwell: Why was it at the lieutenant commander stage then?

Captain Hetu: I don't know. The Navy had been on-again, off-again about sending people to Boston University, and then we were on again. I guess they felt that they owed it to those in the middle grades who hadn't gotten any of this training. I don't know why. It was interesting in the sense that I was the only public affairs specialist in the class. There were four other officers, two aviators and two line officers, ship drivers, which was kind of interesting that they would do that. I can't remember whether they had even had any public affairs tours. I didn't know them before we got to school.

Paul Stillwell: Were they going into that field?

Captain Hetu: Well, yes, a couple of them did, and a couple of them didn't. I remember Norm Campbell was the aviator, and I think he went back to Chinfo and had a tour, but then he used his Chinfo tour to get jet training and made admiral, in fact, as an aviator.[*] Good guy. The other aviator did go into public affairs and, I think, stayed in public

---

[*] Lieutenant Commander Norman D. Campbell, USN.

affairs. Both of the line officers ended up in public affairs, at least for a while. One got out and then went to NASA.*

But they sort of looked to me, I guess, in a way, because I was the only public affairs guy in the group. Early on I got them all together and I said, "You know, one of the bad things that happens here is that people don't get their degrees," and it happened quite often.

Paul Stillwell: Not enough time?

Captain Hetu: Didn't write their thesis, major reason. Just put it off, left the school and didn't ever finish their thesis, which I had always thought the Navy was—I thought it was silly.

Paul Stillwell: They weren't holding people's feet to the fire.

Captain Hetu: No. I thought if you didn't write your thesis and get your degree, which is what the Navy spent a hell of a lot of money on you, that you should have gotten something, a slap on the wrist or a bad fitness report or something. But, anyhow, I said, "A lot of people come here and don't get their degrees, and I would like to get an early-on, let's put our hands in the middle of the ring and vow that we're going to help each other get it and all walk out of here with a master's degree. Otherwise, what the hell are we here for?" And we did. We all got the degree, and we all helped each other, and that was kind of interesting.

Paul Stillwell: Literally cooperate and graduate.

Captain Hetu: We did help each. I remember the summertime when I was trying to write my thesis: five kids and hot and using an old Underwood upright. And discouragement set in occasionally where you'd say, "Oh, God, this is . . ." You're an author, so you know this, but I didn't know that then. The research was a lot of fun. God, I was raking in

---

* NASA—National Aeronautics and Space Administration.

stuff, doing all kinds of surveys, and I went to Washington and met with the guy at the Red Cross who was the—I wrote mine on crisis management, "Public Relations and Peacetime Naval Disasters" was my topic. I did a list in the back of the book of all the peacetime naval disasters since 1775, and I didn't have any idea how many I was thinking about. This was all peacetime stuff, and I ran into some fascinating stories. I'll let you read my thesis, too. It's not very interesting reading, but that part of it was, and I didn't know that I was going to run into all these ships that sank. And you remember those destroyers that went aground in the fog and all those?

Paul Stillwell: Point Honda, right.*

Captain Hetu: I just kept stumbling over all these stories, which sort of was my purpose, was to say in the Navy this happens all the time; they're not always the first time. We've done this for years, we've had a disaster every six months or so.

Paul Stillwell: The Wasp and the Hobson.†

Captain Hetu: Oh, yes, on and on. So I was saying, I got discouraged after I ended up with this room piled high with all this wonderful research and then trying to put it down into a 100-page document was another story. I remember we almost had a "thesis anonymous." [Laughter] We helped each other out. My wife would call Norm, who lived close by, and say, "He's really in a downer. He's about ready to throw the typewriter out the window, literally." And the guys would come over, and we'd all sit around and have a beer and calm each other down, and we went to each other's house. It

---

* On 8 September 1923 seven ships of Destroyer Squadron 11 ran aground in heavy fog at Point Arguello, also known as Point Honda, off Santa Barbara, California. Twenty-two men were killed, and all seven ships were wrecked. For details see Dianne Driever, "Destroyers Down!" Naval History, Spring 1992, pages 20-25.

† On the night of 26 April 1952, during an eastward crossing of the Atlantic, the destroyer minesweeper Hobson (DMS-26) turned in front of the aircraft carrier Wasp (CV-18), collided with her, and sank. Of the Hobson's crew, 176 men were lost, including the commanding officer, Lieutenant Commander W. J. Tierney, USN; 52 were rescued. See Winston Jordan, "Flank Speed to Eternity," Naval History, Spring 1988, pages 12-17.

was just kind of interesting, kind of fun, and we all got them, we all graduated, all got our master's.

Paul Stillwell: What kinds of conclusions did you come to in your thesis?

Captain Hetu: Oh, predictable conclusions and really wrote a disaster plan, crisis management plan for the Navy, which, I don't think was ever adopted, not that I expected it to be. Well, the basic conclusion was that we were in a dangerous business—driving high-powered warships and airplanes, it's just going to happen. You just know it's going to happen, and we tend a lot to stick our heads in the sand and hope it won't happen, and when it does we're never prepared for it. And there are things that you can do to prepare for it.

Paul Stillwell: Such as?

Captain Hetu: About having a disaster plan and knowing who gets called when the balloon goes up and having just a lot of resources available so that when you push—it's not unlike a fire drill or a chemical; that was thought of the thesis. We train for all sorts of accidents and fires and chemical attacks and nuclear attacks, and we never train or think about ship collisions or an airplane crashing, and they do it all the time.

Paul Stillwell: Well, probably one of your points was that you need to get accurate information out as quickly as you can.

Captain Hetu: Oh, yes, all that. The philosophy behind it was, "You tell the truth and tell the whole truth, and don't tell the truth until you know it's the truth. And tell the reporters why you're not telling them. Don't just not tell them." You've got to remember that very often they're as emotionally involved as you are if it happens in their city. Everybody's emotional when they have deadlines and you want the Navy to come out—this stood me in good stead because I handled a couple of serious accidents in Vietnam. I handled the

Evans and Melbourne. I handled all that and the EC-121 that got shot down over Korea; I handled the return of the bodies. So I was able to put a lot of that to good use.

Paul Stillwell: And it was undoubtedly helpful that you had gone through the drill of thinking about such things.

Captain Hetu: Yes, yes, it really was. In our second semester at Boston University, one of our classes formed a student public relations agency; I was elected president of the agency. I think we had 18 people in the class, and we teamed with an undergraduate class, and I became the agency personnel, and we went out and got six actual accounts. They had to be actual accounts; these were not play accounts. We called ourselves Charles River and Associate. And went out and got good accounts. We divided it up into six accounts, I can't remember the word.

Paul Stillwell: Teams.

Captain Hetu: One person got a college that was trying to build a new addition in one of the high-class parts of Boston. The people were fighting this—you know, traffic and all the things that you worry about. And one was trying to keep a mental institution open. One was a dairy farm. These were good. I went and got Eastern Airlines, which was fun. Eastern had just refurbished their airline, had just repainted their airplanes and put out a whole new thing about new meals and all kinds of stuff. So I went to see the VP at the Eastern, and I said, "You know, I'd like to come in a do a program for you."

He was a graduate of the school, and he said, "You know, we've just spent millions of dollars on doing this, and there's not very much you can do for us."

I said, "Well, let me try. Let me come in and noodle around and see what we can find. Maybe we can help you. If we can't, so what? You know, free chance for you." I'd been around a little bit, so he let us do it.

We came up with a program which turned out to be pretty good for Eastern. We called it the Customer of Tomorrow Plan. We said the one group of people you're not looking out for are the young people who are going to be your customers. We were talking about high school and college kids. We did some research and found out at what age people are most impressionable, and if they flew the first time on Eastern, they'd probably return to Eastern throughout their lives if they didn't have any bad experiences.

So we set up this proposal to do student fares, which had never been done before. We made the pitch to the PR guy who came over to the school, and that was part of our final, was to give the pitch. And they liked it so well they asked us to come over and give it to the corporate people. Everybody applauded it, and we got A's, and everybody was happy. The next year I remember reading The New York Times one Sunday and seeing this big ad from Eastern Airlines for student fares and so forth and all. And it was our program, pretty much—refined, of course. Made you feel good. It was fun. I mean, we did something that really happened. We didn't get paid for it, but we got A's. That was okay; that's what it was all about.

Paul Stillwell: Well, it kept the airline going for another 25 years or whatever it was.

Captain Hetu: I don't know. I don't take credit for that, but I mean, at least we planted the seed, I guess. That year, in another class, I did a public relations plan for the state police academy I used to pass every night going home. We were supposed to go out and find some sort of a nonprofit entity and sell them on letting us do a PR plan for them. So I walked in one day into the state police academy, and it was a wonderful time. I went out and spent two weekends there interviewing the state police instructors about the police and all that, it was fun.

Anyway, it was a good year. It made you think about PR; it made you understand that it was a science. I can remember early on I went in to fill out some forms in the office for something or other, parking or whatever. The little box said, what degree you were here to obtain and I put down, MA in public relations and she said, "We don't give an MA in public relations."

I said, "Why am I here? Have I come to the wrong place?"

She said, "No, no, no, it's an MS."

I said, "Master of science? You're kidding. Is it?"

She said, "Yes."

"I guess I didn't even focus on that. I thought it was an MA." I just assumed it was.

She said, "Oh, no, it's a science, not an art."

"Okay, whatever you say."

Paul Stillwell: Well, I think there's some of both in it.

Captain Hetu: Oh, yes. Oh, so do I, but I was surprised that it was an MS.

But you learned some things and some you didn't. I remember the first class, the principles and practice class, we had a woman who turned out to be a good friend and one of my thesis advisers. But she asked us one day, the first day in class, to write out our definition. I was so happy to be going to Boston University, because I thought I would finally get a good succinct definition of PR. I was tired of going to cocktail parties and having everybody say, "What is PR? What do you do?"

"Well, we do this, we do that." Never had a very good answer, and I thought, "Ah, if nothing else, after this year, I'm going to have my answer."

So, anyway, I wrote down, "Public relations is applied horse sense, which is enhanced by your knowledge of the technical tools of communications." That was the best I could get; this was my thing. You know the end of the story already. We went through the whole semester, and the last day of class, Carol Hills said, "Okay, I'm going to hand your papers out now, the ones you wrote the first day in class, and I want you to turn them over and write your definition now." Well, we learned all these great charts and things about identifying the problems, what the goals and missions of the company were, and dah, dah, dah, and the definition was like two pages long by the time we got done with all this stuff.

So I sat down and wrote the same thing down that I had written the first day. And she was going through these papers, happily beaming away that we all learned so much and so forth; some people drew diagrams and everything. She came to mine and turned it over, and it was almost word-for-word the same thing I had written the first day. And she said, "I'm so disappointed. Didn't you learn anything in the class?"

I said, "Well, yes. I learned that my definition's just as good as yours." I had already had my A, was careful not to upset that. I mean, she was good about it. That was probably unfair, in a way, because it did make you think a lot more about public affairs, public relations.

Taught me one important rule, that I guess I knew before I went there pretty much. It was to always write a public relations plan or a public affairs plan. Put it down in writing. That's the one thing I learned there, and I learned how to do it, and I still do it today. Always write a plan; it makes you focus on what it is you think you're going to do. And get it approved by the boss, because it makes the people upstairs focus on what they think they want you to do. When you come to a meeting of the minds, you've got your approved action plan. They know what you're supposed to do, and you know what you're supposed to do.

It also gives you a measure of your progress, and it's your license to operate. If it's in the plan, you don't have to argue with every assistant chief of staff. You say, "Hey, it's in my plan. The admiral says he wants to have this magazine, or he wants to have this whatever the hell it is."

Paul Stillwell: Well, it fosters communication also, to refine those plans.

Captain Hetu: Yes, and focus, yes. And I've done it every place I've ever been.

Paul Stillwell: Well, you've talked about the <u>Evans</u> collision and the EC-121. Are there other applications that you can see in retrospect from that year at Boston that you used in your career?

Captain Hetu: I suppose the two main things that I got out of Boston was, one, the writing of it, putting it on paper, because I had never before formalized sitting down and taking the time when I first got to a new job or a command and say, "What is it we're really trying to do here?" You usually just jump in and start answering press queries and taking things as they come.

The other thing was it gave me a very good idea of conducting research, of surveys and research. I mean, that there's somebody else that's probably done these things. There's probably somebody that's put their thoughts down in a thesis, probably taught me that, and writing plans. So somebody's probably got some pretty good stuff about this somewhere, if you take the time to go look it up. You don't always have to reinvent the wheel.

I learned that from going to the library and doing a lot of research on papers and on the thesis, that there's a lot of material available. You're not a pioneer. There are other people who have done this before you. Take advantage of that and to do public opinion surveys. The Navy doesn't do very much of that. I guess they can't with public funds. But to find out, as best you can, what your audience is and what they think they think. What is it we're trying to tell them? Are we trying to change their minds? Are we trying to enhance what they think? What are we trying to do? You know, sending messages out without a reason to send them out is a lot of waste of time.

Paul Stillwell: Well, in the early '70s, with the advent of the all-volunteer force, the armed services started spending advertising dollars instead of depending on public service, and I suspect, at that point, they also got into market research.

Captain Hetu: They did, yes. And that was perfectly acceptable, because they were going out after recruits, but we couldn't do it in public affairs because that was looked on as propaganda, using government funds to find out what the citizens thought so we could change their minds. It was looked at as somewhat like brainwashing. You're not supposed to do that. The public information officer's role is to put out information and not try to influence thinking.

Paul Stillwell: Yes, but certainly there were some propaganda aspects to it that could have recruiting benefits, for example.

Captain Hetu: Sure. I mean, we were public relations officers, and we obviously told the best side of the story. We always looked for good stories about the Navy. We didn't just sit there waiting for something to happen. We were always trying to think about telling the good side of the Navy. I suppose that's, in the classic of the definition, propaganda in a way, but not propaganda in that we didn't manipulate the message to be untrue or to say something that wasn't honorable or truthful.

Paul Stillwell: Well, it's interesting, in our oral history library is that of Rear Admiral Min Miller who was Chinfo right at the end of World War II.* On his watch he deliberately had the name of the command changed from the Navy Public Relations Office to the Public Information Office.

Captain Hetu: Good thinking. Yes, I mean, that's what we are, and that's a very important part of our mission, to get out information. It's always mind-boggling to me when you see some of the things that come along, the cover-ups and all that. You say, "My God, doesn't anybody learn anything?" It just seems to be like a sine curve where every so often there's another story that comes out that if you would have told the truth in the beginning you could have avoided so much trouble.

Did you ever go to a mystery movie? I used to drive my kids wild, because we'd go to one of these mystery movies and I'd say, "If that guy would pick up the phone right now and call the cops, it would be all over." You know, in the first five minutes of the film.

"Dad!" they'd say. And that's sort of what we do. If you're smart, you pick up that phone within the first five minutes and call the press or whatever, and get it out, get rid of it.

Paul Stillwell: Probably the preeminent case of that is Watergate.† If, in the beginning, the White House had said what the truth was.

---
* See the Naval Institute oral history of Rear Admiral Harold B. Miller, USN (Ret.).
† In June 1972 operatives working indirectly for the Committee to Re-elect the President broke into the headquarters of the Democratic National Committee in the Watergate complex in Washington, D.C. The resulting cover-up led to the August 1974 resignation of President Richard Nixon.

Captain Hetu: You know, that's so true. When I went to CIA with Stan Turner, I can remember we had a case when we first got there.[*] You don't care about the CIA on this tape, but I said to Stan, "You know, what you've got to do is fire those guys now. You know, if Nixon would have hung a couple of those guys on the White House lawn, they would be making gold statues of him. He would have been a hero." What a terrible PR blunder that was. It even brought down the presidency.

Paul Stillwell: Well, going back to this time in the '60s, the Kennedys apparently did that with Secretary of the Navy Korth, rather than have a taint of scandal because of some of his bank dealings in Texas.[†] Do you remember any of that from the Pentagon perspective?

Captain Hetu: No. I don't really. Jim Jenkins was Fred Korth's public affairs officer. No, I didn't know very much about that. I met Korth in the early days, and, in fact, over the years got to know him much better—after the Navy knew him. He's a delightful man, still around town, still works here, and he's in his 80s and he still goes every day to the Army-Navy Club for lunch, I think. I didn't know him then. I'm getting away from the story.

Paul Stillwell: Well, I interviewed his lawyer and he still makes an eloquent defense for Secretary Korth, as is the lawyer's wont.

Captain Hetu: Yes, of course. Well, then there was John Connally.[‡] Jim Jenkins was Connally's public affairs officer.

Paul Stillwell: Well, we've covered a lot of ground today. Any wrap-up thoughts?

---

[*] Admiral Stansfield Turner, USN (Ret.), served as Director of Central Intelligence/Director of the Central Intelligence Agency from 9 March 1977 to 20 January 1981. The first part of his tenure was on active duty, prior to his Navy retirement on 1 January 1979.
[†] Fred H. Korth served as Secretary of the Navy from 4 January 1962 to 1 November 1963. For the perspective of Korth's lawyer, see the Naval Institute oral history of Captain Alex A. Kerr, USN (Ret.).
[‡] John B. Connally served as Secretary of the Navy from 25 January 1961 to 20 December 1961.

Captain Hetu: Geez, here I am. I'm embarrassed because we've talked forever, and I haven't made much progress.

Paul Stillwell: Yes, we have.

Captain Hetu: No. I guess the only thought was what we sort of began with is the fact that public affairs, at least for me, was such a unique wonderful opportunity to do terribly interesting things at a young age, things that other people go their lifetime not meeting the kinds of people and doing the kinds of things we did, Presidents and the movie stars. I think that public affairs officers, at least a lot of the ones I know and I think myself, got to know a lot of admirals on an intimate basis and got comfortable with admirals in a very early time in our career, because we were essentially like aides throughout our career.

I mean, everywhere I went, you were always on the 00 staff and usually on the travel team. A lot of naval officers only do that one time in their lives, one tour. Maybe they get an aide's tour when they're a lieutenant and then chief of staff of something when they're a captain, I don't know, but we did that all our lives. I ended up working for admirals and Secretaries of the Navy, so that you get to be comfortable with people like that, and it's fun. It's also a danger. I mean, you have to be so careful not to wear the boss's stars, and that can be the downfall of people in jobs like ours. Always was extremely careful about that.

I remember in the Secretary of Navy's office, when I would get a new person in the office, a new chief or a lieutenant, part of my welcome-aboard talk was, "You are not the Secretary of the Navy. I am not the Secretary of the Navy. Don't forget that. We work for him, but you'll get a lot of people coming in here, senior people, who will blow smoke because they know we're on the Secretary's staff. Don't bite; you're not."

I was part of the trip-planning team in the Secretary's office. I'm getting way ahead of myself, but I can remember calling and saying, "Well, we're going to go to the Boston Naval Shipyard" or something, or whatever we were going to do. Calling the executive assistant to the BuShips guy or whoever it was and saying, "The Secretary is going. Could you get us a couple pages. I don't need more than that. Don't send me three briefing books, just a little bit. We're only going to be there for a half a day or something."

And the next thing I know, there'd be a vice admiral in my office, you know, saying, "I understand the Secretary's going . . . "

"Yes, sir."

"Tell me again what it is. You talked to my executive assistant."

I always used to think, "Geez, is this guy an idiot? The guy works for you. You can't speak English?" But I didn't want to say that. You have to be careful with that, and you have to say, "Yes, sir," and sit down and talk to him, but remember that you're speaking for the Secretary, and this guy is not there because of Herb Hetu. He's there because of John Warner or John Chafee and don't forget it. You can get yourself in a lot of trouble by overstepping your bounds.

But it was fun. You have to like to work behind the scenes. That's the fun.

Paul Stillwell: Well, we'll get to some of those in a subsequent interview.

Captain Hetu: Yes. That's the fun.

Paul Stillwell: Thank you.

Interview Number 3 with Captain Herbert E. Hetu, U.S. Navy (Retired)
Place: Captain Hetu's home, Alexandria, Virginia
Date: Wednesday, 5 June 1996
Interviewer: Paul Stillwell

Paul Stillwell: Captain, it's great to see you again on a bright sunny morning.

Captain Hetu: Yes, isn't this pretty. What are we doing inside? [Laughter]

Paul Stillwell: Well, we were remembering your career, and we were on the verge of your going to San Juan, Puerto Rico, to take up duty at the Caribbean Sea Frontier, sir. So resume there, please.

Captain Hetu: Oh, yes. That was a double-hatted job. It was the Tenth Naval District and also the Caribbean Sea Frontier, which was sort of the senior half of that command. The reason I got to Puerto Rico was that I had been offered a job in Japan, but I declined because I wanted to do my thesis and get my degree before I left Boston, which we did.

Paul Stillwell: Figuring that was the only way you would get it done.

Captain Hetu: Yes. Anyway, I passed up Japan, which in retrospect was probably a good thing. Of course, that happens all the time in life if you have enough philosophy. So they called me up and said that they had a job in San Juan, Puerto Rico, public affairs officer for the Tenth Naval District/Caribbean Sea Frontier, which was a plus again, because it was my own command again, and never mind. If you're the boss, that's important, because it gives you the opportunity to do all kinds of stuff.

Anyhow, we saddled up five little kids, and wife and moved down to San Juan. It turned out to be a terribly interesting tour, a very short tour but interesting tour. We had lived in Navy quarters at Pearl Harbor, earlier in the '50s, but this was 1965, just after graduation from BU. Got a wonderful set of quarters.

I relieved a Navy commander, still around, Russ Bufkins, whom I had worked for in Chinfo, my first tour of duty as a jaygee. Russ was a commander then, and he was still a commander—a lovely man. The bridge king of the Navy. He always set up bridge clubs wherever he went, and in fact, for the whole year I was in San Juan—or the 11 months, or whatever it was—I got calls every time a ship would come, wanting to know where the bridge game was. I guess it could have been worse; it could have been a crap game or something, but it was funny.

So, anyway, I helped Russ move. Russ was a sweet man, but probably one of the most disorganized people in the world. So his office was papers piled everywhere, and I moved into his house as well, helped him to the airport with his cat, Princess. Why do I remember that? Because it was a terrible morning; that's why. We had to give the cat shots and all that kind of stuff, and I didn't have cats then so I didn't understand. But anyhow, off went Russ, and I took over.

I'm trying to remember the admiral who was there when I arrived.[*] He was there very briefly, because Richard Craighill came in right after I got there.[†] The admiral that was there was a very interesting old-line admiral who brought his dachshund into the briefing every morning, who crawled up and sat in his lap while the briefers gave the briefings. I think the change of command may have taken place when I got there, because Craighill was the admiral.

Paul Stillwell: What do you recall of him?

Captain Hetu: Well, is he still alive?[‡]

Paul Stillwell: I don't know.

---

[*] Rear Admiral Howard H. Caldwell, USN, served as Commandant of the Tenth Naval District from February 1963 to September 1965.
[†] Rear Admiral Richard S. Craighill, USN, served as Commandant of the Tenth Naval District from September 1965 to June 1967.
[‡] Craighill died 7 February 1980.

Captain Hetu: Let me diplomatically set the scene. Puerto Rico was a very sleepy command, shall I say. The people who were there were generally not comers, probably at the end of their career. Not a lot of promotions took place in Puerto Rico.

Paul Stillwell: But a pleasant for a twilight tour.

Captain Hetu: Oh, a lovely place.

Paul Stillwell: If you were in that situation.

Captain Hetu: And we met some lovely people. But a lot of partying went on, and it was our first exposure to things that go on on a base. But it was lovely. We lived a couple blocks from the officers' club and the swimming pool. My kids could walk to school on the base; they went to a base school. So, in that case, it was very lovely. We lived in a great big house. I remember the night we got there. Puerto Rico is hot, and the quarters were not air-conditioned. If you wanted an air-conditioner, you had to go buy it, which was the first thing we did but only after a couple days.

I remember the first morning, we had five small children, and we lived right at the end of the base, next to the Coast Guard runway, which was right outside our window. And we had no idea that these old—they were the big Grumman amphibians.

Paul Stillwell: Well, they had the Albatross for a long time.*

Captain Hetu: Maybe the Albatross, the great big lumbering twin engine—and, boy, the first morning we were there, about 6:00 in the morning, 5:30 in the morning, we heard da-dum, da-dum, da-dum coming down the runway, and nobody knew what it was. Then he parked, did his turnup right outside our window and ran up the engines, and my kids came running in the room. I'll never forget it. The whole house was shaking with this guy running up his engines. But after a while we slept right through that, but the first morning was quite frightening. Anyway, we had a lovely place.

---

* The Coast Guard used the Grumman HU-16 Albatross flying boat for air-sea rescue.

The job was a challenge, to be sure. Puerto Rico, while a commonwealth of the United States, was more like being in a foreign land than anything. The people, for the most part, didn't speak English; they spoke Spanish. We lived on the base.

Paul Stillwell: Did you have bilingual people in your office?

Captain Hetu: Yes, yes. I inherited a wonderful secretary, who I'm still in contact with, Carmen Vasquez, who was a lovely, lovely lady, very dedicated, terrific. Because I started in the first weekend and went in and cleaned the office and took in buckets and cleaned out the files and reorganized, and she was wonderful. Brought in her kids to help reorganize the files. I'm a compulsive neaty and organizer. I can't stand papers piled on desks and stuff.

So, anyhow, we got the place turned around, and it was a great challenge to find programs to start to do. There were a lot of ships came through there, and I thought that one of the things we should be doing was working with the ships, which we started to do. Hometowners and feature stories, getting local television and newspaper people out on the ships. Not a lot had been done there for quite some time, so it was a fertile ground.

I started a morning press briefing, where we read the dispatches, and I got the wire service and so forth. We started as part of the morning brief to do a five- or ten-minute press summary, which was very popular with the admiral and with the staff people.

Paul Stillwell: What was the admiral like to work with?

Captain Hetu: Well, Admiral Craighill was on his twilight tour, like everybody else. I'm not so sure he entirely believed that, but it was kind of a sleepy command. He was not a very articulate guy, as far as press relations and speeches. But, hell, there weren't very many places to give speeches down there anyway except the Navy League once a year. So it was pleasant enough. He was not a bad fellow to work for. He was not very inspiring and pretty much let me do what I wanted to do.

Paul Stillwell: Not very demanding, it sounds like.

Captain Hetu: No, not very demanding at all. But anything I wanted to start up pretty much he would let me do.

Paul Stillwell: Did you continue some of the relationships that Admiral Gallery had set up, such as the band and so forth?[*]

Captain Hetu: Yes, we still have the steel drum band, which was probably the greatest thing we had going for us. It technically came under my office, but we had an officer who ran it all the time, which was fine with me. He knew how to pack them up and send them off. They traveled a lot to various Navy League meetings and conventions, and they were great. I have some of their records around here; we put out records. But I kind of stayed out of that. I had an officer that did that, and I didn't touch him, and he sort of reported through me and the chief of staff, and I never got into that. It was running smoothly.

Paul Stillwell: Why interfere?

Captain Hetu: Yes, particularly with something I didn't know about. I wasn't a musician, and I didn't know about steel drums, and I knew they were successful so—

Paul Stillwell: Was that also a link with the local community?

Captain Hetu: Yes, pretty much. They played a lot around Puerto Rico at schools and so forth. But, of course, steel drums in Puerto Rico were taking coals to Newcastle, in a sense. But they were awfully good, and they were always popular and they played for— see, our big time of the year was for Operation Springboard. See, I was only there for ten

---

[*] Rear Admiral Daniel V. Gallery, Jr., USN, served from 1956 to 1960 as Commandant of the Tenth Naval District and Commander Caribbean Sea Frontier. In 1957 he gained an additional title as Commander Antilles Defense Command. His oral history is in the Naval Institute collection. In it he describes starting a steel drum band.

months, so I went through one of these. It was the Caribbean operation of the year where all the ships came down. We had about three weeks of it, and we did have some NATO participation in that. So that was our busiest time of the year, when the operators on the staff operated. Most of the year was getting ready for Springboard and then writing up after-action reports, and that's about all we did.

The Caribbean Sea Frontier—that was their big operation. Of course, Roosevelt Roads was the big naval air station on the other side of the island, and that was busy. They really were busy. They did things, but that didn't come under us directly.

Paul Stillwell: What things were under the Tenth Naval District hat?

Captain Hetu: Puerto Rico. Guantanamo, technically, was in our area, so I got to Guantanamo several times when I was down there. That was kind of fun. We had a couple things happen. A ship got hijacked. That happened while we were down there. I took a load of newsmen over to Guantanamo. For the most part, the press there were Hispanics, obviously, Puerto Ricans, and some good people, nice people. I took a load of people over there on Good Friday, and I learned a lesson that I didn't know: Puerto Ricans don't like to fly on Friday. It's supposed to be bad luck. I didn't know that.

This was, as I call, it was not only Good Friday, but Friday the 13th, and several people wouldn't come. We got on the airplane, and they couldn't get one of the engines started. It was an old DC-4, a reserve airplane, and they couldn't get one of the engines going.* They finally got it started by taking up the cowl and hitting something with a ball-peen hammer or something. It was a solenoid or something that wouldn't shut. These guys were absolutely terrified. They were sure we were all going to die. I wasn't so sure we weren't either. [Laughter] But we made it, got over to Guantanamo and an interview. I'm trying to remember whether Bulkeley was there then or not. God, my memory is hazy about Puerto Rico. I think John Bulkeley was there, you remember.

Paul Stillwell: He was there a long time.

---

* R5D Skymaster was the Navy designation for the Douglas-built DC-4 commercial airliner.

Captain Hetu: Yes, the guy that turned off the water and so forth.* Anyhow, Puerto Rico was kind of sleepy and hazy in my mind except that it was sort of uneventful. I had a lot of fun there. My family enjoyed living there, and it was a springboard, no pun intended, to bigger and better things for me.

Paul Stillwell: I wonder if you could talk a little more about your family and the involvement with the Puerto Rican culture.

Captain Hetu: Well, we lived inside the base and seldom mixed on the outside, quite frankly. The people we knew that were Puerto Ricans we met really through the Navy League who were all bilingual and sort of the fat cats from Puerto Rico, the bankers and so forth.

The Puerto Rican National Guard and virtually all the reserves and so forth could buy at our exchange and our wine mess, which was always a sore point while we were there, because they were always in line ahead of us and pushing in line. The national sport in Puerto Rico was to get in front of you, both in traffic and in lines and stores and at the exchange. People always trying to get one ahead of you; it drove me crazy.

Paul Stillwell: I have a cousin who's a retired chief petty officer who lives in Puerto Rico, and he met his wife during a traffic jam there.

Captain Hetu: Well, I'm not surprised, probably got married and had children. [Laughter] They were dreadful. I mean, you know, a traffic jam. The other national sport in Puerto Rico was blowing your car horn, which did absolutely no good. But I guess it got rid of their frustrations, because you'd go mad sitting in these traffic jams. And they'd just sit there blowing their horns; nothing happened.

So we didn't get out in town. I mean, we drove around the island and did our sightseeing, went to the rain forest and all of those sorts of things. We went to a

---

* Rear Admiral John D. Bulkeley, USN, served as Commander Naval Base Guantanamo Bay, Cuba, from December 1963 to June 1966. On 17 February 1964 Bulkeley ordered the pipeline cut that previously supplied water to the base in order to refute the charge by Cuban Prime Minister Fidel Castro that the base was stealing water.

wonderful beach. There was an Army base not far from the Navy base that had a lovely officers' beach. We went there every weekend and the kids loved it, and we made some very good friends there on the staff. Jerry McNulty was an intelligence officer; he and his family and our family got very close in a very few months.* I can't remember some of the other people.

It was a good tour; I mean, it showed us the side of the Navy we had never seen. I remember the Army-Navy game, we had a big party, which I was sort of in charge of, with the Army. It was home game for the Navy, so we hosted the party at the officers' club at the naval base, their San Juan Naval Station, and the Army came over there. And they stuck me with goat. I was the new kid on the block, so I didn't realize what was happening, and they had a goat and—this was a big party, it was serious business. At the end of the party, when it was almost cleanup time, they handed me Billy the Goat, and they said, "He's yours."

I said, "What the hell am I going to do with this goat?"

Paul Stillwell: What did you do with him?

Captain Hetu: Well, I talked to the civil engineer officer, who was a friend, and he said, "We'll take him home, we'll tie him up, and we'll decide what the hell to do with him. When we get home, we'll cook him or something." It was a big, mean old goat. The Army guys had either found him or stolen him or something from a farmer, I don't know where they got him, but a big old mean goat. Went and dragged him home. I don't remember how I got him home and tied him up to a tree and went in. About a half an hour, and he was gone. He had escaped, so that was fun.

The civil engineer lived behind me, and so off we went in one of his gray Navy trucks looking for the goat and had the shore patrol and everybody out searching for the goat. We found the goat, finally, and turned him over to the shore patrol. They said they would take care of it. We didn't ask them how or where or why. We said, "Fine, it's your goat."

---

* Commander Gerald McNulty, USN.

Paul Stillwell: You didn't want to know.

Captain Hetu: I had no wish to know what they did with the goat. Got him off my hands.

Paul Stillwell: Were you concerned at all, being with a staff largely of people near the end of their careers, that some of this would rub off on you?

Captain Hetu: Well, yes, sure, that was a concern. I guess I didn't think about it a lot, but I did after I had been there six or seven months that getting a report from the Com 10 was probably not the highlight of my career. But I had a good time, and I started a lot of new things there. I got the office in pretty good shape and got an assistant off one of the ships, and I started to build my little empire, I guess.

So I had a lot of satisfaction. I had a lot of fun. But I hadn't been there very long when I got deep-selected for commander, which was absolutely unheard of. I mean, nobody got promoted, let alone deep selected. Ken Wade, bless his soul, who died not too long ago, was a great pal of mine, but a generation ahead. He was a captain then, and he was in the CNO's office as the CNO's public affairs officer. Friday afternoon was when the lists normally came out, and I wasn't even expecting it. I knew that the commanders' board was meeting, and I knew I was in the deep zone, but I certainly wasn't holding my breath.

I was at the officers' club for happy hour on Friday afternoon, and Ken Wade, bless his soul, called my home. My wife said I was at happy hour, which was early, 4:30 or something on Friday afternoon, and indeed I was. Ken called the bar, and the bartender said, "Is Lieutenant Commander Hetu here?" Loud voice.

I'm about halfway down the bar, I said, "yes."

He said, "You have a call from a captain in the CNO's office." God, this is like E.F. Hutton. The bar stopped dead, and everybody looked at me.

I thought, "Ken did this on purpose, I know." So I walked down and got on the phone and he said, "The board just reported out for commander." Ken had been on the board, and he said, "It's my great pleasure to inform you that you've been selected for commander."

Well, I just about fainted, and really, I said, "Oh, my God, Geez, thanks, Ken, wow, oh, wow."

So everybody was sort of waiting: "What's this call all about from the CNO's office?"

I turned to the bartender and said, "I just got selected for commander, set up the bar. I'm buying." And then called home to my wife and told her the good news and told her to come over and help me celebrate.

I was somewhat of a celebrity, being early selected for commander in San Juan. I'm trying to remember when the commanders' board came out, probably in the spring. Well, in any case, not terribly long thereafter I was selected to go back and relieve Ken as the CNO's public affairs officer, which, again, came as a surprise.

Paul Stillwell: Well, you described him as a generation earlier. Why would they get such a younger officer?

Captain Hetu: I don't know. In all humility, I don't know. I had known Ken a long time. Ken, I guess, had confidence in me.

Paul Stillwell: So he must have recommended you.

Captain Hetu: Oh, yes, absolutely, because that was Admiral McDonald, David L. McDonald.* I was never interviewed by him for the job. I was just told I had been selected, and that it was only going to be for, let's see, about a year, about ten months. I guess it ended up to be over a year, about 16 months, because McDonald was going to retire. And Ken had an opportunity to go to the Seventh Fleet—he was a captain then—in a job that he wanted. He'd had the CNO job and so forth.

So he said, "It won't be for a real long tour, and you've only been where you are for ten months and before that a year at BU, and before that a year in Los Angeles." So I was leaving, hop, skip and jump, you know.

---

* Admiral David L. McDonald, USN, served as Chief of Naval Operations from 1 August 1963 to 1 August 1967. His oral history is in the Naval Institute collection.

I said, "Hey, of course, I'm honored and delighted to take the job."

Of course, Admiral Craighill was stunned by the fact that, (A), I had been selected early, and then (B), selected to go back and work for the CNO. His wife was a bit of a climber, southern belle and treated me very deferentially at parties and so forth. I was a lieutenant commander, dah, dah, dah. My stock in trade went up quickly, and I remember one of the last things that Admiral Craighill said to me, when I was getting ready to leave, the day before. Dick Busby was my relief, and we had a very quick turnover, because I was getting out of there quickly.* The admiral called me in and said, "I hope when you go back and you talk to Admiral McDonald you'll certainly carry the word about the sea frontier down here, the way you've been doing as a public affairs officer."

I said, "Yes, sir, important command."

He said, "Well, you know, we're the shipping center. In case of an emergency, the ships would rally in here [and that was part of one of their missions]. This is a big operation down here, and it's getting bigger and bigger and more important."

I said, "Yes, sir, I know that."

He said, "Of course, it won't affect me necessarily, but I think, and I'm sure you would agree, we've talked about this, that this should be a three-star billet."

I thought, "Oh, my," you know. I said, "Well, sir, I will certainly carry that word back to the CNO."

He said, "Well, you know, it's an important command. It should be three stars. You've got the Roosevelt Roads over here and Guantanamo and, dah, dah, dah. We're only the Eastern Sea Frontier and the Caribbean Sea Frontier." He went through this little dog-and-pony show and, of course, it was clear what was happening.

I said, "Well, yes, sir, I'll certainly carry that word back."

Paul Stillwell: History records it did not get upgraded to three stars.

Captain Hetu: No, no. Probably my fault. I forgot to mention it to Admiral McDonald. [Laughter] But, anyhow, that was sort of the end of Puerto Rico. I enjoyed Puerto Rico,

---

* Lieutenant Commander Richard E. Busby, USN, a public affairs specialist.

I met some interesting people there, but it was a short tour and just about long enough. I was just starting to get a little bored, under a year, sort of had made all of the changes and was kind of—I like to party, but I don't like to party every night, and there was a lot of that going on.

Paul Stillwell: Well, you stepped into a much more hectic atmosphere and environment then when you got to Washington.

Captain Hetu: Oh, boy, yes. I've had so many great jobs, but working for Admiral McDonald was really a wonderful experience, and I was not yet—

[Telephone interruption]

Captain Hetu: Anyway, we arrived in Washington, moving again, packing up again. We had gotten a house in Vienna, so we were able to have our renters move. They weren't too happy, although actually we got another house in the interim, but that's another whole story. That's standard for all Navy families, I guess, moving all the time, getting new houses.

Anyhow, I came to Washington, Ken Wade took me in to meet the admiral. I was still a lieutenant commander. I had not been frocked yet or made my number.[*] We went in the first morning to the admiral. Admiral McDonald did a lineup, fairly customary, with the aides. The Marine aide, the personal aide, the executive assistant, and the public affairs officer stood at the lineup every morning. When we got the word that the admiral was inbound, why, we'd all scurry into his office, and Admiral McDonald would waltz in. I shouldn't say waltz; that doesn't sound right. He made an entry. He was a great guy. He was one of the old-school admirals, and I really loved him to death.

Paul Stillwell: I understand he was a thoroughgoing gentleman.

---

[*] "Frocking" a naval officer refers to the practice of allowing him to wear the insignia and assume the title for which he was recently selected. The officer does not receive the pay for the higher rank until a vacancy appears on the lineal list so he can be officially promoted.

Captain Hetu: Absolutely, southern gentleman all the way. A tough guy, but always a gentleman.

Paul Stillwell: Tough in what ways?

Captain Hetu: Very opinionated and not at all afraid to speak his mind.

Paul Stillwell: Also parochial about aviation.

Captain Hetu: Yes. Well, he was an aviator and, of course, he had relieved Admiral Anderson, who everybody remembers only had two years as CNO, and he got cross-wise with McNamara.*

Paul Stillwell: What were your specific duties?

Captain Hetu: Obviously, they were to represent the CNO with the press and to be the focal point for anybody that wanted to talk to him, interviews. I helped write the speeches. I didn't write them, but I helped formulate them. I handled all the correspondence for his public appearances. He got a lot of invitations, and when we'd get an invitation to do a speech or do an appearance or whatever, I would sort of check it out and write him a recommendation if his calendar was open. He was a very orderly guy. We'd put a note on it, and it would come back "Okay" or "No," or "Let's discuss."

Paul Stillwell: How comfortable was he with the media and in public appearances?

Captain Hetu: Well, I was going to say, the interesting thing was, the first morning, here I was, standing there, the heir apparent to Ken Wade, never had met Admiral McDonald. I had been selected for this job and had never even talked to the man and had never been

---

* The Chief of Naval Operations, Admiral George W. Anderson, Jr., USN, disagreed openly with Secretary of Defense Robert McNamara about disposition of U.S. ships during the Cuban Missile Crisis in 1962. For that reason and others, Anderson's tenure as CNO was cut short after one two-year term. For Anderson's side of the story, see his Naval Institute oral history.

that close to a CNO in my life, and here I was in the office and standing there. And in he walked. He welcomed me to the staff and said, "Glad to have you here, Commander, and Ken tells me you're the best and so forth."

So after he went through the lineup, he would take out his overnight work papers and put them in the out basket or whatever, or give them to the aides if they needed more work and talked about the schedule for the day, what was coming up and dah, dah, dah. It was very quick, very businesslike, and then he would dismiss everybody. At the end of the first morning he said, "Ken, you and Herb stay a minute." So everybody trooped out, and he said, "Just so you know, I don't like the media and I don't like talking to the media, and I wish it wasn't necessary."

I thought to myself, "My God, what am I doing here?"

He said, "But I understand that it's necessary, and it's required in our society the way that our country is run. It's something I've got to do. It's something I don't necessarily like to do, but I know it's important, or you wouldn't be here. Ken tells me you're the best guy for the job to relieve him, and you've got big shoes to fill. But you should know that I feel your job's important and when you tell me I should see somebody, I'll see him. I won't debate it with you—usually." So he said, "It's an important job. I rely on you to tell me what I should do in public affairs, because I don't like it, and you're the expert and you'll tell me what to do. So welcome aboard and glad to have you here." And that was it.

Paul Stillwell: How did it work out in practice with the media?

Captain Hetu: Absolutely terrific. He was good to his word. When I felt that it was important that he see somebody, or I knew that somebody was a straight shooter, he would do it, and he was great. He was a good speaker. He was very good in Q&A sessions and in news conferences, things like that. He was terrific, very studied. We would give him what I used to call "mind-joggers." When we were going someplace, I always kept a book of dirty questions and answers, which changed daily or monthly or weekly, whenever they needed to. And then local questions if we were going to visit a

Navy command, if they had had a problem there or something that had gone--the local people would brief me pretty well.

So he was always well briefed, and he paid attention. He knew it was important, and my press book always went in with the traveling bag for him to study on the airplane, and he did, and he was terrific. And he would ask me questions. It was a great job, because I knew that he depended on me, and for that reason you work double hard. I would get briefed by the local PAO and the press there and if there were any troublemakers and that sort of thing. Very often, when we would arrive at a place, he would always go in and visit with the commander there, the admiral, or whoever it happened to be. That was usually the first thing we would do, and always we would have the local public affairs officer in that meeting, which they thought was terrific. It increased their stock, and I told the admiral I thought it was important that they be there just to tell him if there were any local land mines to watch out for. So it worked out well. He was a great, wonderful guy to work for.

Paul Stillwell: I presume the business of the dirty questions included things that you anticipated would come up, and you at least wanted him to think about them before he had to answer.

Captain Hetu: Exactly. We used to call them "dirty questions and clean answers." [Laughter]

Paul Stillwell: Do you remember any examples of how these briefings worked and your preparation of him for those?

Captain Hetu: Probably the most intense period, we went to Australia and New Zealand for the Coral Sea Celebration that year, which was the last time a military representative from the United States went down there for that.*

---

* The Battle of the Coral Sea took place in early May 1942. It was a standoff tactically but a strategic victory for the United States, because it prevented the Japanese from landing in Port Moresby, New Guinea, which would have been a good jumping-off place for invading Australia.

Paul Stillwell: Probably the 25th anniversary.

Captain Hetu: That's right. And after that they had U.S. representatives, but it was generally a State Department person or somebody like that, but no longer military. They were trying to change the emphasis. But, as you know, the Australians and the New Zealanders, Australians mostly, I guess, felt that we really saved them in the Battle of the Coral Sea. Debatable but probably—

Paul Stillwell: Well, I think that's a legitimate claim.

Captain Hetu: Yes. Oh, we weren't going to dissuade them on that. That wasn't our mission. But I went down in advance and went to all the capital cities in Australia, every place but Darwin, and I went to each city for two or three days and met with all the local people. There was a parade, there were news conferences, there were wreath layings, there was visiting. The veterans organizations' parade, a black-tie ball in every location. I mean, it was a killer. I went down ahead, and, of course, they wined and dined me. I had never been to Australia and, good Lord, they really like Americans there. Boy, they were terrific. I mean, people would literally invite you home from the airport for dinner and stuff. I just couldn't believe it. It was marvelous.

Paul Stillwell: Well, I think they're just inherently friendly people.

Captain Hetu: Yes. And they liked Americans, and it was quite a thing for me to experience. I mean, to be sitting in an airport, and I was in civilian clothes the first time. I didn't wear my uniform, and they'd hear me order a drink at the bar and say, "Ah, are you a Yank?"

I'd say, "Yes, I am."

"Oh, well, come on. Hey, Harry, here's a Yank."

The first time it happened, I thought, "Geez, what's going to happen here? Am I going to get beat up or something?" No, you got beat up with hospitality. The first thing you knew, you had three drinks sitting in front of you. They were just incredible people.

But then I finished that. I didn't go back to Washington. I wrote up a fairly good report on each city and some of the press problems that were likely to occur. Some were frivolous, and some were important. The nuclear question was then big in Australia about whether or not we had nukes on our carriers or on our ships.

There had been a woman stowaway on one of the American ships, and this was big. This was back in 1967. The Australians loved this story. This was a woman who went aboard a frigate, and the crew kept her on board for something like six days, and she wasn't found. They had her in a sailor suit and fed her, and the Australians just loved it. It was just on the front page of every paper for days and weeks. And, of course, the serious implications were if you could do this with a woman on a ship with nuclear weapons, then our security was not very good. So that was sort of the serious side of that, but the frivolous side was that the Australians just loved this business. And she became a national heroine for some time.

One of the few times in my life that I was silly enough to make a comment as a public affairs officer, representing myself, was in—I guess we were in Sydney, and the press guy asked me, he said, "How do you like Australia? Are you having a good time, Commander?"

I said, "Yes, I think I'm going to stow away under the mayor's desk and stay here when my boss leaves for America." Well, I got all over the place—the Navy commander is going to stow away in the mayor's office, which was treated lightly, but it wasn't a smart thing to do. You're never too old to learn.

Paul Stillwell: Well, that raises the question, then. How much can you speak for the admiral?

Captain Hetu: Well, in this case, I was speaking for myself.

Paul Stillwell: But there are situations certainly where you are his spokesman.

Captain Hetu: Sure, oh, yes. Sometimes, obviously, when he can't speak to everybody about everything, but if you agree on a statement that he would agree to, sure, on occasion you would say, "The admiral feels so and so and so and so," and not go beyond that. Then you don't start trying to define for the newsman what it is the admiral really means by that. That's fraught with—that's a slippery slope. If you start down that way, you're in trouble.

Paul Stillwell: Well, working that closely with him, you were familiar with his thinking on a variety of issues.

Captain Hetu: That's right. I was going to make the point earlier, and if I did, excise it. But one of the roles of a public affairs officer is to sort of interpret to the admiral or to your command, or whoever it is, what the press really wants to know. There were so many people that I met in the Navy, particularly old-line officers, who would say, "Now, how exactly did he word the question?"

I'd say, "That's not the point here. I know what he wants to know, and you know what he wants to know. You don't want to dance around this guy, because he said 'gray' instead of 'dark gray.' I mean, come on."

Very often, when a newsman would call with a query, I would interview the newsman to find out exactly what he wanted to know and write the query accordingly, not try to tape a guy and say, "Ah ha, he said so and so, so we don't have to answer the second half of the question." I mean, that's ridiculous; that's not the way you play the game.

Paul Stillwell: Well, that can backfire, because if the media people perceive that you're playing a game with them, that makes them more suspicious.

Captain Hetu: Oh, then you spend days while they come back with a second question. I always felt it was better to interview the newsman really, in a sense, find out what he really was after and then get it out of the way once and for all. Answer all the questions as soon as you can and get it behind.

But, yes, you do a lot of talking about the admiral. I didn't necessarily talk for him as much as I would talk obliquely. You know, you get to know the guy. Obviously we're PR people; you can't get away from that. I didn't talk about his warts voluntarily. I talked about how strong I thought he was and what a good leader he was, and he was. I thought he was great. So, sure, a lot of times I would background newsmen on the admiral, what kind of person he was, and how he felt about certain things. I knew how he felt, sure, but not quotable. "You know, you can't quote me as putting the words in the admiral's mouth."

You know, the Australian ship—I went back to Fiji and briefed him on the whole thing. We spent a day on Fiji, and he was a great; he did his homework. He was a serious guy. I mean, he liked to play, but he was very serious about what he did, and this was a twilight tour. This was right before he retired and it was a fun trip, but he knew he was representing the United States and he did, and his wife Tommie, who was a lovely, lovely lady. They were a great couple. I mean, they were a handsome couple, and gracious and nice and both smart.

Paul Stillwell: Well, he was the kind of guy on appearance that Central Casting would send over for the Chief of Naval Operations role.

Captain Hetu: Oh, yes. He was just spiffy, and in civilian clothes he was a spiffy dresser. I haven't seen him for several years, but he's still a crisp dresser and starched shirts. He was my hero. I still wear a white handkerchief in my pocket to this day; it's sort of my trademark. He wore a white handkerchief in his pocket always, in his uniform pocket, with is blues, I guess.

Paul Stillwell: Which was unusual.

Captain Hetu: I guess he was one of the last naval officers to do that. I think Admiral King did it.*

Paul Stillwell: Yes.

---

* Admiral Ernest J. King, USN, served as Chief of Naval Operations from 26 March 1942 to 15 December 1945 and as Commander in Chief U.S. Fleet from 20 December 1941 to 2 September 1945; he was promoted to the rank of fleet admiral in December 1944.

Captain Hetu: I had many photographers come up to me and say, "The admiral's got a white—does he know he has white handkerchief sticking out of his pocket?"

I said, "Uh-huh, he put it there."

"Really? Can they wear it, can they have . . . ?

I said, "He's the Chief of Naval Operations. He can wear it any way he wants to."

He was the guy that made wearing collar insignias optional when I was there. And of course, all the aides had to go out and get new shirts because our shirts all had holes in the collars. But he didn't care. I mean, he was the kind of guy really, truthfully, that he made it optional, and if we wanted to wear collar insignia we could; he didn't care. You know, a lot of admirals and all their staff would have to do it. Generally, we didn't, but one day, we were doing something, and I asked him one day when we were talking about why he had taken the stars off his collar. I don't remember how we got onto it, but I sort of said, "You know, didn't you like the way they looked?"

He said, "No, the reason I did it was they were tearing the hell out of my uniform coats. The coats were getting all frazzled. You know, he's an old Scotchman, and he said, "I don't care if anybody else wants to wear them. I just was tearing up my coats, and I was tired of buying new uniform coats."

Paul Stillwell: This would be the service dress khakis.

Captain Hetu: Khakis, yes. So that's why he did it.

Paul Stillwell: How large on your radar screen and his was Vietnam during this period?

Captain Hetu: Not very large in those days. It was there. "Veet-nam," as the admiral used to say. But even when we went to Australia, we didn't divert and go off to Vietnam or anything. I guess Vietnam was cooking, but I don't remember it being real high visibility. McDonald was not a fan of McNamara's, didn't like him.

Paul Stillwell: Do you remember any specifics in that regard?

Captain Hetu: [Chuckle]

Paul Stillwell: Obviously you do, please tell.

Captain Hetu: Well, I can't remember specifics. I remember he would say things in the car when I was riding with him, going from here to there, and he'd come out of a meeting all steamed up. He'd say things about McNamara and I would kind of wish I hadn't heard that, and I'd say, "Admiral . . .

But he said to me one day, he said, "You probably wonder if I feel this way, why I don't just say something publicly."

I said, "Well, I don't think it would be a very good idea, but, yes, I sort of do wonder."

He said, "Well, I'll tell you what. If I ever got into a disagreement with McNamara that I felt strongly enough to quit, I would resign. I think that would be bad for the Navy to do that, and I think I have more influence and more chance of changing it by staying where I am than quitting in a huff. But if I ever got into any sort of moral or ethical corner where we just couldn't resolve it, I would resign rather than stay on." He never did, but pretty good philosophy. But he said, "It would be very bad for the Navy for me to do that. I wouldn't want to do that."

Paul Stillwell: Did you get the sense that his relationship with Secretary McNamara was one of frustration, because he was being directed by somebody who didn't really understand the profession?

Captain Hetu: Oh, yes, definitely, yes. And, of course, following on Anderson's footsteps, I don't think they ever had a real—that I know of—confrontation like Anderson was supposed to have had in the op center, I guess, is the story that goes along.

Paul Stillwell: During the Cuban Missile Crisis.

Captain Hetu: Yes. But, McDonald said, and said until the end, that he never really wanted it, never really wanted to be CNO necessarily. He had had a slight heart attack at one point before he was CNO. I don't remember whether it was in London or where, not anything debilitating, but I guess a slight heart condition. He was in London as CinCUSNavEur, which was not necessarily a stepping-stone upward.[*] It was usually a twilight tour.

Paul Stillwell: But a very pleasant place to be.

Captain Hetu: Oh, yes. That's where I went next. I was just going to say, McDonald was probably one of the last of the old-line, wonderful guys. He was very pragmatic about things, I recall, and he knew the way that things were. He didn't try to change things he couldn't change. But he tried to represent the Navy in the very best way. I think he probably, I would hope, be remembered as a good CNO. I think he was a good CNO, probably not as flamboyant and charismatic as some CNOs. I mean, he was not a favorite of the sailors probably—probably didn't know who the hell he was, for the most part. But he was a wonderful representative of the United States that trip in Australia and New Zealand. It was very soon. It was April and then he retired in August. He was relieved by Moorer.[†]

Paul Stillwell: One of the issues that spring was the reactivation of the battleship, and he opposed that vociferously, and so it was announced the day of his retirement that the New Jersey would be brought back.[‡]

Captain Hetu: That's right, yes, with Admiral McDonald jumping up and down. Yes, that's right, it was. I had forgotten that. That's right, the day we were in Annapolis at the

---

[*] Admiral David L. McDonald, USN, served as Commander in Chief U.S. Naval Forces Eastern Atlantic and Mediterranean (CinCNELM), U.S. Commander Eastern Atlantic, and Commander in Chief U.S. Naval Forces Europe (CinCUSNavEur) from April 1963 to June 1963.
[†] Admiral Thomas H. Moorer, USN, served as Chief of Naval Operations from 1 August 1967 to 1 July 1970. His oral history is in the Naval Institute collection.
[‡] For details, see Paul Stillwell, "The Battleship Battle, 1964-1967," Marine Corps Gazette, August 1981, pages 38-46.

change of command. That's an interesting feeling, at the change of command. Talk about the king is dead, long live the king.

Paul Stillwell: Well, please describe it.

Captain Hetu: Boy, well, he went down in the limousine and so forth, or whatever car they drove him down in. You go down as a CNO and you leave a citizen, and he did. He put on his suit and sort of zipped out the back door and drove himself home. Of course, the rest of the staff were all standing there, sort of the ins and the outs. It's kind of sad.

Paul Stillwell: Did you have a feeling that he had a sense of relief over making that transition?

Captain Hetu: Oh, sure. Yes, he did it gracefully. I think he was pleased that Tom Moorer, another aviator, came in behind him. He liked Moorer, and Moorer was very qualified for that job. I think Moorer had had what, the LantFlt and PacFlt?

Paul Stillwell: Yes, he had both major fleets. He had been groomed, not only for CNO but for Chairman of the Joint Chiefs.

Captain Hetu: Yes, and it worked.

Paul Stillwell: It worked.

Captain Hetu: But McDonald had not had a fleet command. He had had the Sixth Fleet, but he had not had Atlantic or Pacific.* He got his fourth star at CinCUSNavEur.

So Moorer came in; in fact, I was Moorer's personal aide for several weeks. His aide was coming, a guy named Nick Pope, I think, was an aviator coming from Vietnam and got sick on the way back and he had to be hospitalized, I forget, it was in Hawaii or where. Had a heart murmur or something, and so all of a sudden the brand-new CNO

---

* Vice Admiral David L. McDonald, USN, commanded the Sixth Fleet from July 1961 to March 1963.

had no personal aide. They knew Nick was coming back, or they had hoped that he would get a clean bill of health and come back and take the job, so they stuck me in the job as the aide for three or four weeks, which was fun.

Paul Stillwell: What do you remember about working that closely with Admiral Moorer?

Captain Hetu: Well, I just sort of kept the machinery oiled. I mean, they all knew that the other guy was coming in and had me there because I knew the routine. Of course, Admiral McDonald's aide, Tom Bigley, had gotten another job.[*] I forget where Tom went from there, I think a command. Jerry King was the executive assistant, and he stayed on with Moorer.[†] I guess it was Jerry that suggested to the admiral that I sort of sit in and keep the seat warm for a couple weeks and help Mrs. Moorer in the transition. And they had welcome parties and stuff like that that I helped with.

So I didn't work that closely with Admiral Moorer. I was in the lineup in the morning and so forth, but I didn't get involved in policy matters and things, because they knew the new guy was coming, and there was no sense of me getting all up to my armpits in stuff like that. Not only that, I was a public affairs officer; I wasn't a line officer. But Moorer was very gracious and nice and thanked me when I left, and so forth. And I was looking for a job.

Paul Stillwell: Well, before that, one of the events of that spring was the attack on the Liberty.[‡] What do you remember about the reaction in Washington?

Captain Hetu: Yes, yes. That was with McDonald.

---

[*] Commander Thomas J. Bigley, USN.
[†] Captain Jerome H. King, Jr., USN, served from 13 May 1966 to 24 May 1968 as the executive assistant and senior aide to the Chief of Naval Operations. The oral history of King, who retired as a vice admiral, is in the Naval Institute collection.
[‡] On Thursday, 8 June 1967, during the Six-Day War between Israel and Egypt, Israeli aircraft and torpedo boats made a number of attacks on the U.S. communications intelligence ship Liberty (AGTR-5). Of the ship's crew of 297, 34 were killed and 171 wounded. Israel claimed that the attack on the Liberty was a case of mistaken identity. Many in the ship's crew were skeptical of the claim.

Paul Stillwell: Yes, it was. It was in June, as a matter of fact, just about this date 29 years ago.

Captain Hetu: Admiral McDonald—have you done him, have you interviewed McDonald?

Paul Stillwell: No, my predecessor interviewed Admiral McDonald.

Captain Hetu: My recollection is that Admiral McDonald was the acting Chairman, was the duty Chairman. A lot of stuff was going on that I was not privy to, because I didn't need to know and he was doing his acting Chairman. He released the first messages that went out ordering the air strikes and stuff. He was the guy that did that. It was my recollection, that I learned later, I didn't actually know it that day because I just was unaware of it.

Paul Stillwell: What do you remember about the public relations fallout?

Captain Hetu: I didn't do a lot, because most of that was done in DoD and the White House, and I didn't personally get involved in that—hardly at all—and the CNO didn't do a lot of talking. All the talking about that was done by the Secretary of Defense, and I'm trying to remember—I don't even think the admiral was involved in the briefings. My recollection is that we sort of stayed out of it; it was handled downstairs by the big guys. He didn't do any one-on-one interviews, to the best of my recollection. We were just sort of not told; we were just sort of elbowed out of the way. It was a little bigger than just a Navy problem; it was a national problem.

Paul Stillwell: You said earlier that in your role as a PR man you were not in a position to discuss Admiral McDonald's warts. Are there any now that you can discuss all these years later?

Captain Hetu: Yes, I guess, and I'm not playing the PR man now, I can't really think of any. I remember one disappointment. First of all, nobody got any medals or anything when he left.

Paul Stillwell: You mean of the immediate staff.

Captain Hetu: Yes. I don't mean that as a disappointment. I don't think anybody expected a medal, but very often when the guy would retire and his staff was going to go off to other places, they would hand out some green wienies or something, and that didn't happen. He gave us nice fitness reports. This is not a criticism; that's the way he was. I mean, if you did your job and you did a good job, you got a good fitness report. You didn't get a medal for doing a good job. I mean, if you did something different, you got a medal. But he didn't do that. And I ascribe to that, I think—he was the old school.

I remember one disappointment I had. Tom Bigley used to write the inscriptions on all the photographs by hand, and then the Admiral would sign them. He didn't inscribe any photographs himself. What we would do, if somebody wanted a photo, whoever it might be, we would write a proposed inscription, tack it to the top of the photo that would go in. He would just approve it, and then somebody would write it on the picture, and then he'd sign the bottom.

Paul Stillwell: So Bigley was pretty good at imitating his handwriting?

Captain Hetu: Yes. And I got my picture; that was the one thing we all did want. Of course, I don't even know; they're all in a box someplace now. All the admirals you worked for, you get their picture. My picture came, and I was so disappointed, I said, "He didn't even write it to me." Bigley wrote my inscription, admiral signed it, but Bigley wrote it. One of the down sides of being on the inside.

Paul Stillwell: What relations, if any, do you remember with congressmen?

Captain Hetu: I don't remember very many. I don't remember him doing an awful lot with Congress. I know he had some friends from the South. I don't remember him doing very much. I guess he did, but I didn't get involved in that. I remember the first—this is kind of a stupid story, but when Ken Wade was leaving and I was taking over, the admiral had a going-away dinner party for Ken and had a lot of newsmen there, some of the old-timers that covered the Pentagon in those days. Jack Raymond from The New York Times and Charlie Cordry and Elton Fay from the AP and the guy from the Baltimore Sun, Watson.

Anyway, a premier party, small dinner party, maybe 12 people and me and the admiral and Ken Wade. It was a bachelor party. I had never been to the admiral's house, and I didn't know how to get there. I took the wrong turn going across the Memorial Bridge or something and I got lost, and I got there late. I missed the cocktail hour, and they were sitting down to dinner when I walked in. Talk about being mortified—I mean, my first public thing with the admiral and I was about 35, 40 minutes late. And he was very gracious. He said something, I don't remember what he said, I was too terrified. [Laughter] I thought I was stupid, I felt so—talk about, you know, going to a nudist colony with your clothes off. Everybody else has their clothes on. God almighty, I felt stupid. But he was very gracious. I thought he'd probably fire me; I thought I'd lost the job.

Anyhow, I wanted to do a big sendoff for him when he retired. Jerry King was then the executive assistant, and Jerry was a very serious, taciturn sort of guy. He and I became very good friends, because I learned early on that he had a pretty good sense of humor but never let on. I used to do things to kind of tickle his funny bone. Sometimes, we'd get stupid letters from people. I answered all the stupid letters, too, tried to be diplomatic answers to dumb letters. Sometimes I would write a funny letter on top telling the guy to go to hell or something and see if I could get it by Jerry King. Never did, of course.

I'd slip one in just every so often just to sort of catch him off guard, and he thought it was pretty funny. I said, "One of these days I'm going to get one by you, and the admiral's not going to think it's too funny." I wrote a comic press release for Jerry, when he made admiral, and I wrote it and sent it in to him. We got along really well, and he was a fun guy. I wrote a sort of parody on his life and that the Navy was shocked when he was selected. They didn't understand how he made it, didn't go to the Naval Academy and so forth.

Paul Stillwell: Was there a fair degree of camaraderie among that immediate staff?

Captain Hetu: Yes. Had to be; you had to count on each other. We had an interesting group, Jerry King and Tom Bigley. Jerry went on to make three stars, and Tom did as well. I still see Tom occasionally. Our Marine aide was a guy named Bill Holmberg, who was really a character for a Marine.[*] He was out to save the world. Bill was always doing do-gooder things for groups around the world, sending old school desks on LSTs to schools in South America, and he was always doing something. Bill sent an anchor to a VFW place in West Virginia, up in the mountains.[†] How he got involved in that, I can't remember, but Bill was always doing something like that, always had some crazy thing going on. A fun guy, a nice guy. Bill never made colonel. He had a heart attack and got cashiered out of the Marine Corps. The last I heard he was selling ethanol or something, he was always trying to save the world. But we were close, yes.

Paul Stillwell: We hear about the legendary long working hours that people like Admiral Burke and Secretary McNamara put in. What was it like on McDonald's staff?

Captain Hetu: Well, McDonald came in early, I think, about 7:30, something like that, in the morning, and he left at 5:00, 6:00 o'clock, unless there was a meeting or something going on in the Joint Chiefs or something. No, Admiral McDonald went home when it was time to go home and if there was nothing to keep you. He wasn't around trying to let people know that he was staying until midnight or something. He didn't do that. He took work home every night and he did it, did his homework and came in in the morning and had everything done. He was great. The aides loved him, because he was a guy who went through his basket, made decisions, and got it done. Didn't have a hold basket.

---
[*] Lieutenant Colonel William C. Holmberg, USMC.
[†] VFW—Veterans of Foreign Wars.

Admiral McDonald used to write a letter to his mother every Sunday night, literally every Sunday night.

Paul Stillwell: Typed it himself.

Captain Hetu: Yes. And he'd come in on a Monday morning, and usually the last thing out of his briefcase was the letter; we used to call it the letter to mother. We'd always sort of look at each other and laugh, "There's the letter to mother."

Oh, one event that I remember which was—you know, you learn these lessons as you go along, over and over, unfortunately. Admiral McDonald was pinning the first Navy astronaut wings on the Navy astronauts; it was the first time. I don't think he was very much in favor of it, but they altered the Navy wings. Over the center of the wings they put a space ship in orbit, a small one, but they were astronaut wings and the Air Force had done it so the Navy followed suit, and Admiral McDonald agreed to pin the first astronaut wings. I'm having a mental lapse again about who the first Navy astronauts were, who they were then.

Paul Stillwell: Shepard, Wally Schirra, Scott Carpenter.[*]

Captain Hetu: Yes, that sounds right. I think they were the three or four that—we did it in the CNO's office and had the press, it was jammed and the astronauts. I was sort of orchestrating all this, and I had a lot of press and had cameras and all kinds of stuff. And Bill Holmberg, the Marine aide, was sort of in charge of the hardware and so forth, but I guess we hadn't spelled that out too carefully.

So we were in there and the astronauts came in, and Bill Holmberg turned to me. We were standing in the back, and he said, "You got the wings?"

I said, "No, I don't have the wings. You mean the astronaut wings?"

He said, "Yes, where are they?

---

[*] Captain Alan B. Shepard, USN; Captain Walter M. Schirra, USN; Commander Malcolm Scott Carpenter, USN.

I said, "Hell, I don't know. That wasn't on my checkoff list. I was to get the press in here and write the statement and stuff, and that's all I was to do. Hell, I don't do the hardware. I don't get the medals when we give medals. What the hell are you talking about? I don't have the wings."

He said, "Jesus Christ, where are they?"

I said, "They're over in the secretariat office," which is on the D-ring, and we were on the E-ring.* So, God, slip a note to Jerry King, said, "Tell the admiral we're off to get the wings. We don't have the wings. Tell him to keep talking." So off we went. It was lunchtime and in the office, there was nobody there, and the safes were locked with the wings in them. Oh, my God, what do you do?

So we said, "Well, we can't get the wings. I mean, what are we going to do?" We went out in the hall, and I don't even remember who these officers were. There were three aviators out in the hall and we said, "We have to have your wings."

They said, "What?"

"We have to have your wings, we have to give the admiral wings to pin on the astronauts We'll explain it later. We'll give you your wings back, but right now we've got to have them." And so we took their wings.

Paul Stillwell: But these were regular wings.

Captain Hetu: Yes, oh, yes. We didn't know what else to do. We had to go through the motions of taking off the original wings and putting some other wings on.

Paul Stillwell: And the new wings were just like the ones they'd been wearing.

Captain Hetu: Yes, the same wings. So we took the wings, and the admiral was in there. I thought, "By now he's probably in trouble talking about the Liberty, and God knows what he's talking about in there trying to keep going." Just at that point, the guy who had the wings in the safe came back from lunch. And this was the Keystone Cops, I'm not

---

* The Pentagon has lettered corridors, going from A at the innermost to E at the outermost. E-ring offices, which go around the perimeter of the building, are considered the most prestigious.

kidding. I don't even remember whether these three were admirals or what the hell they were, thought we were all nuts, and we were. They finally got the wings out of the safe, the admiral's talking, we gave the wings back to these guys. They said, "What the hell is going on?" You know, just ran in and we had the astronaut wings and did it.

It was a nightmare; it was a dream you would have. You know what I mean? I mean, it was really a dream. We ran in at the last minute, slipped the wings over to Jerry King, or whoever was standing next to the admiral, and it worked. Went a little long, but we got the wings. [Laughter] But, boy, I'm deadly. People who have worked for me hate me, because I always do things in advance, and anytime there's something like that, I always get ready a day in advance, because I always tell them Hetu's Law: "Something will turn to crap without—trust me, something will go wrong." There'll be a lightning strike, or something will go bad. You've got to be ready. And here I am in the CNO's office, thinking to myself, "God almighty, why didn't we check to make sure that this was taken care of?"

Paul Stillwell: So you didn't follow your own law?

Captain Hetu: No. Well, it truly wasn't my job to get the wings, and I know that's a copout, obviously, but I should have viewed them, because I always did that. But, generally, if we were going to give a medal to somebody, I didn't go make sure the medal was on the table. I assumed it would be there. Bad word. I tell everybody that ever worked for me, "Don't ever use two words in my presence, 'assume' or 'presume.' Don't ever do that."

Oh, the end of Admiral McDonald. God, I'm afraid this is going to go into two volumes the way I'm shooting my mouth.

Paul Stillwell: Not to worry.

Captain Hetu: I went to King and I said, "You know, we've got to do something special for this guy. I mean, the change of command and all that is pretty standard, and that'll be

. . ." I did get involved in that, but I didn't run it. I said, "I'd like to do a lunch, I mean, super-duper big lunch. This guy deserves a really nifty sendoff."

Jerry said, "Well, you know, the admiral doesn't like too much fuss."

I said, "So what the hell's he going to do? What can he do to us now? Come on, let me see what I can come up with. I'll get the Navy League to sponsor it or somebody, and we'll have a big one up at the Shoreham and Navy Band and just have a hell of a lunch and get the Joint Chiefs and some good speakers."

"He said, okay, see what you can come up with."

So we got Bob Hope to be the emcee, and he was then making a Navy movie, and Hal Bishop was working on the movie.[*] Hal was at BuPers, sort of an adjunct public affairs officer. Hal was a good guy, but he didn't come up through the affairs side of the house. But he was working at BuPers, and he was working on this movie, and I'll have to try and think of what it was. But the Navy was giving cooperation, and it was a Hope movie.

So we got Hope to emcee it, and he didn't do that lightly. We went to the admiral's hometown in Georgia. I called the newspaper there, the Atlanta Constitution. Anyway, I asked them to print me up a big headline on their masthead, which we used to put together the program. I still have that stuff here somewhere. Then we had it blown up as a banner, which was behind the head table, something like "McDonald Retires, Navy Hero." That was the banner behind, and then we had Hope and we had the Joint Chiefs there, and we really had a great lunch. It was a super lunch.

The admiral was pleased, I mean, he really was, and Hope did his normal shtick and did his monologue all about McDonald, and it was funny and it was well attended. I don't remember how many hundred people we had there. The admiral was really touched, and we were pleased, we were all pleased. My recollection we went back to work that day, after the lunch, maybe about 2:30 or 3:00 o'clock. The admiral called me in by myself and thanked me for the lunch, which was very touching. He didn't do that very often.

---

[*] Bob Hope, who for many years entertained U.S. servicemen and women, appeared in a 1968 movie, The Private Navy of Sgt. O'Farrell.

Paul Stillwell: So that probably meant as much or more than giving you an end-of-tour medal.

Captain Hetu: Oh, yes, oh, sure. Yes, I didn't mean to imply that I was looking for a medal. No, getting a face-to-face attaboy from McDonald was like getting a Medal of Honor. Nobody else really knew about it. I guess Jerry King did, because he asked Jerry to get me over and said, "I want to thank Herb for that lunch." He said, "I guess Herb really orchestrated that lunch," or something; Jerry told me after.

Jerry said, "Yes, he did." We were a little worried. We did surprise him. I mean, he knew it was lunch, but he didn't realize how big it was going to be and that Bob Hope was going to be there and all that.

Paul Stillwell: Did the staff feed Hope some material about the admiral?

Captain Hetu: Oh, sure. Yes, I did. Well, his jokes were generic jokes about military people and stuff. I still have the monologue; I've kept it. I have it in my files. But it was funny, and, of course, Hope could say "Good morning," and everybody would laugh. It was nice, the admiral was pleased, and we were pleased because it was nice to make him feel happy. So that was that.

Paul Stillwell: Was there any prospect that you would be held over into the Moorer administration, or was it an automatic departure?

Captain Hetu: No, Moorer had his own public affairs guy, Bob Brett, who had been with him for a long time.* It was a given that Bob would come in and be his public affairs officer. Bob was a pal, and he thought it was great, hilarious, that I was Moorer's aide while he was the public affairs officer. We used to kid around. I'd say, "Sorry, Bob, you can't see the admiral today. He's really busy. [Laughter] Just tell me what you want, and I'll take care of it."

He'd say, "You SOB," and we'd laugh; it was fun, yes.

---

* Captain Robert P. Brett, USN, a public affairs specialist.

But then I got orders. I forget, there were a couple of things cooking, but all of a sudden Admiral McCain in London fired his public affairs officer summarily, phfff, "Get off the seventh floor, and you're out of here. Go pack your bags and go home."*

Paul Stillwell: Had he done some egregious thing to inspire that?

Captain Hetu: Something, I don't remember what it was. You didn't have to do very much to piss off McCain. Anyway, he was a commander, I'm trying to remember; I think he was a reserve. McCain always surrounded himself with a strange crew. I had worked him, I told you earlier, in Chinfo, not directly, because I was a branch chief and he was the Chief of Information.† But he was ultimately my boss, and I had a fair amount to do with him in Chinfo.

So they were searching around for a place to send me when all of a sudden, pop, the London job opened up overnight, you might say. They asked me if I'd like to go to London and work for McCain, and McCain was then, of course, four stars and I said, "Hey, terrific, good job: CinCUSNavEur, family get to live in London, and wow, okay, yes, I'll do it, you bet."

So it was a whirlwind change for me. I remember Admiral Rivero was then the Vice Chief, and he was going to London for a trip, for some conference or something. I don't even remember what it was, except I hitchhiked on his plane and went in and said, "Admiral, I'm getting transferred." I knew Rivero because he was Vice Chief with McDonald.‡

Paul Stillwell: Highly respected also.

Captain Hetu: Yes Great guy, Puerto Rican, yes, a nice little man, very nice man. He said, "Sure, yes, come on." So I went to London with him. Found a house miraculously. I won't go into all that, but found a really nifty house out in Stanmore, in Middlesex, that

---
* Admiral John S. McCain, Jr., USN, served as Commander in Chief U.S. Naval Forces Europe and Commander in Chief U.S. Naval Forces Eastern Atlantic from May 1967 to July 1968.
† As a rear admiral, McCain served as the Navy's Chief of Information from August 1962 to August 1963.
‡ Admiral Horacio Rivero, USN, served as Vice Chief of Naval Operations from 31 July 1964 to 17 January 1968. His oral history is in the Naval Institute collection.

was just coming empty. It's hard to find quarters in London, very difficult. I never was quite sure why this house opened up. To tell you the truth, I think the guy who owned it, he and his wife had some kind of strange separation, and the neighbors would never tell us. I had all sorts of things I thought were going on in that house, but I don't know.

Anyway, I went over and miraculously found this house and went to the CinCUSNavEur staff and said, "I'm coming."

One of the guys lived there and said, "I just heard about a house." We went over, signed up the house, went back to Washington and got the family packed up, movers. All this happened in a week or ten days, and off we went to London. My next great adventure.

We flew overnight, five kids. We flew out of Dulles, 8:00 o'clock at night—sitting in steerage with five kids—and we arrived at London Heathrow at 8:00 o'clock the next morning. I had worn my uniform, because in those days if you flew commercial you had to wear a uniform. I don't remember why, but you did, which was okay. I was a commander, and we arrived at the airport, and I was met by a Navy, I guess he was a jaygee then, Erv Sharp, who was the junior officer in the public affairs office.* He met me with two cars, and he said, "One car is to take your family home to your house."

I said, "Erv, my wife's never even seen the house. She doesn't know where it is."

"Admiral McCain wants you at the headquarters immediately. Send your family home. I'll have the driver take her by the commissary, so she can pick up some issue for food and stuff and then take her to the house." I gave her the key, and the driver knew where it was. My wife and family went off to the house. I thought I was going to have a week off or something to get somewhat squared away. The house was partially furnished, and the Navy had given us some furniture, beds and stuff. Erv had gotten the house livable for us, terrific guy.

Erv Sharp, by the way, had been a chief journalist and had transitioned into an officer. He was a jaygee, I guess, when I was there. Later I helped him change his

---

* Lieutenant (junior grade) Erwin A. Sharp, USN.

designator while I was there to 1650, and then he subsequently made captain, very proud of Erv. Retired in the Joint Chiefs; he worked for Colin Powell.* Anyways, I digress.

But, anyway, I went into the headquarters, and McCain was waiting for me. He was having an interview that morning with a correspondent from the Chicago Sun-Times, whom I didn't really know, and he wanted to know from me what he should say to this guy. I just got off the airplane. [Laughter] I'd never even been in the headquarters building.

Paul Stillwell: And you hadn't gotten up to speed on the command.

Captain Hetu: No, or the issues or anything. So thank God for Erv Sharp. The other guy had left; I mean, the guy I was relieving was gone. We never even shook hands, and Erv had been carrying the weight. He said, "God, am I glad to see you." So he briefed me on the way in about the questions and answers, and he had written up some Q's and A's that he had given to the admiral and explained his rationale and said, "But he wants to hear it from you. I told him this, but he said he wants to talk to you before he talks to the newsman."

"Okay." Went in to see the admiral, and he sort of welcomed me aboard, "Okay, boy, glad you're here, now, let's get down to this interview." That was my welcome, no how's your family, go to hell, or nothing. "You know this guy?" [Laughter]

I said, "I know him, Admiral. I know him by reputation, dah, dah, dah. And I think these are the important questions and so forth."

He said, "Why don't you just sit in, now, you jump in if you think I'm making a mistake."

I said, "Okay, yes, sir." I was tired, I'd been up all night. So I sat in on the interview, and I don't even remember what the hell it was about. I was half jet lag and everything else. But that was McCain, and that was the forerunner to a very interesting tour with Admiral John Sidney McCain.

---

* General Colin L. Powell, USA, served as Chairman of the Joint Chiefs of Staff from 1 October 1989 to 30 September 1993. In 2001 he became Secretary of State.

Paul Stillwell: Well, that's curious, because he was a former Chinfo himself, and you almost got the impression he was his own public affairs officer too.

Captain Hetu: Admiral McCain never did anything without checking with ten people all over the world. I don't say ten, but I mean, every decision he ever made he was calling people all over the world. He was always on the phone with this guy and that guy and Congress people and State Department people and everything. He was just a wild man. I don't say every decision, but virtually every important decision I can remember him making, and I don't even remember what they were.

The Sixth Fleet was down there, and he had a monkey on his back all the time, and I didn't know that at the time. I don't think he was shooting for CinCPac quite that soon, but I guess he was always on his way up. McCain is an enigmatic guy.

Paul Stillwell: What do you mean by monkey on his back?

Captain Hetu: Oh, he was always driven. He never sat still; he'd drive you crazy. He was forever pacing up and down, smoking a cigar, and fidgeting. And, God, he was an interesting man, and he's always had to be doing something 80 hours a day. He never sat still. He was tough on his staff, very tough. He had big aide, a personal aide named Max, and I can't remember Max's last name. Max was a very big guy, 6-2 and big, football big. And the admiral used to just tear him to pieces, tear him to pieces.

Going off on a trip, "Max, did you send this message to the people telling them we were coming, dah, dah, dah, dah?"

"Yes, sir."

"Don't say, 'Yes, sir!' to me like that. It's yessir.'" He said, "Don't say it like you knew I was going to ask you that, and you're sort of telling me that you're smarter than I am, because you're not smarter than I am."

This guy would stand there, and I'd say, "Oh, my God." And McCain came up to his chest, you know.

I used to call him "Blue Max;" that's why I can't remember his name.

Paul Stillwell: There was a movie by that title around then.

Captain Hetu: Yes. That was about the German medal, the Blue Max, but I used to call Max Blue, because he always looked like a beaten puppy. I said to Max a couple times, "Why don't you just pick him up and shake him one time? You know, he'll never touch you again. Just pick him up and shake him once or twice when he does that to you."

Max said, "Oh, I'd like to."

I thought, "Some day he's going to do it." He never did.

Paul Stillwell: How did the admiral treat you personally?

Captain Hetu: Well, it was a love/hate relationship. Max was the, I guess, executive assistant, and the flag lieutenant was a lieutenant commander named Nicholas Brown, of the Brown Browns.[*] His brother was the head of the National Gallery, Carter Brown, and Nick was a Naval Academy graduate and very rich, married to a French lady. What a way to be a naval officer. I mean, Nick was a nice guy; I liked Nick.

Paul Stillwell: His father had been Assistant Secretary of the Navy.

Captain Hetu: Yes, richest man in the world or something at one time. Nick went to the Naval Academy, and he lived, I remember, in London. They bought a double flat and had a hole knocked through and had nannies for their children and maids and stuff. That was the way to be a naval officer in London—or anywhere. But, I mean, he didn't make it stink. He was a good guy. So it was always fun to be around Nick and, of course, Nick played off the admiral. The admiral sort of treated Nick with kid gloves, in a sense, because Nick was very well connected.

Paul Stillwell: Max apparently wasn't.

---

[*] Lieutenant Commander Nicholas Brown, USN. The Brown family is prominent in Rhode Island and has a strong connection with Brown University in Providence. The father of Nicholas Brown was John Nicholas Brown, who served in the Navy in World War I and was later Assistant Secretary of the Navy for Air from 1946 to 1949.

Captain Hetu: No, Max wasn't. Boy, Max was always disconnected. Poor Max.

Paul Stillwell: Well, how would you describe this love/hate relationship? What would be examples?

Captain Hetu: I just meant to mention, he had a guy that had been with him for, I guess, ever, named Bill Dailey, who was a lieutenant commander. I think Bill retired as a lieutenant commander, which always sort of surprised me that McCain was unable to get this guy promoted. He was a mustang. His job was not very well defined. He was just the old shoe around and just sort of did odd jobs, nice man.

And he was sort of the family—how do you . . . ?

Paul Stillwell: Handyman.

Captain Hetu: Yes, I guess so. That's kind of demeaning, but yes, he did odd jobs and did things for the admiral and Mrs. McCain. These were the days, I guess, when you could do that kind of stuff. But a nice man; he traveled with us usually, not always. I'm trying to decide what to say. The admiral didn't drink but occasionally, and when he did, he couldn't handle it. I don't know if you ever knew that or . . .

Paul Stillwell: No.

Captain Hetu: I don't want to get into that, just occasionally he would disappear and not—and Bill would find him.

Paul Stillwell: Well, how was he from a public affairs standpoint in dealing with the media?

Captain Hetu: McCain couldn't drink, I should just say in his defense, because he drank like he did everything else. You know, he couldn't sip a drink.

Paul Stillwell: He did everything enthusiastically.

Captain Hetu: Yes. He would do it like he did everything else. If he had a drink he'd chug-a-lug it, and nobody can drink like that. I can't drink like that, and I've been known to have a few.

Anyway, the love/hate relationship. I guess I was one of the inner circle, you might say, because McCain was very attuned to public affairs. He knew that public affairs, in one sense or another, was largely responsible for his success. He came from OP-09D as a captain, where I am told—I didn't know him then, that nobody ever expected him to make admiral, and he made admiral out of the 09D job and he was a consummate politician.

Paul Stillwell: Mr. Sea Power.

Captain Hetu: Mr. Sea Power, the sea power presentation, which he gave a million times before three people, if they'd sit still for a half an hour. And he was very enthusiastic about it. One of my major jobs when I was there that the admiral called me not long after I had been there and said that he wanted to change the sea power presentation. He wanted to give it on the Russians and on the Russian Navy, wanted to change the thrust of it from just sea power. You remember the 75% of the world was water, and dah, dah, dah. He wanted to change the thrust of it to focus on the Soviet Union as the major threat, and that they were really a peninsula surrounded by water and talk about their fleets and why the U.S. Navy was the major counter to the Soviet threat.

So we worked many months putting together a new presentation, and if you don't think that was a chore. I mean, this guy was so comfortable with the sea power presentation over the years that he could do it in his sleep virtually. We changed slides occasionally just so update numbers and things, but it was pretty much in. So we had start really from scratch, and, God, he brought in people, reserve officers for active duty and all kinds of people to help with this presentation, which drove me mad. Because just when we would get to the place where we were kind of getting it shaped up, then he'd bring in somebody new who would have another idea and the admiral would say, "Great idea, boy, let's go and try that." And we'd go off in another direction. I was about to go crazy.

He had a woman lieutenant, whose name I cannot remember, who was supposedly a graphics expert, and she wasn't really. Anyway, that was a very frustrating time in my life, because it was an important command and we did have a fair amount of things going on. My pal Pickett Lumpkin was then over at Stuttgart as the CinCEur PAO, and I loved Pickett to death.* I'm sure I've said that earlier, more than once. And Pickett was a great guy to get you involved in things. He'd get me over to Stuttgart often. I was on the <u>Stars and Stripes</u> advisory board, and we would have a meeting every quarter for that, and then he'd get me over there for other PAO conferences.† I was going to Stuttgart every six weeks or so and seeing Pickett and having a hell of a time, good time.

Then there were things going on at CinCUSNavEur, because McCain was there, and he kept things going. But then overlaid on this was this new presentation. Good God, oh. He spent a lot of time on that and was very demanding and wanted things done overnight. It was during this period that when tensions were running high, that he accused me one day when I was in the office with him—I hesitate to say things, but he accused me of being a spy for the CNO's office. He said, "I know you're over here watching over my shoulder [or some words to that effect]. You worked for the CNO, and then you worked for Moorer." And he pretty much accused me of being—I don't know if spy is the right word, but reporting back to Washington, that I had been sent from Washington.

I blew up. There were only two of us in the office, and I told him, "Go screw yourself. I won't take that." He impugned my honesty and my integrity. "And you can talk about anything else but not that, and I have been loyal to you. I've been working 14 hours a day on this damn presentation, and I've been working on this command and I've been as loyal as anybody you'll ever meet in your life. And to accuse me of something like that, I'm out of here. Get yourself another boy. I don't want the job. I'm of no value

---

* Lumpkin by this time was a captain. CinCEur—Commander in Chief Europe.
† <u>Stars and Stripes</u> was a daily newspaper produced by the U.S. armed services mainly for reading by service members. It had separate European and Pacific editions.

to you if that's what you think about me. I'll take my kids and my wife and get the hell out of here and go back somewhere. I want out."

That was, I guess, the best thing I could have done. Well, it was the only thing I could have done, in my mind. God, he was stunned into silence, I remember. Came over and put his arm around me, and said, "Now, now, boy, I didn't impugn your honesty or integrity."

I said, "Yes, you did. Of course you did, if you think I'm spying on you or lying to you, you certainly did. You can't do that. I just can't stand for that."

He said, "No, I didn't do that, I'm sorry." Apologized all over the place and said, "You don't want to leave."

I said, "Well, no, I don't. I think it's an important place and so forth. But, good God, we've got to put this behind us because if I'm thinking all the time you're thinking that I'm not loyal to you, then we can't work together. I can't work for you."

He said, "No, no, I was upset and distraught, and dah, dah, dah." I don't remember exactly what he said, but he apologized and we shook hands or something, and I stayed, obviously.

Paul Stillwell: Did the relationship change after that?

Captain Hetu: Yes, yes, yes. This was, I guess, probably about the time I started to tell the Blue Max he ought to shake him once or twice. I never told anybody about that. I mean, I never told anybody on the staff certainly ever, that that had happened.

Paul Stillwell: Did you perceive after that that he had more confidence in you?

Captain Hetu: Yes. Oh, he never even danced up to that line again, no. I remember he said, "We want to showcase this. We want to premiere this new presentation of mine someplace important. I want to kick this off at a big to-do."

I said, "Okay, let me work on it." So I got the Overseas Press Club in New York and got him as the speaker at the Overseas Press Club, which was a pretty prestigious place and a lot of international press and so forth, ballyhooed it, quite honestly as a new presentation about the Soviet Navy and that there would be new stuff it in, which there was. We got cleared some tidbits about numbers of submarines or something, new statistics.

Paul Stillwell: Did you have to coordinate this through Washington?

Captain Hetu: DoD. Yes, did it through Chinfo and really worked with the Department of Defense getting it all cleared. That was another interesting thing—taking all the slides back and getting everything cleared by DoD. And the admiral was calling every day to see if it was cleared. I didn't have to do that; he did that.

Paul Stillwell: Well, this was timely, because that's when the Soviet Navy really was emerging.

Captain Hetu: Oh, yes. It was big stuff. But two things happened in New York. No, one thing happened in New York, one thing happened in the world. The morning of the night that we were to give the speech at the Overseas Press Club the Pueblo was captured, taken over by the Koreans.*

Paul Stillwell: Yes, indeed it was.

Captain Hetu: Yes. Of course, the balloon went up and I got a call from Dan Henkin, who said, "Will you tell your boss not to say a goddamn word about this. We are telling every four-star in the world not to respond to queries about this, and we know he's going to speak at the Overseas Press Club tonight, that there are going to be press up the buckets. And he's the only guy on the stump, person that's . . ."†

I said, "Oh, my God. Oh, my God." Oh, you better talk to the admiral, Dan. He better hear this from you or from somebody higher up that he can't say a word because

---

* USS Pueblo (AGER-2), an electronic intelligence ship, was seized on 23 January 1968 in the Sea of Japan by North Korean naval forces. The ship's crew members were held as prisoners until 23 December of that year. Of the 83 officers and men on board, 28 were intelligence specialists.
† Daniel Z. Henkin was Deputy Assistant Secretary of Defense (Public Affairs), 1967-69, and Assistant Secretary of Defense (Public Affairs), 1969-73

he's a good sailor. He'll say, 'Aye, aye,' but boy we're going to be under the gun." Good God, because DoD was saying very little at that stage, trying to decide what to do. You remember that. I'm sure it was Dan; yes, I think so. So I got the admiral on the phone with him, and the admiral said, "Yes, I understand."

"They're going to beat you to death on this thing tonight at the Overseas Press Club," but it was too late to cancel. So after all these months of working and all these days and weeks of getting the Overseas Press Club and figuring we were going to make a big splash with this new thing on the Russian Navy, the Pueblo got captured, so we were back on Page 7 or something.

Another lesson you learn as a public affairs officer. All your work can go down the tube in one day, if something else happens that pushes you off the front page, and it sure as hell did.

Another interesting thing happened at that point. It was a busy day. I had a good pal at CBS who was a producer over there, Dave Buxbaum, and I had known Dave for many years. He had produced the—I don't think I even mentioned—I think I did earlier when I was in the audio-visual branch we did the Thresher story.

Paul Stillwell: No, I don't think you talked about that specifically.

Captain Hetu: Oh, gee, that was an interesting time. We did a story with CBS on the Thresher, and Dave had been the producer. I had known Dave a long time. I can do the Thresher later, if you want to, or we can just forget about it.

But I had called Dave and said I was coming to New York from London and so forth. He called me and he said, "I've got some film from the French interview with Johnny McCain in a prison camp. They're trying to sell it, but we're not going to buy it. But I thought maybe the admiral would like to see it while he's here."[*]

I said, "What's it like?"

He said, "Oh, tough stuff, very emotional. You want to see it?"

---

[*] Lieutenant Commander John S. McCain III, USN, a naval aviator, was a prisoner in North Vietnam from 1967 to 1973. He retired as a captain in 1981. He became a member of the U.S. House of Representatives in 1983 and the U.S. Senate in 1987. He described his experiences in Faith of My Fathers (New York: Random House, 1999). McCain used material from Captain Hetu's oral history in the book.

I said, "Yes."

"Slip out, come over and look at it."

So I went over and looked at it and said, "Oh, I can't show this to him today, with this speech tonight and the Pueblo, wow. I'm afraid it would uncork him, you know, can't do it." I said, "How long have you got the footage?"

He said, "I'm supposed to give it back tonight, but I'll just delay them, tell them we're still thinking about buying it and so forth."

I said, "Okay, I'll get the admiral over in the morning. But I've got it tough. I don't want to tell him that you have it until after the speech. If I tell him before, I'm afraid it will be on his mind and that and the Pueblo and the new presentation, God knows what will happen. I don't know, the guy could blow sky high."

So I didn't tell him and told the aide and said, "After the speech get with the admiral and tell him about this film and they're going to hold it and we'll take him over to CBS tomorrow. I'm sure he'll want to see it."

So obviously he did and took him over with Mrs. McCain and put him in a theater. Nobody went in, and I don't remember what happened. I think I said to the admiral, "I think you and Mrs. McCain ought to see this by yourselves, and you don't want anybody else in there." So that's the way they watched it, and it was a very emotional piece of film, as you may remember.

Paul Stillwell: I saw it later.

Captain Hetu: Well, it was on the newscasts, and they'd show it occasionally. Johnny was all encased in bandages and, you know, his arms were broken . . .

Paul Stillwell: Casts.

Captain Hetu: . . . casts. He was a mess, and he cried during the interview. He was a gallant guy, but he was hurting so bad that he could hardly talk. Oh, boy, tough one. So, anyhow, we got through that.

Paul Stillwell: How did the admiral react?

Captain Hetu: Very emotional, but never talked to us about it. I mean, he never thanked me or thanked Dave for seeing it. I think they looked at it twice.

Paul Stillwell: Well, some things are just too painful.

Captain Hetu: Yes, he couldn't—nothing to say. But, he never knew, I'm sure, that I delayed it or anything, and that was a very hard decision to make. That wasn't a great heroic decision. That was the only decision you could make.

So, anyway, we went back to London after that and started off on talking about the Russian Navy, somewhat disappointed that we didn't get the big splash we wanted to get, but he understood. Nothing I could do about the Pueblo.

Paul Stillwell: Some things are just beyond your control.

Captain Hetu: Yes, that's right.

Paul Stillwell: What do you remember about the relationship with the British in that job?

Captain Hetu: Oh, lovely. You know, for all his sort of rough edges and craziness, he could be a very charming guy, and he was very intense. McCain wasn't what I would call a fun guy. He could be charming, but he couldn't maintain it too long.

Paul Stillwell: But very dedicated to the job.

Captain Hetu: Absolutely, yes, that's right, and to the United States and he was a patriot certainly.

Paul Stillwell: Was there a common bond in dealing with the professional sailors of the Royal Navy?

Captain Hetu: Yes. Yes, they liked him. The Brits liked Admiral McCain to my recollection, like the Congress did. He was little and feisty and a submariner and had a lot of medals and tough talking, little tough guy.

Paul Stillwell: Almost a stereotype, or a caricature.

Captain Hetu: Oh, boy, a caricature, really. I've seen him throw his cigar when he got mad, and we used to laugh, because he always had a big long cigar and always used a wooden pointer when he would give his presentations, so he was forever switching hands. He'd put the cigar in one hand and the pointer, and then he'd put the cigar in that hand, and put the pointer—and we thought some day he was going to stick that pointer in his mouth.

He was funny. He had a tough mouth but never around women. I don't think I ever heard him swear in front of a woman. He may have, but I never heard him. But he was pretty tough talking around men. I remember one of the things he used to say to you was, "God bless you, goddammit. God bless you, goddammit." It was sort of a double whammy. But he was an interesting guy.

Towards the end, he became so driven. I guess he then knew that he was in contention for the CinCPac job, mindboggling. I didn't know that. I mean, he was on the phone more than ever, and he was always on the phone back to connections and people and talking with congressmen. He was very well plugged in to the Congress. And, you know, that was how he—he went from OLA job as two stars, and I think he went from there to the Eastern Sea Frontier, where he got his third star, and everybody was sure the Eastern Sea Frontier was the last.[*]

Paul Stillwell: Well, he was ComPhibLant for a while.

---

[*] As a rear admiral, McCain was the chief legislative liaison officer for the Secretary of the Navy, 1958-60. OLA—Office of Legislative Affairs. As a vice admiral He was Commander Amphibious Force Atlantic Fleet, 1963-65, and Commander Eastern Sea Frontier, 1965-67.

Captain Hetu: PhibLant and then the Eastern Sea Frontier. But I remember that he was a smart guy. One of the lesser known jobs at Eastern Sea Frontier was the naval adviser to the United Nations ambassador, which nobody ever did anything about. I mean, it was just sort of one of your several titles. Well, he parlayed that, and I think Goldberg was then the U.N. Ambassador, and McCain drove that horse hard; he was always with Goldberg.[*] But a lot of people felt that was how he got his fourth star, to London, which surprised a great many people, that he ever made four stars.

Paul Stillwell: Would you describe him as an opportunist?

Captain Hetu: Well, he sure knew how to play the game, and he was very successful at it. I remember the middle of the night a guy from ABC that I knew in New York called me in London; it was five hours' difference, I guess. That was 3:00 in the morning or something like that and got me out of a sound sleep and said, "My God, it's just been announced here; we just found out that your boss is going to be CinCPac."

I said, "Oh, my God, really?"

He said, "Yes, CinCPac. What do you think about that?"

I said, "Is this a dream? Am I awake?"

He said, "No, he's going to go to CinCPac."

Well, the next morning, the admiral was dancing around. He was as relaxed as I'd ever seen him. Finally that monkey was off his back when he was named CinCPac.[†] I'm trying to remember how long he was there, several weeks, didn't go right out. I don't remember whom he relieved.

Paul Stillwell: Admiral Sharp.[‡]

Captain Hetu: Sharp, yes, that's right. Kept all the chairs at the same level. Sharp was a little guy like McCain. Anyway, he was asking very few people to go with him to be on

---

[*] Arthur J. Goldberg was U.S. representative to the United Nations from 1965 to 1968.
[†] Admiral McCain served as Commander in Chief Pacific from 31 July 1968 to 1 September 1972.
[‡] Admiral Ulysses S. Grant Sharp, USN, served as Commander in Chief Pacific from 30 June 1964 to 31 July 1968. His oral history is in the Naval Institute collection.

the staff—Johnny Butts and I think the intelligence guy, not very many people.* I was scared to death he was going to ask me to go. [Laughter] I remember telling my wife Peggy, "God, I hope he doesn't ask me, I don't really want to go. I've about had all the McCain I can handle, I think. I need to go to Vietnam anyway." I wanted to get a Vietnam tour. I hadn't had one, and I wanted to go.

So one Saturday morning we were working away and getting close to his departure time and the change of command. I don't think Admiral Wendt was on board yet by then.† No, he wasn't, that was a week away or something. Saturday morning McCain called me into the office, or I went in to do something with him, and he said, "Listen, boy, how would you like to go to CinCPac with me?" And he said, "I don't want a big long answer. I just want a yes or no. Don't give me a lot of crap," or whatever he said, "just a yes or no answer."

I said, "No, sir."

He said, "What? Why not?"

I sort of laughed. I said, "Well, the real reason, Admiral, is that the CinCPac PAO is now an Air Force brigadier general, and I'm too junior to get the top job. Here I had my own sort of four-star command, and it was good for my career, and I want to go to Vietnam next. If I went to CinCPac, I'd be way down in the pecking order. I'd have one of the branches in the public affairs office or something like that. I really don't want to do that I wouldn't be working directly for you, really."

He said, "Yes, that makes sense, okay. Well, but what if I took you out there as sort of my special assistant, like you were with Admiral McDonald?" He said, "You know, he had Chinfo, but then you were McDonald's special assistant. You would come out and be my special assistant for public affairs. We'd have the general down there running the shop." Oh, my God. Oh, I wasn't ready for that.

Paul Stillwell: That would be awkward.

---

* Captain John L. Butts, Jr., USN.
† Admiral Waldemar F. A. Wendt, USN, served as Commander in Chief U.S. Naval Forces Europe and Commander in Chief U.S. Naval Forces Eastern Atlantic from July 1968 to June 1971.

Captain Hetu: That's what I told him. I thought, "Oh, God, now what do I do? How do I escape from this?" I don't know if I said awkward, but I said, "Admiral, I think that's probably not a good idea. If you're going to joint command and taking a Navy commander as your public affairs spokesman might be viewed by the other commands as you'd be sort of isolating yourself, and I don't think you want to do that. It's joint, and you're going to have all these other services working with you, probably ought to keep the general there. I want to go to Vietnam and then maybe at the end of the Vietnam tour I can come back and work for you there."

I knew damn well he'd forget in 15 minutes. He said, "Okay, okay, boy. Yes, I understand. Okay, that makes sense, okay. Well, just wanted you to know that I wanted you to come."

I said, "Well, I'm flattered, of course," and dah, dah, dah, and get out of here. So, anyway, off he went to CinCPac, and Admiral Wendt came in to be CinCUSNavEur. I didn't know very much about him. I don't think anybody knew very much about Admiral Wendt.

Paul Stillwell: He'd been OP-06.

Captain Hetu: Yes. A nice man, a prince of a fellow and I really enjoyed working for him. A great big guy.

Paul Stillwell: Also I heard he had a pretty good sense of humor.

Captain Hetu: Good sense of humor, nice wife. Yes, I loved working for Admiral Wendt; I wrote speeches for him. I didn't like to write speeches. McCain you didn't have to write a speech for because he always gave the sea power presentation, or some form of it. But Wendt I wrote speeches for. He didn't do a lot of speaking, but I wrote those he did give, and he liked public affairs. I went with him everywhere, and we just really hit it off personally, and I liked him a lot.

Then I had a chance to go to Vietnam. The Det Charlie job came up in Vietnam, the Seventh Fleet in-country detachment.* I thought that was the best public affairs job you could get in Vietnam, and so it came open and I really wanted it. So I told Chinfo that I'd really like to get that job. I went in to see Admiral Wendt, whom I hadn't been working for terribly long. I said that I had this opportunity to go to Vietnam, and I really wanted to do it.

He tried to talk me out of it and he said, "It's not really important to you. You don't have to do it. You'll make captain, and you're doing a good job. You've had four-star commands and worked for the CNO. Hell, you're in good shape." He said, "I didn't go to Vietnam." He said, "Look at the . . . " Wendt didn't have a lot of medals. He said, "I didn't do a lot of that stuff, and I made four stars. Don't worry about it; you'll be all right, getting good fitness reports here."

I said, "Well, I really do want to go to this job." He would not have kept me if I didn't want to stay, certainly, but I remember at a cocktail party that night or a day later, my then wife said to him, "Admiral, if you keep Herb here and don't let him go to Vietnam, I'll never speak to you again." [Laughter]

Mrs. Wendt was there, and they sort of laughed and said, "Why is that, Peggy?"

She said, "Because he will never let me alone if he doesn't go. All he talks about is going to Vietnam, and if he doesn't go to Vietnam and you don't let him go, I'm not going to talk to you again either because he won't be fit to live with."

The admiral said, "Okay, Herb, go to Vietnam."

I said, "Thank you, Admiral." We all laughed and had a drink, and then I went to Vietnam.

Paul Stillwell: Well, a couple more questions before that. Who was Admiral McCain's deputy at CinCUSNavEur, and did he serve as kind of a moderating influence?

Captain Hetu: God, what a question. I should know that instantly, and I can't remember who his deputy was.

---

* For background on the development and role of Det Charlie during the Vietnam War, see Commander Harry E. Padgett, USN, and Lieutenant Commander Jack A. Garrow, USN, "Saigon—the Navy Reported Today . . . ," U.S. Naval Institute Proceedings, April 1969, pages 132-137.

Paul Stillwell: Presumably he was an aviator, because McCain was a submariner.

Captain Hetu: Well, I'm trying to remember. I don't remember us having a three-star.

Paul Stillwell: Well, probably a two-star.

Captain Hetu: Yes, we had a chief of staff and then Johnny Butts, who was an aviator, really sort of was—in fact, McCain took Butts with him to CinCPac, and he got two stars. I think he was either the chief of staff at CinCPac or 03 or something like that. Butts was very in with admiral at CinCUSNavEur. Butts and I weren't very close. I don't know whether he saw me as a threat or quite what, but I didn't much like Admiral Butts. He was a captain then, I was a commander. We didn't get along real well. In fact, he marked my fitness report, and I'll tell you that story later on. Marked me down one notch in one thing, and I had been getting 4.0's for forever, and I didn't even learn about it until I went back after Vietnam to be the Secretary's public affairs officer. But that's another story I'll tell you later, because I confronted McCain with that.

Paul Stillwell: Well, the other thing I was curious about, were there any Sixth Fleet issues during your time in London?

Captain Hetu: I don't remember any real crunch issues with the Sixth Fleet. We went and visited the Sixth Fleet a couple of times. He liked to get out on board ship.

Paul Stillwell: Had the dust settled on the move from France to Italy by then?

Captain Hetu: Yes. I can't even remember who the Sixth Fleet commander was there. Admiral McCain didn't have very much to do with the Sixth Fleet at all. I mean, I guess we did operationally, but I didn't public affairs-wise.

Paul Stillwell: Well, it had been Admiral Martin, and then Admiral Richardson took over from him.

Captain Hetu: Yes. I'm trying to think maybe Martin was there.* Yes, I think so, because I think George Rodgers was the public affairs officer, Captain George Rodgers, who was not a PAO but a nice guy and an aviator.† George Rodgers died a couple of years ago. We didn't have a lot to do with the Sixth Fleet. I mean, I think he exercised his control over it, but I don't remember any issues overriding. I wasn't in London all that long either. I wasn't here two years; I was only there a year and a half.

Paul Stillwell: Well, then off you went to Saigon. Was Ken Wade still on the flagship?

Captain Hetu: I'm trying to remember. I think Ken was by then the deputy Chinfo, and the Seventh Fleet public affairs officer was—I can see his—

Paul Stillwell: Ralph Slawson was out there for a while.‡

Captain Hetu: Ralph Slawson, that's right. Good old Ralph.

Paul Stillwell: A nice guy.

Captain Hetu: Very nice guy, very decent man. He's around Washington someplace; I see him occasionally. Yes, I relieved Bill Stierman.§ Well, on the way out we had a little bit of an interesting—I was in Pearl Harbor with Brayton Harris, who was going to MACV, Navy commander.** We were together in Pearl Harbor when the EC-121 got shot down by the Koreans.††

Paul Stillwell: April 1969.

---

* Vice Admiral William I. Martin, USN, commanded the Sixth Fleet from April 1967 to 14 August 1968. His oral history is in the Naval Institute collection.
† Captain George F. Rodgers, USNR.
‡ Commander Ralph L. Slawson, USN, a public affairs specialist.
§ Commander Joseph William Stierman, USN, a public affairs specialist.
** Commander Brayton R. Harris, USNR, a public affairs specialist. MACV—Military Assistance Command Vietnam.
†† A U.S. Navy EC-121 electronic reconnaissance aircraft with 31 crewmen on board was short down 14 April 1969 by North Korean aircraft. The incident took place approximately 90 miles off the coast of North Korea. The entire U.S. crew was lost.

Captain Hetu: Yes, and we were dispatched from Pearl Harbor to Sasebo, Japan. What happened was the Russians found the bodies of the aviators.* There was also some pucker time there, because they were going to nuclear alert and all kinds of stuff when the Koreans shot this plane down, Navy reconnaissance plane.

Paul Stillwell: And the New Jersey, which was on its way home from Vietnam, got turned around and sent to WestPac.†

Captain Hetu: Right. We didn't know whether we were going to go to war or what the hell was going to go on. We weren't sure at CinCPac whether we were going to get sent to Saigon or to Seoul or where we were going to go. Vince Thomas was then the public affairs officer at CinCPacFlt, and McCain was at CinCPac.‡ I went up and called on him, said hello. Finally it sort of settled down, and they said that the bodies had been found: The Russians had them, and they zipped us out to Sasebo to handle the press bringing the bodies ashore.

The Russians transferred the bodies to an American destroyer. We got there about the time that all this was taking place, and why they decided on Sasebo, I can't remember—location, obviously.§ It was a couple days off when we got sent, because the ships were steaming around up there picking up debris and bodies. Then they were going to bring him into Sasebo, and that's where the press was going to come together to view the bodies coming ashore. There wasn't very much anybody could say about the shootdown; that was happening other places.

---

* On this point Captain Hetu's memory varies from contemporary press reports and from the recollection of Captain Sheldon Kully, USN (Ret.), who was commanding officer of a U.S. destroyer that recovered two bodies of EC-121 crew members and some debris from the aircraft. Kully's recollection, which coincides with media accounts, is that the Soviets recovered no corpses from the lost aircraft.
† WestPac—Western Pacific.
‡ Captain Vincent C. Thomas, Jr., USNR, a public affairs specialist.
§ The destroyer Henry W. Tucker (DD-875) recovered the body of one officer and one enlisted man from the EC-121 on 17 April 1969. On 18 April the Henry W. Tucker rendezvoused with the Soviet destroyer Vodokhnovenny, which had also recovered debris. The Soviet ship then sent a motor whaleboat to transfer debris from to a motor whaleboat from the Henry W. Tucker. The U.S. ship departed the search area that day en route Sasebo, Japan.

But returning the bodies was a big event, and I think—I'm trying to remember how many bodies there, 10 or 12.

Paul Stillwell: I thought there was a crew of about 30, and all were dead.

Captain Hetu: Yes, but they didn't find them all. Anyway, Brayton and I got to Sasebo and started to set up the arrival arrangements and all the things you had to do to take care of the press and talking to the skipper on the destroyer, who was a good guy.* I wish I could remember his name, because he was a joy to work with, a neat, nice guy. We kept him over the horizon until the morning. We didn't want to bring these bodies in at night in all the shroud of darkness and all that stuff, wanted it to be at least a bright sunshiny day.

Three things I can remember that were different, and the one thing was we didn't want to bring them off in body bags, terrible.

Paul Stillwell: Bad image.

Captain Hetu: Bad image, terrible. So we wanted to get these big metal caskets, body holders, and they had them up in Tokyo. The Army had them in a mortuary up there, and the Army wouldn't give them to us. I mean, it was just bullshit. You know, "Well, you don't have a requisition and all this."

"Come on, we've got to get these out to a ship. We've got to send them out by a tug, and we want to keep the ship over the horizon until we can get the things out there and we've got to send some mortuary people out to help them put the bodies in." They were keeping them in a freezer out on the ship.

So I called Dan Henkin in Washington, I guess, Dan. Yes, Dan was still there, and I knew Dan. I had known him from the old days when he worked for the <u>Armed Forces Journal</u>. So I called Dan from Sasebo and said, "Dan, I'm having trouble with the Army pukes up in Tokyo." I think it was outside of Tokyo, wherever it was. I said, "They

---

* Commander Sheldon D. Kully, USN, commanded the destroyer <u>Henry W. Tucker</u> (DD-875) from July 1967 to July 1969.

won't give me these caskets. I've got to have them." He immediately—you know, didn't take but three minutes to understand what was going on. I said, "We can't bring these guys off in body bags."

He said, "Hey, never mind, hold on." Dan called Tokyo or the joint commander or somebody, CinCPac or whoever it was. I don't know how he did it, but in about an hour we had our caskets shipped down by the fastest truck they could find. Loaded them on a fleet tug and sent them out to find the destroyer.

Paul Stillwell: Did they go by air from Tokyo to Sasebo?

Captain Hetu: I'm trying to remember, they got them down there right quick. I guess they did bring them down by air. They would have had to to get them there.

Paul Stillwell: That's a pretty good haul.

Captain Hetu: That's a haul. Yes, I think you're right. Yes, they couldn't have brought them by truck. Whatever Dan did, we had them within hours, not days, but hours, and then got them on a tug and got them sent out to the destroyer with a couple of—I don't remember whether they were Army mortuary people or Navy people, but sent some people out to help the corpsman, who were taxed.

We talked to the ship, and the skipper was terrific. I remember we were talking Navy regulations by long distance, Navy regs about getting his guys in dress blues with white gloves, and I think he had enough white gloves. I think the officers all had enough white gloves so that the pallbearers bringing these caskets off the ship would be in dress blues with white gloves. We wanted this to look like the Navy takes care of its own.

Paul Stillwell: Dignified.

Captain Hetu: You bet. So we got everything going; everything is set. We were sitting around, I remember, at the base commander's house the night before the ship was supposed to come in the next morning—I think 8:00 o'clock or something, sunup, so forth. We were sitting around having a drink, sort of running through the whole scenario in our minds and I don't know, but I think it was me, maybe Brayton, or maybe both of us, said, "Wait a minute. Do you have a wide brow?"* We were going through it in our minds: "My God, they're going to have just a normal brow to bring the caskets off with these pallbearers on each side. It's going to look like the Keystone Cops. I mean, they can't get them down, they'll have to slide it down or something."

The captain, the CO of the naval base said, "God, I see what you're saying." So he called in the public works officer, got him out of bed, I think, and said, "We've got to have a wide brow. So they went down and cut one down the middle, and overnight they made a wide one. They made it six feet wide or something and painted it and got it down there. So the next morning they just marched off this thing. God, that was close that we remembered that.

Paul Stillwell: The devil is in the details, as they say.

Captain Hetu: Always. Well, that wasn't the end of the details. We went down in the morning; they had the dock cleared for the ship. We went down at first light, 5:30 or so. I don't even know if we went to bed. The press was out at the gate. We didn't want them mushing around until about an hour before and get them set up. Then I suddenly looked over, and right behind the place where the destroyer was coming in was the Pueblo's sister ship.

Paul Stillwell: The Banner.

Captain Hetu: Yes, sitting right there. We said, "Oh, my God, what a great backdrop, huh? Here's this EC-121 get shot down, the spy plane, and the ship's going to come in and the bow's going to be here, and right behind the people coming down with the bodies is going to be the Banner. Oh, my God." So we had to shift ships, and I don't recall how we did it, but we had to move one or two ships to free it up on the other side so that when

---

* A brow is a portable wooden bridge or ramp between the ship and a wharf, pier, or dock. It is usually fitted with wheels at the shore end.

it came it they would see just shipyard or whatever it was behind there. But that was a long day; that was a long 24 hours. You know what, thinking back, I think we moved the Banner; that's what we did, got it under way.

Paul Stillwell: That would be the easiest thing to do.

Captain Hetu: Yes. And it sort of just disappeared, steamed out into the sunset. Yes.

Paul Stillwell: Well, there was a PR fiasco associated with that on the West Coast, because the word could not be put out in Long Beach that the New Jersey would not get back from deployment on schedule. The families were frantic, going to meet the crew members who were not coming in to meet them. So it was a mess in Long Beach.

Captain Hetu: Oh, yes. We were far removed from that. Anyhow, in came the bodies, and the skipper on the ship—I had flown out the night before, I guess, and spent a couple hours with him and came back, and he was a neat guy. I really wish I could remember. He just did everything beautifully and the Navy really looked good, as good as we could, because it wasn't an accident, it wasn't something we had done wrong. Got shot down by the bad guys. But we thought the Navy came out treating these people with dignity, and that was the whole thing. It was a picture story. They did interview the captain of the ship, because he was the one who had picked up the bodies from the Russians. It was kind of an interesting sidebar that the Russians had found these people and turned them over to our ships.

Paul Stillwell: Well, this illustrated the concept that the Navy takes care of its own.

Captain Hetu: Yes.

Paul Stillwell: What other recollections do you have of Brayton Harris?

Captain Hetu: Brayton and I are still friends. We had a lot of fun together. He's a real pro. Do you know Brayton?

Paul Stillwell: Yes.

Captain Hetu: Yes, a real pro.

Paul Stillwell: Interesting, he stayed in USNR his whole career.

Captain Hetu: Yes, that's right. So he never had to worry about being a double-dipper when he went to work for the government, always pissed me off.* [Laughter] He had one or two government jobs after he retired—with the Selective Service and somebody else.

You get to know people better after retirement than you do on active duty, because you're very seldom with people of your own rank, except if you're in Chinfo or in a big command someplace, so Brayton and I—the only place we had ever been together was Vietnam. In fact, there he was in another command, although I saw him often. He worked for MACV, running the accreditation business there in Vietnam.

But we had a good time in Sasebo and cemented our relationship probably forever just working those two or three days together and had a lot of fun doing it. And tired, and drank a lot of scotch, but we survived. Brayton and I did that, and then we went to Vietnam. I went to the Det Charlie job, and he went to MACV. I was in the Rex Hotel, which is downtown Saigon. The Seventh Fleet office was there and traditionally, over the years, the Seventh Fleet Det Charlie guy and the NavForV public affairs officer lived together at the Rex.† You always had to pull strings and bribe sergeants or whatever the hell we had to do, because you're just supposed to come in and get next on line for the next billet available, but we were always able to do it, so that I got Bill Stierman's bunk in the Rex. And it was an interesting time.

---

* Retired officers of the regular Navy receive reduced pension benefits when serving in government jobs. That would not apply to Harris since he was a reserve officer rather than a regular.
† NavForV—U.S. Naval Forces Vietnam.

Bill Stierman is still around Washington. Bill's an iconoclast guy, marches to a different drummer.

Paul Stillwell: Who was the NavForV PAO?

Captain Hetu: When I first got there, it was Jack Davey and then Jack White.* Jack Davey was my roommate. Admiral Zumwalt was ComNavForV.† So the job was pretty much—not much innovation, I mean; it was pretty much in concrete what you were doing and plenty to do, and there was nothing to change, really.

Paul Stillwell: Well, it would be useful to explain the role of Det Charlie, vis-à-vis the Seventh Fleet PAO per se.

Captain Hetu: And vis-à-vis the in-country people from the other commands, because we were very autonomous. That was one of the great fun jobs; that was why it was such a great job. The Seventh Fleet Detachment Charlie was a double-hatted detachment in a sense. We had a captain who was in charge of the detachment out at Tan Son Nhut, aviators, and their major job was to liaison with the Seventh Air Force, to make sure that our planes didn't bump into each other flying air strikes, putting it very simply.‡ [Laughter]

Then the other half of the Seventh Fleet detachment was the public affairs side of the detachment. I was OinC or something of the public affairs side of the detachment, although I reported to the captain out at Tan Son Nhut, and he reported to the Seventh Fleet commander. We were very autonomous. I mean, the Seventh Fleet public affairs officer and I talked a lot, but he had his own problems with the whole fleet, and I had my sort of role in country.

In the Seventh Fleet public affairs detachment we must have had 50 or so people and about six officers, six or seven, several chiefs, and then a lot of photographers and

---
* Commander John R. Davey, Jr., USN, and Commander Jack M. White, USN, both public affairs specialists.
† Vice Admiral Elmo R. Zumwalt, Jr., USN, served as Commander U.S. Naval Forces Vietnam from September 1968 to May 1970.
‡ Tan Son Nhut was the name of the U.S. Air Force base at Saigon, South Vietnam.

journalists. We divided them up into teams; two-thirds of the public affairs detachment was in Saigon and one-third over in Subic Bay. What we did was rotate teams through Subic, photojournalist teams, journalist or two and a photographer. They would ride the ships, get on the ships going through Subic, coming on-line, do fleet hometown photo stories on everybody aboard and then jump off, maybe do a couple others on station and then come back in country, and then we'd send another team. Just kept a daisy chain running.

It was great, because I could go to Subic and do all kinds of stuff. We were autonomous in country, in the sense that we didn't report to MACV. We were there, but we didn't report to them, which kind of pissed them off.

Paul Stillwell: Nor to ComNavForV.

Captain Hetu: No. And, in fact, we didn't wear greens. We were issued greens, and we had them and so forth, but we almost never wore them. We always wore khakis with the piss-cutters, and that made them mad, because all the Army guys and Air Force guys always wore greens and wore combat boots and stuff.[*] We always wore our khakis, which were more comfortable and more realistic.

Paul Stillwell: Did you have to go through SERE training before you went to Saigon?[†]

Captain Hetu: No. A lot did; I escaped somehow. I guess, to get me there on time, they sort of deferred that. No, I never did go through that. I was not looking forward to it, so I didn't miss anything.

Paul Stillwell: Wasn't the point of this operation that it was harder to get journalists out to the fleet, so you would bring the news people to them rather than the other way?

---

[*] "Piss cutter" is the nickname for the fore-and-aft garrison cap.
[†] SERE—survival, evasion, resistance, and escape.

Captain Hetu: Well, we had two airplanes, two CODs, the old Grummans, props.* We didn't have the turboprops, the old Spad, and we flew press out to the carriers with those. And it was the Yankee Station Press Special, YSPS.

Paul Stillwell: So you coordinated those embarks.

Captain Hetu: Yes, yes. And filled up the planes and took them out for a couple days. Then we'd go out and pick them up and bring them back, take out mail. That was what was so wonderful about the job. Anytime I sort of got an itch and go out and visit a carrier, I'd just go, get on one of the Spads and fly out, and then I really could either stay a day or two and come back with them, or I could just fly back in the—usually we went into Danang, someplace like that, and go up and down the coast and stop at a couple places. Saw all kinds of places. Wonderful job, great job.

Paul Stillwell: Well, you issued a lot of press releases, too, didn't you?

Captain Hetu: Every day we put out both written and radio releases on the air strikes and on the shore bombardment. We did that every day, and we did actualities back to radio stations in the States. I don't remember how many; we had several hundred, as I recall, radio stations in the States who were on our little network that we would send back these reports, you know, by wire. Not by wire, but by short wave, I guess, or however we did it then; there were not satellites then.

You know, this was before all this modern technology, although we thought we were doing pretty well. But in those days we had to worry about getting the film off the ships and getting it on planes to Hong Kong to get it back to New York. You know, no satellites, no videotape. We were always running the press special, and we would go every day to the 5:00 O'clock Follies, which was across the street.† The 5:00 O'clock Follies being the MACV body count brief.

---

* COD—carrier on-board delivery, an aircraft configured for carrier takeoffs and landings, dedicated to transporting personnel and cargo between ship and shore.
† The foundation of reporting in Vietnam was the famous—or infamous—"5 O'clock Follies," the daily briefing where military officials provided news releases and verbal accounts of battlefield and air activity.

Paul Stillwell: So you had a representative at that each day?

Captain Hetu: We went and sat in the audience.

Paul Stillwell: Oh, I see.

Captain Hetu: Part of their briefing was our gunfire report, but, no, they were MACV spokesmen, although several Navy guys were there. Haig Cartozian was one of the briefers.* Haig lived next door to me in the Rex and worked for MACV as a briefer and we've become great friends, in retirement as well. Yes, the 5:00 O'clock Follies, we'd go over and watch those. Those were really remarkable. The press was antagonistic and mad. The nutty part of it was that the 5:00 O'clock Follies were held in an old theater around the corner from us. It was not air-conditioned, it was hot, there were rats running around the floor, I mean, literally run under your feet, and it was just terrible.

A block away they had the air-conditioned briefing theater in the MACV building, which was next to the Rex Hotel, but they couldn't use it because it was an American theater, and they wanted to do it a Vietnamese theater. So every day we hiked over to this terrible-smelling, awful, ratty place with the folding chairs that were all beat up, you know, dirty. A couple of Vietnamese families lived in this place at night, so it always smelled of nuc mom and other things. It was awful. But that's where the briefing was. See, the Vietnamese would always get up first and introduce the briefing, and then we, the Americans, were sort of the guests, but obviously it was our briefing.

But the Vietnamese Army briefed, too; they had briefers as well. And a real mixed bag of correspondents and Vietnamese, and French and foreign correspondents, Americans. It was an interesting time.

Paul Stillwell: Were there any prominent journalists that you remember dealing with in that capacity?

---

* Lieutenant Commander Haig O. Cartozian, Jr., USNR, a public affairs specialist.

Captain Hetu: Yes. Well, a lot of them were in and out, and then there was the cadre of people that stayed there. The guy from the New York Daily News, AP guy—trying to pull names out of my head.

Paul Stillwell: Well, The New York Times kept somebody there, didn't they?

Captain Hetu: The New York Times, Time magazine. We used to party with those guys at night and then deal with them during the day. We could always kind of watch that from a little distance, because we really weren't involved in the body count war and all that stuff. We were pretty much aloof to that. The correspondents did like to go out to the carriers occasionally, because that was always a respite and there was always a good story, and it was always comfortable and good food. Although there was good food in Saigon. Saigon was a comfortable place to be in, and it was not a war zone by any means. Well, it was, but it wasn't.

Paul Stillwell: Well, there were occasional personal dangers, weren't there?

Captain Hetu: Oh, yes. Oh, sure. Yes, rocket attacks and throwing satchel charges every so often around the place. But, I don't know, I never got shot at that I know of. I got a combat V, by the way; it's on my citation, which I always thought was kind of humor, got a kick out of that.

Paul Stillwell: Well, this is one of the few times you were separated from your family, wasn't it?

Captain Hetu: Yes. Yes, indeed, that's right.

Paul Stillwell: Which is a normal lot in life for line officers, really.

Captain Hetu: That's right, yes, that's absolutely right. Yes, the only time, really, that I had a tour away from the family. That was tough.

Paul Stillwell: What do you remember about that aspect of it?

Captain Hetu: Well, the family stayed in London. I left London and flew back to the States and so forth and then off, dah, dah, dah. Saw my parents, and Peggy and I had made arrangements for Peggy and the five kids to come back on the United States, on the ship, and I thought that she had a lot of courage to do that.* She wanted to do it. We could have all flown back to Washington, but our house would not have been ready, because we had to tell the people who were renting it to leave, which was difficult to do. But that was in our lease, of course.

I left in April, March, end of March or something, and she stayed on in London for another five or six weeks, and they got her space on the United States, which was legitimate. So the kids had a nice trip coming back across the Atlantic on a super ship, which was nice. It was a lonely time, the first time I had ever been away from my kids and stuff—I mean, for any real long time.

I remember it was difficult. I remember Mike was in high school; he was the only one. I think he was a freshman in high school. He wrote me a letter once and said the kids in school were sort of giving him a tough time because I was in Vietnam. Vietnam, as you remember, wasn't very popular about 1969. He sort of wanted to know what he should tell them. Surprised me, tough letter.

So I wrote him a letter back. I don't remember precisely what I said, but the sense of it was, "Mike, you know, there are people who complain about things but don't do anything to make them better. All I would tell you to do is ask these kids who give you a bad time about Vietnam, ask them what their solution to this problem is. It's a very complex situation. It's not a great war. I don't enjoy being here, but it's our country. I am a career naval officer, and this is where I am, and this is what I signed up to do. You can't have the bad times with the good times."

I guess it worked. He said that he used that simplistic approach saying, "Well, if you can come up with a better solution, why, you tell me about it or write the President.

---

* SS United States was a 990-foot-long passenger liner that went into service 1952. At 53,329 gross tons, she was the third largest liner in the world. Her top speed of more than 38 knots was considered a potential military asset. She was removed from service by the United States Lines in late 1969.

I'm sure the President would love to hear from you if you tell him how to get out of this mess, and if they have a solution, tell them to write to the President. I'm sure he'll be glad to hear about it, if they can tell him how to get out of here."

But I enjoyed it. It was a great job. I was, like I say, very autonomous, very my own person and just had freedom to do things. It was so much fun. I could release messages; I was CTU 77.7.7, I think it was. We were way down, but we were enough that I was able to release a message. One of the nifty things that Bill Stierman passed onto me is, he said, "You can request Rapid Air." And Rapid Air was a little airline that the Air Force flew with executive jets all over the Pacific. He said, "As a CTU, you can release a request for Rapid Air, so when you go to Subic and back, don't dare go out to Tan Son Nhut and fly C-130s or something. Fly Rapid Air."

And I did. And I had no time. I could fly whenever they could get me on board. I would just say, I forget what it was, Category III or something, which was almost like space available, when you have an empty flight going this way and that way. I flew back and forth, I don't how many times on it. I usually was by myself, because it was always the down leg of a trip. I'd go to Subic, and my two missions were to, of course, spend a couple days with my detachment people there—I had a lieutenant commander over there, rotated the two. I had two lieutenant commanders; one would be in Subic and one in Saigon, and we'd rotate.

I had three missions: check out the detachment over there, make sure everything was going okay, which it always was. Secondly, to bring back photo supplies to our photo lab in Saigon, which was always running low on this or that, and I had a photo lab also in Subic, so these guys would send back. And the third thing was to get olives for the martinis. [Laughter] You could not buy olives in Saigon; you could buy everything else but olives. So I used to come back with a case of olives, usually with onions in the center of the olives; they loved them. So that was my important mission in life.

Paul Stillwell: Was Craig Whitney still with Det Charlie?[*]

---

[*] Lieutenant (junior grade) Craig R. Whitney, USNR.

Captain Hetu: I had three ensigns, and one was Craig Whitney, now with The New York Times.

Paul Stillwell: He went to the Times that year, in fact, 1969.

Captain Hetu: Yes, when he got out of the Navy. Yes, Craig Whitney was one of my guys. Kenny Pease was there on his first tour of duty out of the Naval Academy. Ensign Pease, now Rear Admiral Pease and another great big guy, Mahoney, who got out of the Navy.* He's now a lawyer for NBC, I think, here in town. But they were all great big guys, you know, Whitney's tall, not very big, but Kenny is a big guy, and Mahoney was a big guy. These used to be my bodyguards. I could tell you some great stories about these guys.

Paul Stillwell: Well, please do.

Captain Hetu: Two stories on Ken. You know, Ken hasn't changed much; he still looks a lot like he did then. He was a big, good-looking guy and tough, and a nice young man; still a nice young man, even though he's an admiral. But a couple stories. My office was, I think, on the second floor, and the room was on the third floor of the Rex. So we had integrated our social and our professional life. And in the room that I shared then with Jack Davey and then Jack White, we had an anteroom, probably as big as this office, probably 10 by 10, a little smaller than this, which we predictably made into a bar, and it was the Det Charlie Bar, very famous. Had a refrigerator, bar, couch, three or four bar stools. Every night, after the last whistle blew, why, we would go up there and drink martinis.

We required everybody that came in to check their weapons, like a western bar. There's nothing more dangerous than public affairs officers drinking martinis with a loaded gun on their hip. So we had sort of like a coat rack with the pegs in them, and everybody who came in had to hang up their weapons, so we checked the guns and drank

---

* Ensign Kendall M. Pease, Jr., USN, a public affairs specialist. He was the Navy's Chief of Information at the time of this interview.

martinis. Up along the top of the wall was a—I can't ever remember the name of the French name for indirect lighting with a . . .

Paul Stillwell: I don't know.

Captain Hetu: Like a thing that went all the way around; there was a name for it and I can't think of it. We put empty Beefeater bottles on that, so that after not too long the whole room was Beefeater bottles all around the ceiling. When you turned the lights on, it looked like a shrine. You'd turn them on, and all these Beefeater bottles would light up with the lights behind them.

Paul Stillwell: So you were drinking the good stuff.

Captain Hetu: Oh, well, it was only $2.00 a bottle or something. Oh, yes, no sense drinking anything but, and we drank a lot of it. But never got into any real trouble, except the one night. There was this little Army lieutenant colonel down the corridor who was sort of a martinet; maybe he was a bird colonel, because there weren't very many lieutenant colonels in the Rex. There were some, but the two Navy 0-5s, you know, that's where I learned 0-5 and 0-6; that's the Army terminology.*

Anyway, this guy used to give us fits and putting us on report for making too much noise in the bar and all that stuff. Came down one night, and he read us all out. He hammered on the door and yelled at us and so forth and so on, and he was going to put us on report and all these people, and blah, blah, blah. So he left and went away, and we all sort of giggled about that. So Kenny and Mahoney, these two enormous guys, and I don't know if Craig was there that night or not, but Mahoney and Pease went down to the colonel's room, where he had his girlfriend in the room with him. They knocked on the door, and the colonel came to the door, and they took the colonel and pulled him out into the hallway, ran into his room and locked the door, so that they were in there with his girlfriend. [Laughter] He went ballistic and knocked the door down, a la, you know—

---

* Pay grade O-5 is a commander in the Navy, lieutenant colonel in the Army; O-6 is a captain in the Navy, colonel in the Army.

Paul Stillwell: Arnold Schwarzenegger.

Captain Hetu: Yes, movie-ville. This guy knocked his own door down, went through the door. [Laughter] Hilarious, and the girl was screaming, and the guys were yelling. I just thought, "Oh, God, I wonder what's going on." I ran down, and Kenny and Mahoney had the colonel by the ankles and were holding him out the window and, oh, God, I said, "Don't drop him. Don't drop him."

"Oh, we won't drop him, Commander. We're just teaching him a lesson."

I said, "Oh, God, pull him in, pull him in." So they pulled him in, and the guy was white, of course, scared to death. [Laughter] I played the game and said, "Okay, you guys, get out, go to my room. I said, "Colonel, I'll take care of this. I'm really sorry about this. You know, we certainly don't want to have to tell anybody what happened here with your girlfriend and the door being broken down."

He said, "Oh, no, no, I don't want to do that."

I said, "Listen, let me take care of those guys. I promise you I will put those guys in hack for the rest of their tour in Vietnam. You can rest assured, boy, that they'll never make first lieutenant, and blah, blah, blah, blah."

He said, "Okay, okay, Commander, all right.

Shook hands sort of, and I said, you know, "Come have a drink."

"No, no, I don't want a drink." So we went away and he got his door fixed, and we never saw the colonel again.

Mahoney and I just about died laughing. Did have to sort of try to reprimand them a little bit without smiling too much; it was a funny shtick. [Laughter]

Paul Stillwell: Obviously it didn't stunt Pease's career.

Captain Hetu: No, no.

I remember the night they said they were Viet Cong roaming the streets in Saigon this particular night and said we should all be careful in our rooms. And, of course, we'd all just come down from the roof bar where we had all had plenty to drink, and I was alone. Jack was down in the Delta or something, but I didn't have a roommate that night. I had a .45, and I foolishly put a round in the chamber. And, of course, what I had forgotten was when you do that, it cocks the hammer. I opened the door to look out into the hall. I was looking at all the other drunks, and all were looking back and forth at each other. "Any Viet Cong?" You know, dumbest thing you could ever do.

So I couldn't get it uncocked. I forgot how to let the hammer down. Hell, I never took it out of the holster, and so I thought, "I know what I'm going to do; I'm going to kill myself if I'm not careful. So I laid the thing in the middle of the vacant bed and left it there and got up in the morning and called down to the office, and Pease was there. And I said, "Pease."

He said, "Yes, sir?"

I said, "Come up to my room. I have a chore for you."

He said, "Okay," and he came up.

I said, "Kenny, that damn gun, I got that thing cocked. It just won't uncock. I've done everything they told me to do, and I can't get it uncocked."

He said, "Oh, yes, sir." Kenny took it and in about eight seconds went click, click, and handed it back to me and said, "There you go, Commander."

I said, "Well, I'll be damned." He knew damn well I had no idea how to get that thing uncocked.

Then the great Kenny Pease story was we had a weather bureau worked for AFN, Armed Forces—AFRNTN, I guess it was, in Saigon. She was a big, buxom blonde gal and was dating this, I think it was, a major that ran the station over there. But big boobs and always wore a short, teeny skirt. We always wanted her to bend over and tell us what's happening in Australia. So we decided to take her out on to one of the press specials. She was technically a press person, and we would take her out to one of the carriers and give the guys a thrill and let her stay out there for a couple hours and come back with the flight later in the day.

Kenny was the escort officer, sent him off to the carrier, and I can't remember which one it was. You'd probably be able to tell me; Kent Lee was the skipper.[*]

---

[*] Captain Kent L. Lee, USN, commanded the aircraft carrier Enterprise (CVAN-65) from 11 July 1967 to 8 July 1969. The oral history of Lee, who became a vice admiral, is in the Naval Institute collection.

Paul Stillwell: The Enterprise.

Captain Hetu: Enterprise. And Kent Lee was not known for his sense of humor. When this gal stepped off the plane, he went bananas. He went bananas, called Kenny up to the bridge, chewed his ass out, "Get that woman back on that airplane. Get her the hell off this ship." The crew was going nuts, of course, and she had walked around a little bit before Kent spotted her.

So he sent Kenny back and put Kenny on report. Wanted to know who Kenny's boss was—me. He wrote a back-channel message to the commander of the Seventh Fleet and put me on report, raised hell about this woman, dah, dah, dah, dah, showing off her body and all this kind of stuff. It was written like a Holy Roller preacher.

So, the next thing I know, I get a rocket from CinCPacFlt: "What the hell's going on out there?"

Then I talked Ralph Slawson at Seventh Fleet, and I talked to Thomas at CinCPacFlt. I said, "Hey, you know. She works for AFN and sent her out to give the boys a thrill, and it's not Kenny's fault. Hell, I told Kenny to take her out there. It's my fault, lack of judgment, whatever, I don't know, sort of stupid. We just thought, she was well known in Vietnam, and everybody knew who the weather girl was. So do whatever you have to do."

Slawson gave me a back channel and said, "Don't worry about it. The admiral thinks it's hilarious or something." Thought Kent Lee was crazy.

I said, "Okay." So that passed.

One of the great adventures of my tour in Vietnam was the sinking of the Evans, which happened on my watch. If you recall, the Melbourne was the Australian carrier that cut the Evans in two, right between the stacks.[*]

Paul Stillwell: That was early June of '69.

---

[*] At 3:15 on the morning of 3 June 1969, during a SEATO naval exercise in the South China Sea, about 650 nautical miles southwest of Manila, the U.S. destroyer Frank E. Evans (DD-754) was struck and cut in two by the Australian aircraft carrier Melbourne. The bow section of the destroyer sank within two minutes of the collision, resulting in the loss of 74 of her 273 crew members. The bow of the carrier was damaged, but she suffered no personnel casualties.

Captain Hetu: That's right. I hadn't been there terribly long. The forward part of the Evans went down, which was the part with the bridge. It was top-heavy because it cut it, and she just capsized and went down, with 74 souls. Jerry King was the ASW group commander on Kearsarge.* He knew that I was in Saigon with the Seventh Fleet and sent a rocket in and asked me if I would come out to the ship, help them get ready for the inevitable press thing.† I said, "Yes, indeed." Flew out within hours. I have a whole report on that, as a matter of fact, that we did because it was a long, involved case.

Anyhow, we got out to the carrier, flew out, and the carrier had the survivors on board. The skipper was a guy named Al McLemore, nice guy.‡ The survivors were all in pretty much shock, and so we knew that there were going to be a lot of press when they got to Subic. We spent a day or two on the ship; that's a little vague. I forget what time of night we got there. This all sort of ran together, but I talked with the admiral and the captain of the destroyer and so forth. Spent a lot of hours talking about how to handle this and had a lawyer, a legal officer, and briefed the captain, briefed the exec, and then briefed the survivors.

Got them all together on one of the flight decks, I guess it was, to tell them what their rights were and what they could and couldn't do, could and should not do with the press. There'd be a lot of press waiting for them in Subic. And told them, "You know, you don't have to speak to the press. There's nothing anywhere that says you have to talk to the press if you don't want to. If you do, be very careful not to voice opinions about what you thought happened. Generally, most people were asleep. You don't know what happened. There will be a court of inquiry and probably court-martials, and anything you say could—don't try to help your skipper or anybody. Just say you don't know what happened; that's all. Don't voice any opinion whatever about what happened. If you have an opinion, it'll come out in the court of inquiry.

---

* Rear Admiral Jerome H. King, Jr., USN, , served as Commander Anti-Submarine Warfare Group One from 30 June 1968 to 26 September 1969, on board the USS Kearsarge (CVS-33). The oral history of King, who retired as a vice admiral, is in the Naval Institute collection. It contains Admiral King's extensive discussion of this case.
† This stemmed from King's previous association with Hetu in the CNO's office.
‡ Commander Albert S. McLemore, USN, was the commanding officer of the Frank E. Evans (DD-754) at the time of the collision.

"If you do want to tell stories, from what I've heard just talking to some of you guys, there's some real heroics that went on, people helping people out the dark, out in the middle of the night. People helping other people off the ship and in the water, dark water. It was terrible. And those stories, you can't tell enough of those."

Paul Stillwell: Human interest.

Captain Hetu: Human interest, and heroics and the fact that you took care of your own people. Spent a lot of time cleaning the crew up. They didn't have any clothes, just what they had on, and a lot of them were in skivvies when they were picked up. So we got them outfitted, and I said, "I really want everybody here in a good, clean, fresh uniform. Dungarees is fine, but they've got to look good, white hats. You know, everybody is expecting that they're going to see like in the movies, these guys come out with blankets wrapped around them and, you know, arms in slings and all kinds of stuff. When these guys march off that ship, there'll be a lot of press there, cameras rolling; we've got to make them look like the Navy takes care of their own people. These kids look good and they're walking straight."

So I spent some time flying back and forth to Subic, talking to the press, talking to the base, getting the base all set up, because we had to find a place to put all these kids. I knew how many were killed—I'm trying to remember how many survivors, 150, 160.[*] There were a lot of people, and they had to be put up. Happily, there was a brand-new barracks that had just been completed in Subic; nobody had moved into it. It was just getting ready to receive the first shipment of people. So we had a brand-new barracks with new bunks, new everything, great.

So that's where the crew went, and they had buses and had all the logistics associated with bringing these people off the ship. Then I had to brief the press and set up ground rules to say, "No talking to these kids when they come off the ship. I will have a press conference with the admiral who found them, Jerry King. The commanding officer and the exec will be available in the press conference to talk. The people on the crew will be available to talk to you after the press conference. But these kids have been

---

[*] The crew at the time of the collision comprised 273 officers and enlisted men; of those 199 survived.

through a hell of a traumatic experience, and I don't want anybody sticking microphones in their faces on the bus or trying to grab them aside and all that stuff. If you do, I'll lift your credentials and throw your ass off the base."

They listened, and it worked. Brought the crew in. Had a news conference in the theater and had telephones. The base was terrific. We had something like 20 telephones set up, which was not easy to do in the Philippines. I mean, it was easy to set the phones up, but it wasn't that easy to get the lines through, so that these kids could call home, call their families mostly back in Long Beach. The ship was homeported in Long Beach.

So we had that done, and then we let the press into the center place where the phones were, to photograph the kids talking on the phone. I thought that was a pretty good story, the fact that they were in these banks of phones. And the press was very good. I remember one television guy tried to stick a microphone over a kid's shoulder talking on the telephone at home, and I pulled his power plug. [Laughter] That's accepted journalism, I guess, today, but then it wasn't, and that was an invasion of privacy, so I pulled his plug.

Paul Stillwell: Well, indeed, it was an invasion of privacy.

Captain Hetu: Yes. He was pissed, but he knew he was wrong. And it went pretty smoothly. I mean, the stories were as accurate as they could be. Immediately, within a day or two, they named a board of inquiry headed up by Jerry King, and it was very unusual because they had a joint board. They had Australians and U.S. Navy, of comparable rank. They had two rear admirals, and I have pictures of those.

Paul Stillwell: One aspect of that story, I think, there were three brothers from one family lost in the Evans.

Captain Hetu: Yes, I think that's true, and I thought that they weren't supposed to do that since the sinking of the Sullivans or something.[*]

---

[*] Five brothers from the Sullivan family of Waterloo, Iowa, were lost when the light cruiser Juneau (CL-52) was sunk off Guadalcanal on 13 November 1942.

Paul Stillwell: Right.

Captain Hetu: That's true.

Paul Stillwell: They highlighted for the public.

Captain Hetu: Yes, that's right, you're quite right. But that was a wartime order and not peacetime. That's right, there were three brothers. So then Jerry King kept me on to do the public affairs for the board of inquiry, and there was a lot of press. Boy, we had press from Australia, well, all over the place, from Vietnam, must have had 50, 60 press show up. So we were very fortunate. It was summertime, and we used the school as the headquarters for the board of inquiry and for the press center.

So it couldn't have been more perfect. In a sense, we had classrooms for briefing rooms. I turned a couple of classrooms into press working areas, where the press could write their stories. I had a briefing center where we had our desks and I had three or four officers—in fact, Brent Baker was one of the officers that came in off one of the carriers to be my assistant. He was then a lieutenant, went on to be Chinfo later.[*]

We had daily press briefings. We had to accredit the press to permit them to cover the hearings. They were open, for the most part. They had some classified, very few closed sessions. Complicated by the fact that the wife of the skipper of the Melbourne showed up as accredited to an Australian magazine. This caused all kinds of consternation, because the captain of the carrier was, of course, one of the principals of the investigation.[†] His wife showed up to cover all the sessions, take notes, tell the husband, presumably, what was going on every day. He wasn't privy to sit in the hearings. So we let her in finally. I said, "You know, it's kind of crazy, because any other of the newsmen out there could do the same thing if they wanted to. We can't get any sort of agreement from them not to tell anybody what they're seeing. That's why they

---

[*] Rear Admiral Brent Baker, USN, served as the Navy's Chief of Information from July 1989 to July 1992.
[†] The commanding officer of HMAS Melbourne at the time of the accident was Captain John Stevenson, RAN. His wife Jo has written several books.

are there, to tell people what they're seeing. So, anyway, she covered it, so there she was, and then she was sitting in the front row every day. She became a story unto herself.

It was interesting, because we had to put out sort of Australian-American lexicon, because there were Australians there who didn't understand a lot of the terms that we use on ships and that they use. So we had to put out sort of a list of sayings and what they were side by side. We put out all kinds of lists of the survivors and the dead on the American ship and the witnesses, all the witnesses and their names and jobs and so forth. The Australians were very sensitive, because this same carrier had cut an Australian destroyer in two about like two years before that, maybe not even that long before. Because I think the Melbourne had just really come back on the line, pretty much, after having her bow rearranged from hitting one of her own destroyers in almost precisely the same way, at a nighttime ASW exercise.

Paul Stillwell: Well, in this case it was the Frank E. Evans that was at fault.

Captain Hetu: Yes, it was.

Paul Stillwell: Cutting across the bow.

Captain Hetu: Yes, well, that was a complicated scenario, very difficult, the lights. This caused us a little bit of trouble after several weeks, because the press started to change. The same people didn't stay forever. They would leave, and then new people would come in and they'd come in and say, "Tell us what's happened. What's going on?"

You'd say, "Oh, my God, it's very complicated."

I was searching, trying to figure a way to describe what was going on, so a—I think he was a former RAF pilot, and I think he was Australian, but he worked for the Times of London.* He and I sat down, and between my somewhat knowledge of maneuvering boards and his background as a pilot, we concocted a chart to show where the ships had been and what the testimony had shown what had happened. I still have it somewhere here, drew it on a big piece of drawing paper, and we used it as a briefing

---

* RAF—Royal Air Force.

chart to show new newsmen coming in what had gone on, and then finally even Jerry King was using it. They didn't use it officially, but they were using it to refresh their memories about the testimony. We just took testimony and concocted this briefing.

Paul Stillwell: Sort of a surface plot, really.

Captain Hetu: Yes, exactly. To show what had happened and the screen changing and the ship cut and so forth. He thought the light was here and the light was there and the OD went the wrong way. The skipper, Al McLemore, was terrific guy. I got to know him very well.

Paul Stillwell: He was not summoned to the bridge. As I remember, he was watching a movie.

Captain Hetu: No. No, he was asleep.

Paul Stillwell: Oh, asleep?

Captain Hetu: Yes. They'd been on this exercise for several days. He hadn't been asleep for 38 hours or something and finally just went down and went to sleep, and he did not get called to the bridge. He got court-martialed and got found guilty. Boy, that was tough one, and I felt bad about that. This board, of course, only recommended. They didn't do the court-martials; this was just a board of inquiry. But then Al subsequently was court-martialed and lost numbers, I guess, and retired as a commander, never got promoted.

Incidentally, Thor Hanson had the Evans before, and Thor and I became friends years later when Thor was the executive aide to the Secretary of the Navy and went on to make three stars.[*] So, anyway, that was a pretty interesting time, lasted several weeks and sort of a classic CIB operation.[†] My thesis from Boston University on "Public

---

[*] Captain Carl Thor Hanson, USN.
[†] CIB—crisis information bureau.

Affairs in Crisis Situations" lent itself. This was really, in a sense, a peacetime naval disaster. Although there was a war going on, they weren't involved in Vietnam; they were in a SEATO exercise, but it was a tough one.[*]

---

[*] SEATO—Southeast Asia Treaty Organization.

Interview Number 4 with Captain Herbert E. Hetu, U.S. Navy (Retired)
Place: Captain Hetu's home, Alexandria, Virginia
Date: Thursday, 20 June 1996
Interviewer: Paul Stillwell

Paul Stillwell: Well, Captain, as we start on the last lap for this oral history, I think we should go back briefly and talk about the film coverage you did on the sinking of the Thresher, which occurred in April 1963.*

Captain Hetu: Yes. After the Thresher went down, there were a great many stories trying to figure out what happened, and since the Navy didn't know, it left it wide open for virtually anybody to speculate. There were stories about giant octopi.

Paul Stillwell: And this was the first-ever loss of a nuclear submarine.

Captain Hetu: Yes. And that it had been sunk by a Russian submarine, that it had had an underwater collision. There were just wild, wild stories. You may remember the Navy searched and searched for a long time, which kept the story going and going and going. They finally did find the remains of the Thresher and, I guess, brought up some of the pieces.† But it was too deep to do very much with.

I guess about the time they found it, I was then head of the audio-visual branch, radio-television, Navy. CBS came and wanted to do an hour special on the Thresher, and this was not well received.

Paul Stillwell: By whom?

---

* The attack submarine Thresher (SSN-593) was lost with all hands on 10 April 1963 while operating east of Cape Cod. The presumed cause was a reactor shutdown during a dive.
† On 24 August 1963 the bathyscaph Trieste recovered a length of copper tubing and a fitting with markings from the Thresher.

Captain Hetu: Well, by the submariners, didn't want to do a post-mortem, and, in fact, the Chief of Naval Operations, then Admiral Anderson, didn't want to do anything about it. So I was a lieutenant commander swimming upstream. My television officer then was Bob Sims, who went on to be a captain, was the Secretary's public affairs officer, went to the White House and became Assistant Secretary of Defense for Public Affairs.

Anyway, Bob had known Anderson, because Bob had been on the Sixth Fleet staff, which was good, although Bob, I think, was a jaygee or a lieutenant.[*] He wasn't very senior, but he knew Anderson, and we went to the Chief of Information and said, you know, "Really, they're going to do this—with us or without us—and we think that if we can cooperate with CBS, we could at least get a positive spin on the story, at least get some of our messages into it."

The Chief of Information was then Bill Mack.[†] With his support we went to see Anderson to lay out the fact that we thought that we were convinced that CBS was going to do it, and that it would leave it open to all sorts of wild stories if we didn't help them. We should at least try and point them in the right direction. Admiral Anderson finally agreed and we wrote a message from the CNO to everybody in the chain of command, telling them to cooperate. That's what you need in a case like this. You've got to have somebody from that level tell everybody to open the door for you: "Whether you want to or not, they're coming."

Paul Stillwell: "Aye, aye, sir."

Captain Hetu: Yes. And cooperate to the best of your ability. The reason I give all this preamble is that this is where I first met a guy named Dave Buxbaum, who was a very young producer at CBS, and, in fact, after this we became very fast friends. Fred Friendly was the overall producer, but Dave Buxbaum was going to produce this show,

---

[*] Vice Admiral George W. Anderson, Jr., USN, commanded the Sixth Fleet from September 1959 to July 1961. The oral history of Anderson, who retired as a four-star admiral, is in the Naval Institute collection.
[†] Rear Admiral William P. Mack, USN, had become Chief of Information on 22 August 1963.

which was his first solo production, which meant that CBS thought he was a real comer, of course.*

Paul Stillwell: And Fred Friendly was already a legend by that time.

Captain Hetu: Yes. Anyhow, when they were trying to get a handle on what sort of a theme to use for this show, we kept emphasizing that we could not have saved the people on the submarine even if we had known they were alive, and we didn't have the real tools to go down and find out precisely what happened. We turned the emphasis of the show to oceanography and the lack of oceanographic expertise that the Navy had. It was a very low priority budget item.

Anyhow, the show turned out to be about oceanography, with the Thresher as the vehicle to carry the oceanography theme through, and the title of the show turned out to be "The Legacy of the Thresher," which we thought was a lot more positive than it could have been. The bottom line was that came out was that the Navy and the nation needed more attention given to oceanography, and 75% of the earth's surface is covered water, etc., etc. We were able to turn the thing around. I mean, I always thought that was quite a victory for the Navy, not for me personally, but for all of us. Bob Sims, I guess, me, and certainly the fact that the Chief of Information and the CNO were smart enough and forward looking enough to do something like that and not just say, "To hell with it. Let them say whatever they want, and we'll just hunker down and take our licks," which is sometimes what people want to do in a case like this, and it's not the good thing to do. Anyway, I think it turned out pretty well.

Paul Stillwell: What you just described is often the stereotypical reaction for a line officer.

Captain Hetu: Yes, put your head in the ground, and they'll go away eventually. They'll get tired of beating on you.

---

* From 1959 to 1964 Fred W. Friendly was executive producer of "CBS Reports," putting out several landmark programs. He later served as president of CBS News from March 1964 to February 1966.

Paul Stillwell: Anything you remember about the mechanics of actually putting the program together? Did you provide interviewees?

Captain Hetu: Yes. The key to this, once the CNO says he's on board, then everybody's on board, and we got virtually anybody we wanted on the tube to talk about it, to set the record pretty well straight. I think they came to the conclusion that it was an unavoidable accident, that it was just that these are very complicated, dangerous machines, and that these things happen, like airplane crashes. Thank God, they don't happen quite as often, but it served me well.

I, in later years, was the communications counselor for the space shuttle disaster, the Challenger, and it was the same sort of mentality.* One of the things we learned in the Challenger, and I don't want to digress, but was that NASA had an extraordinary public affairs plan in every minute detail in the event something like that happened. And they never even opened the book, never used it. I mean, there was that feeling of inconceivability that this could not have happened. They were reading their own newspaper clippings, and they had convinced themselves that an accident couldn't happen.

Paul Stillwell: To what extent did you have to steer them away from classified material, such as crush depths and test depths and what have you?

Captain Hetu: I don't remember that as being a problem. They were very cooperative, and I don't remember us getting into any confrontations on stuff like that. We'd just tell them, "We can't go into that."

They'd say. "Fine, let's move on to something else." One of the reasons that Dave Buxbaum and I became pals is because we had a mutual respect. He knew I was shooting straight with him, and he responded in kind. In later years, when I went to the CIA, CBS "60 Minutes" was the first program ever to come inside the CIA with a camera. Dave

---

* On 29 January 1986, the space shuttle Challenger exploded 79 seconds after launching from Cape Canaveral, Florida. All seven astronauts on board were killed.

Buxbaum was the reason, because I trusted him and he trusted me. That's another story, but the day I suggested, at the morning meeting of all the senior people at CIA, that we bring Dan Rather and the "60 Minutes" inside there, there was a deathly silence. But we did it anyway.

Paul Stillwell: The sound of jaws dropping. Admiral Anderson was relieved within a few months after that. Did Admiral McDonald just pick up the level of support from him?

Captain Hetu: Yes. There was never a hitch.

Paul Stillwell: Were there any eventual long-term affects from this, such as did Sea Lab get a boost because of this program?

Captain Hetu: I don't know, but I think so. I mean, we used this program, repeats of it. If people on the Hill hadn't seen it, our legislative people were certain that they did see it.[*] It was interesting, and I think it was a classic case of turning something around that could have been pretty bad for the Navy, because people were willing to believe anything, because we couldn't tell them otherwise.

Paul Stillwell: The other thing is that this illustrates a point you've made a number of times—that if you meet the media halfway, they will come the other halfway.

Captain Hetu: One of the things that we emphasized, that came in the show, was that it had not been a nuclear explosion, that there was no evidence of nuclear material and that the reactor hadn't exploded. That was a plus, because a lot of the anti-nukes were spreading the stories that the reactor had exploded, and that part of the ocean would be contaminated forever and all that stuff.

---

[*] "The Hill" refers to Capitol Hill in Washington, D.C., that is, the U.S. Congress.

Paul Stillwell: Did Admiral Rickover have any input to the program?*

Captain Hetu: I don't remember him having any input.

Paul Stillwell: He probably wanted to keep a low profile at that point.

Captain Hetu: Yes, I think he wasn't sure what had happened either. He was pretty much told to cooperate, and I don't even remember whether he was interviewed; I don't think so. I don't even know if I have a tape of that anymore. This process we're going through makes you realize how you're always too busy going through life to keep all this stuff somewhere, on a bookshelf or something. I haven't done that; I wish I had.

Paul Stillwell: There's a great quote, "Life is what happens while you're in the midst of making plans."

Captain Hetu: [Laughter] Yes, isn't that the truth?

Paul Stillwell: Well, are we ready to move on to SecNav's office?

Captain Hetu: Yes, on and out.

Paul Stillwell: Did your friend Ken Wade have a hand in that assignment for you?

Captain Hetu: No, I don't think so. Well, I don't know that he didn't, but it was Bill Thompson.† Bill was the Secretary's public affairs officer, and he was getting ready to go to Harvard for the advanced business course that Harvard gives to senior executives from companies. They go for three or four months, I think it is, and live together and work

---

* Vice Admiral Hyman G. Rickover, USN, was head of the Navy's nuclear power program.
† Captain William Thompson, USN, a public affairs specialist.

together. Bill had been selected for that and was getting ready to go. He then was working for John Chafee.*

Paul Stillwell: Had you known Captain Thompson before then?

Captain Hetu: Oh, yes, Bill and I had known each other for 100 years. We met, I think, way back in the '50s when I was at Pearl Harbor. Bill was a lieutenant commander, I guess, and I was a lieutenant. Yes, we've known each other forever. I got the word that I was under consideration for the job in SecNav's office. Let's see, I went to Vietnam in April, and this was in the fall of that same year.

Paul Stillwell: Were you still a commander at that point?

Captain Hetu: Commander, yes. And I was brought back for a quick trip back to the States to be interviewed by Chafee for the job. Captain Stan Turner was then the executive assistant to Chafee, and Stan was very forthcoming.† When I was interviewed, I guess I came out of the Secretary's office and was interviewed by Stan as well. He said, "Well, you've got a terrific record and we're all very pleased that you're here and so forth. We have one little problem and that is that Admiral McCain marked you down in one category. You've had 4.0s for many years, and all of a sudden there's one little blip."

I said, "McCain? You've got to be kidding."

"No."

I said, "I'll be damned. I can't believe that that happened." Then I thought, "Oh, I have a feeling I know how that happened, that McCain didn't write the fitness reports himself." Admiral McCain was then CinCPac, but he was in Washington visiting, and I knew that, so I called his aide. It was Johnny Butts, who was the guy who had gone with him from CinCUSNavEur, who I suspect was the guy who wrote the fitness reports.

Butts was, by then, I think, a rear admiral and was in town, was McCain's executive assistant or something. I called up and said I was back from Vietnam, and it

---
* John H. Chafee served as Secretary of the Navy from 31 January 1969 to 4 May 1972.
† Captain Stansfield Turner, USN, later a four-star admiral.

was urgent that I see Admiral McCain. I had to see him now, soon, today, and I got in to see him. He was very warm and welcomed me, "How are things going in Vietnam?" I had gone to see him in CinCPac on my way out to Vietnam to make a call on him. So he said, "What can I do for you?" or something like that.

I said, "Well, Admiral, I am in danger of losing a very great job that I really want to have because of a fitness report you gave me."

He went, "What? I don't know. What? What?"

I said, "Well, the only bad mark I've had in 20 years or something is"—and I don't ever remember what one he marked, I don't even remember what box it was that he marked down, to tell you the truth. It was not a substantive box. It was something like "Does he brush his teeth three times a day?" or something, I don't know. But in those days, that's all it took.

I said, "I don't know why you did that. If I had not pleased you or done something wrong, nobody told me and you didn't tell me. You told me I was doing a great job and so forth."

He said, "You did do a great job. I wanted to take you with me, remember?"

I said, "Yes, I remember. And I was going to come work for you after Vietnam, too, but now I have a chance to go in the Secretary's office."

He said, "Oh, great job, you'd be perfect for that."

I said, "Well, Stan Turner, the executive assistant, tells me the one thing that could keep me out of that job is your fitness report."

He said, "Oh, my God, boy." He picked up the phone and called Turner, wanted to see the Secretary and said that I was there and so forth and said he wanted to go up and talk to Chafee and so forth. And so he did, to his credit. I kind of suspected he might; that's the kind of guy he was. So, anyway, he went and saw Turner and went and saw the Secretary and said that this had been a mistake. I don't know what he told them, I wasn't in there when he told them. Anyway, he said that it was an oversight and, dah, dah, dah. To my knowledge, it was never changed and I didn't care. But, anyhow, I got the job.

I went back to Vietnam, and I can remember all the way back in the airplane I kept saying to myself, one F, two E's.

Paul Stillwell: Oh, the spelling of his name.

Captain Hetu: Yes, Chafee.

Paul Stillwell: I take it you had had a favorable impression of Secretary Chafee during your meeting with him.

Captain Hetu: Oh, yes, I thought he was a terrific guy. He was a very genuine, down-to-earth guy. I don't even remember whether he asked me about my career and where I'd been, what I'd done and was impressed with the people that I had worked for and so forth. He asked how I felt about the press and what my philosophical feelings were about the press. We just went through sort of a, "You never lie, you know. I think you should be open with the press, not talk to them every day but often and so forth."

Anyway, we got along fine, I thought, and I went back to Vietnam and was back there a month or so when I got a message from Thompson to me, personal. I remember our communications officer out at Tan Son Nhut called me one morning and said, "Boy, congratulations, you're going to go work for the Secretary of the Navy and stuff. Got the job."

I said, "Wow, okay."

So they ordered me back before Christmas. I went back in December, which was bittersweet for me. I really had hoped that I would be able to finish out my year tour. I mean, I had it made by there. I'd had eight months and I was on the downward slope, and I enjoyed the job. I really did. I was kind of disappointed. Certainly wanted to go home, and I wanted to be home with my family for Christmas, but, on the other hand, I was mentally ready to stay until April, and I didn't stay. So I had my Vietnam tour, but it was shortened. Some of my friends, in a good way, never let me forget that I didn't finish out my whole tour there, that I was in Vietnam, but I wasn't one of the real guys. It wasn't because of anything I did.

Paul Stillwell: Well, he asked you about your view on the media. I would think that, by the nature of the job, a politician such as he would be more adept at dealing with media than most admirals.

Captain Hetu: Oh, yes. Well, John had come from being governor of Rhode Island, and he was a consummate politician. In fact, it was after I came back and took the job and was relieving Bill Thompson when I went in the office one day and there was a seaman, a JOSN, in the office with the Secretary. He was standing there behind him saying, "John, you can't do that. We have to do this, dah, dah, dah."

I said, "Did I just hear that seaman call the Secretary of the Navy by his first name?"

They went on and on, and they were discussing something in sort of a forthright manner. I said to Thompson, "Who in the hell is that? What's this all about?"

He said, "Well, that's Jerry Whitcomb."

I said, "Who is Jerry Whitcomb?"

"Well, he's a friend of Mel Laird's. He's from Michigan, and he's well plugged in politically. Jerry was in the reserves and got called up to go on active duty and, I guess, Laird called Chafee and said, 'I got this guy who's a very bright guy and he joined the reserves and the closest thing they could come up with was a journalist rating, and maybe you have something he could do in Washington. He'll do anything.'"[*] To Jerry's credit, he didn't try to get out of going anywhere.

So Bill Thompson said, "Yes, I can use him here with Chafee." We had two worlds with Chafee. One was Rhode Island and then there was the rest of the world. So Jerry handled Rhode Island, and I handled all the rest of the world. That was the agreement we came to and, of course, there was some disagreement about which was most important. [Laughter] But I was a commander, and Jerry was a seaman—he was a good guy. Chafee was paying a lot of attention to Rhode Island, because he obviously had his sights on running for the Senate.

Paul Stillwell: Which he did successfully later.

---

[*] Melvin R. Laird served as Secretary of Defense from 22 January 1969 to 29 January 1973.

Captain Hetu: Well, the first time he didn't. He got his butt handed to him the first time. He ran against Pell, which was a death.*

Anyhow, I had an interesting office after I finally took over, with Jerry, the seaman there, and I had a chief and we had a small office. The public affairs staff was a small staff. There was myself, a secretary who came with Bill Thompson, Lois Fleeger who was terrific; the seaman; a chief; and I needed a lieutenant to be sort of a speechwriter. Speechwriting was always a problem.

Paul Stillwell: Why do you say that?

Captain Hetu: Just getting somebody who could write speeches the way the Secretary wanted to talk. Getting speechwriters was always a problem—it always has been for me, in any case—to get somebody who can walk the fine line of agreeing with the policies, of course, of the organization that he's working for and putting it in the boss's words, getting inside his head and putting it so the boss is comfortable reading those words. That's tough. Very often, in my experience, you get a speech writer who's very knowledgeable about things—Ed Stafford comes to mind—but wants to impart his own ideas through the Secretary's speech, sort of get his own policy views.† And you can't do that, you just cannot do that.

Paul Stillwell: When did you have connections with Ed Stafford?

Captain Hetu: In the Secretary's office.

Paul Stillwell: At that time?

---

* Claiborne D. Pell, a Democrat, served in the U.S. Senate from 3 January 1961 to 3 January 1997. Chafee was unsuccessful candidate for election to the Senate in 1972. He was elected as a Republican to the Senate in November 1976. He was subsequently appointed by the Governor, 29 December 1976, to fill the vacancy caused by the resignation of John Pastore for the term ending 3 January 1977. Chafee was reelected in 1982, 1988, and 1994, and served until his death of heart failure on 24 October 1999.
† Commander Edward P. Stafford, USN (Ret.), who has written several Navy books, notably the history of the aircraft carrier Enterprise (CV-6).

Captain Hetu: Yes. Ed's a good writer.

Paul Stillwell: Excellent.

Captain Hetu: Yes, a super writer. I liked Ed very much, but he, on occasion, got his own ideas mixed up with the Secretary's, and that was somewhat of a problem.

Paul Stillwell: Did he fill that role at the time?

Captain Hetu: Yes, he was there, but then he left to do something else and I needed some help. He worked with Bill Thompson. So I went to BuPers and sort of gave them the profile of the kind of officer I was looking for. Chinfo didn't have anybody in mind, and I wasn't getting very much response. So I just sort of decided that for once I'd use the Secretary's mantle and go to BuPers and say, "I'm looking for a lieutenant, a bright young lieutenant. It would be a hell of a job for him, a good two-year tour for a young officer, really see how the Navy works and if you got any comers, why, send me one."

A guy fell out of the computer—I guess they used cards then—Steve Pfeiffer.[*] Steve is now a very senior lawyer with Fulbright and Jaworski. At that time Steve was just finishing up his tour at Oxford. He was a Rhodes scholar and somebody in the Navy, for one of the few times in my recollection, in the personnel area, had used their head. Steve wanted to be a naval officer. He wanted to serve his time. So he had applied for OCS out of college and was selected for OCS. Almost simultaneously he was selected as a Rhodes Scholar, not by the Navy, but independently.

So he went to the Navy and said, "I would like to serve, but I also don't want to turn down my Rhodes Scholarship. How can we work this out?" So the Navy sent him to OCS, commissioned him, put him in the inactive reserve, and let him go to England with the promise that he would serve his active duty when he came back. So I got a lieutenant who has not been on active duty, right out of a Rhodes Scholarship.

Paul Stillwell: With a relatively limited knowledge of the Navy.

---

[*] Lieutenant Steven B. Pfeiffer, USNR, served as a special assistant to the Secretary of the Navy, 1973-74.

Captain Hetu: Relatively, but an extraordinarily bright young man. He had not yet gone to law school. He went to law school after he finished his Navy tour.

Paul Stillwell: And probably a quick study.

Captain Hetu: Oh, just terrific. And, of course, Stan Turner had been a Rhodes Scholar, so that didn't hurt anything.

Paul Stillwell: How did he work out in practice?

Captain Hetu: Oh, sensational. You know, what a find this guy was. He was smart and had a great sense of humor, and we got along really well. In fact, we remain friends to this day. I still see Steve.

Paul Stillwell: What can you say about Secretary Chafee's working style and your relationship with him?

Captain Hetu: Chafee was a joy to work for. John Chafee is a genuinely nice man, and he's very personnel conscious. I mean, he worries about people. Just a nice man to be around. He had a wonderful sense of humor; he liked to laugh, and I used to like to make him laugh. I traveled everywhere with him. He was very frugal. John was the old Rhode Island family. He had a wonderful family. I remember his dad was sort of a wonderful old craggy sea captain-looking guy, and a nice mother.

Anyhow, I thoroughly enjoyed working for John Chafee. John Chafee was the kind of guy who always took you with him wherever he went, and I learned a lot about politics working for John. I ran his slide show in back rooms of Italian restaurants in Rhode Island and traveled with him. He was not running for office but was certainly keeping his contacts alive in Rhode Island, and one of my great disappointments was soon after I came to work for Chafee, I thought, "Boy, oh, boy, now I get to ride in one of these big limousines." In those days, the Secretary had a limousine and a driver, and he had traded the limousine with Warner, who was then the Under Secretary because he felt that the limousine was too ostentatious.* He didn't want to ride around in a limousine, so we drove around in a little Chevy or Dodge, I don't remember, Plymouth, maybe. He decided that he was going to have this car—John was big on the ecology then, the environment, and, remember, this was 1970.

Paul Stillwell: The first Earth Day, I think.

Captain Hetu: This was a little before it was politically correct. Anyhow, he had his car converted to propane. [Laughter] This was a long time ago, and this meant that they had to put propane tanks in the trunk, which scared the hell of me, and had to move his radio and everything out of there so there wouldn't be any sparks. They were afraid the car would blow up. So they had to put his two-way radio in the front seat on the floor. So I spent a good deal of my time in those days riding the shotgun spot in the front seat with my knees up under my chin on top of the radio. So this wasn't quite what I had pictured working in the Secretary's office. [Laughter]

The propane didn't last very long. Poor old Wash, who was the driver—Washington was a sweet black man—had to go over to the Navy yard about twice a day to fill up the propane tanks. It had a switch, I remember, on the dashboard so you could switch to the gas tank so you wouldn't run out of petrol or you wouldn't get stranded someplace. But poor old Wash was running back and forth to the Navy Yard twice a day to fill up the propane tanks, because it took a lot of propane to run a car in those days. [Laughter]

Paul Stillwell: What would be examples of Chafee's frugality?

Captain Hetu: I mean, I offer these in the very best sense, because he was a fun, wonderful guy to be around. When we would go on trips and stay in a hotel, generally the hotel bill was paid by the host, if it was a speaking engagement or whatever—usually, not always, but very often. Very often they would have a couple of bottles in the room, a

---

* John W. Warner served as Under Secretary of the Navy from 11 February 1969 to 4 May 1972.

bottle of scotch, a bottle of bourbon, some glasses and ice. We always took the bottles when we left, and John would give me the scotch because he knew I was a scotch drinker and he'd usually take the bourbon, I guess. And he took the soap. He had a bunch of kids. The Secretary of Navy made money, but he wasn't making a million dollars, certainly. I don't remember what the Secretary of Navy made then, but it wasn't all that much money.

Paul Stillwell: I don't know.

Captain Hetu: He had five children.* Before I got there one of his daughters was killed by a horse, got kicked in the head in a stable that they had that horse, which was very terrible in his life and hurt him deeply. I remember we went to Guantanamo for an inspection tour, and went to the hospital to walk through. There was a young girl in the hospital, laying in the bed with her head bandaged. He stopped in to say hello to this young lady, and the doctor was going through. And he said, "What happened to you?"

She said, "I got kicked by a horse." And, you know, I just saw the color drain out of him. I mean, it was almost like he had to catch himself. It was just a bad moment for him.

Paul Stillwell: Understandably.

Captain Hetu: Yes, but he recovered. He didn't say anything about it, and I guess the doctor said to me afterwards, "The Secretary looked like he was going to get sick."

I said, "Yes, there was no way to head this off, and I didn't even know this and you didn't know it, but his daughter got killed a year or two years ago, got kicked by a horse."

"Oh, God."

I said, "Don't worry about it."

He said, "Oh, I should tell him how sorry I am."

---

* Lincoln D. Chafee was appointed to the United States Senate on 2 November 1999 to fill the vacancy caused by the death of his father, John H. Chafee. Lincoln Chafee was then elected as a Republican to the U.S. Senate in 2000 for the term ending January 3, 2007.

I said, "I wouldn't say anything if I were you. I mean, just leave it alone."

Paul Stillwell: You don't want to remind him again.

Captain Hetu: Yes. "He doesn't hold grudges. I mean, he wouldn't be mad at you in a million years. He knows that you wouldn't do something like that on purpose."

But we traveled a fair amount. One of the greatest trips we took was to Antarctica.

Paul Stillwell: That was in January 1972.

Captain Hetu: Yes, and we went with a group of people. I'm trying to remember how many guests we had on that trip, about eight or ten, and a very interesting group it was. [Laughter] We had the Buckley brothers, the senator and the writer.* We had Barry Goldwater and his son.† We had a guy named Kirkpatrick or Kilpatrick, Kilpatrick who had been the chairman of one of the early studies on the Defense Department, the Kilpatrick Study. Anyway, it was a very interesting group that we had.

Paul Stillwell: What was the purpose of it?

Captain Hetu: Just to go down and visit Operation Deep Freeze, see what was going on on the ice. We spent a couple weeks down there. Went to New Zealand, of course, and went out of Christchurch. Absolutely incredible trip, one of the great trips of my entire life.

Paul Stillwell: What made it so?

---

* James L. Buckley served in the U.S. Senate from 3 January 1971 to 3 January 1977; his brother, William F. Buckley, is a prominent author, magazine editor, and television commentator.
† Barry M. Goldwater, a Republican from Arizona, served in the U.S. Senate 3 January 1953 to 3 January 1965; did not seek reelection to the Senate in 1964; unsuccessful Republican nominee for President in 1964; again served in the Senate from 3 January 1969 to 3 January 1987. Barry M. Goldwater, Jr., a Republican from California, served in the House of Representatives from 29 April 1969 to 3 January 1983.

Captain Hetu: Oh, the people on the trip were incredible people. But the beauty of that place, and we went everywhere. We went to the South Pole, we went to Vostok, the Russian station. We had a scientist there, a Navy civilian who had wintered over with the Russians. We were just after the winter season; we were going in right after the place had opened up, after it had been closed for the winter, the darkness, the dark season. When we got there the sun was up 24 hours a day, going around like this in the sky.

Paul Stillwell: January is summer in the southern hemisphere.

Captain Hetu: Oh, yes. Well, and it never got dark the whole time we were there. I mean, it was light 24 hours a day—incredible. Went out at 10:00 at night riding icebreakers, and it was hard to get your system acclimated to this, because it didn't seem like you should be going to sleep. You were tired as hell but you didn't know why.

The trip to Vostok, the Russian station—and I can't remember the name of the scientist who had wintered over with the Russians, but he was like a vegetable by the time we got there. Boy, was he glad to see us. He wanted to get out of there in the worst damn way. There was a Russian airplane, in fact, the first one that had come in when we arrived. We were on a C-130 with skis, and there was a Russian plane there that looked like a DC-3. It had two engines, had flown from the Soviet Union and they let us go aboard it, and they had these great big tanks. You know like tanks outside of a farmhouse that they keep oil in, they had tanks like that. They had those up in the cabin of the airplane they flew and they had—oh, my, primitive.

This guy told us some wild stories on the way back. The Russians were left a winter's supply of vodka but had not sense to ration it. So for the first two or three weeks everybody was drunk all the time, and they drank it up in three weeks or something like that. Then they didn't have any more vodka for the rest of the winter. And these people, by then, were at each other's throats. He was in a sort of cabin or whatever it was with three other Russians or something, and he finally moved out and built himself some sort of a bivouac place away from the Russians, so he slept by himself.

Paul Stillwell: What nationality was he, American?

Captain Hetu: American, yes. And, boy, he was a nut case almost by the time we got there. The Russians were having a party, and I remember we were drinking vodka out of Mason jars. And it was high; Vostok was 8,000 or 9,000 feet because of the thickness of the ice. As you well know, Antarctica is a continent, but it's covered with a very thick covering of ice. Vostok, I think was 9,000 or 10,000 feet, and so you almost had to take oxygen, and you forget about that. I remember I smoked then, before I stopped, and you couldn't get your cigarette lit. I mean, you'd light it, and it would go out because there wasn't enough oxygen. You'd be sucking on your cigarette, and you couldn't get any smoke through it.

And that with drinking vodka at that altitude, man. The Russians were just having a hell of a time, boy, they were. We were exchanging hats and pins and all kinds of stuff. I got myself a Russian hat down there, one of those fur hats. That was an interesting trip. We had to leave the engines going all the time, because you couldn't shut them down. We were scared to death if you shut the engines on the C-130 down that you'd never get them started again. So the whole time we were there they were running, sitting out there cranking over.

We went to the dry valleys, which is an anomaly—a topographical mistake. I don't know what you'd call it, but it was totally dry and warm. It had a stream going through it. We would find seals that they were telling us were 100 years old, that were mummified, and so forth. We went to Shackleton's camp, and we went to all the old camps that were still there, exactly the way they had been in the early 1900s.[*] Their animals were still there, mummified, the horses were mummified.

You couldn't take anything, obviously, but they still had canned goods there and all sorts of things. It was so dry and so no humidity; everything stayed pretty much the way it was. The shacks were all in the same; they were still in perfect condition, even some of the livery, the reins and things from the horses were there. God, it was just fascinating.

Paul Stillwell: And presumably no bacteria either.

---

[*] Sir Ernest Henry Shackleton, a British explorer, made several trips to Antarctica early in the 20th century.

Captain Hetu: No, that's right. We went to a huge penguin rookery and walked through this rookery. It was just like being on another planet. The penguins were totally oblivious to us and had no fear at all. We walked through thousands of these birds. The only time they'd come up and peck on your leg is if you got too close to one of their nests where they had eggs, and then they'd come up. They didn't hurt you, but they'd peck on your leg.

Paul Stillwell: Just to get your attention.

Captain Hetu: Get you out of there, yes. Oh, what an extraordinary adventure that was; it really was. And the Buckley brothers were characters. We went to the South Pole, and the senator decided to have his brother take a picture of him holding up the world. So he got on his head and did this. We were at the South Pole, and he was holding up the world. Of course, take the picture and turn it upside down. James was the senator, and Bill was the author/writer. Bill shot off a rocket. He wanted to shoot a rocket with an American flag and he did, but it misfired and scooted along the ice and hit his brother right next to the eye. God, it was a tense moment. We thought he had hit him in the eye with this rocket. It cut his face superficially and scared the hell out of everybody. I don't know why I remember that except that it . . .

Paul Stillwell: Spectacular.

Captain Hetu: Yes. They had done an ice core, so the Buckleys asked the scientists if they have a couple feet of this ice core that they weren't going to use; it was from the time of Christ. Apparently they were able to do that, and they took it back with them when we went back to the station, the staging area, the staging station. Good Lord, where did we fly to from New Zealand? To McMurdo, and another interesting story. When we embarked to go down to McMurdo, the Buckleys brought aboard three cases which looked terribly like wine cases, and that's what they were. Nobody said anything to them, and every night at the mess, which is pretty Spartan at McMurdo, the Buckleys would bring a bottle of wine to dinner. And I remember Bill Buckley, ever the preppy, wore a button-down white shirt under his Antarctic garb that we were issued. So he'd wear his white button-down shirt and had a bottle of French wine with dinner, which he shared with us.

Paul Stillwell: What was the outcome of the ice sample? Was it preserved in some kind of freezer?

Captain Hetu: Well, no. The ice sample we brought back to McMurdo and melted it in a clean bucket. They had brought small, little bottles about the size of eye drop bottles, and I have one someplace, I don't know where. It has a little sign on it saying that this was water taken from an ice sample from the time of Christ, from the year 0001 or whatever. And they handed these out. I don't know how many hundreds of them they had, but I can remember them sitting in their quarters; we stayed in a BOQ-like arrangement. I was there the night that they poured the water. They were pouring the water into these bottles and capping them. And we were drinking scotch; I think it was Chivas, as a matter of fact, that they had brought along. We were drinking scotch and water from the time of Christ.

Paul Stillwell: Oh, gee. [Laughter]

Captain Hetu: It was a big thing of ice water from the core and, of course, we were drinking that with our scotch. So it was kind of an interesting evening, pouring this water into little bottles and drinking scotch and water from the time of Christ.

Paul Stillwell: Something that would stick in your memory, obviously.

Captain Hetu: Yes, yes.

Paul Stillwell: Well, now the public has this perception of some of these fact-finding trips as boondoggles. What would be your justification for them as the public affairs officer?

Captain Hetu: Oh, there was very little known about Antarctica. Of course, the Navy was just in a support role down there to the National Science Foundation. Oh, I thought it gave people a tremendous understanding for the place. It gave them an appreciation that what the Navy was doing was very important down there. And you learn so much. I mean, it's total immersion, no pun intended, for ten days or however long we were there. And these people all came back, I'm sure, supporters not just of the Navy, but of what we were trying to do with Antarctica, and that it was sort of one of the last frontiers of pristine environment. There were rules, of course, then that you couldn't dump waste down there. You had to take even bodily waste out in drums and all kinds of stuff.

We went and visited the New Zealand camp, and they had dog sleds at the New Zealand camp. They still were using dog sleds. Like I said, the Russians, dry valleys, we just immersed in Antarctica, flew in helicopters all over the place. The scenery is unbelievably gorgeous, still have an active volcano. I don't know, have you ever been there?

Paul Stillwell: No.

Captain Hetu: Boy, go, if you can.

Paul Stillwell: Was the Secretary inclined to visit the fleet?

Captain Hetu: Oh, yes, yes. You know, a little of that politician rubbed off, I suppose. He wasn't campaigning on the ships, but he liked people, and as a politician he was a warm person, and I think that comes through. He liked to be with the enlisted people. He liked to be shaking hands and talking with people. He was very easy to talk to, and I think he did a tremendous good for the Navy getting around. Did I tell you the story about going to Harvard?

Paul Stillwell: I don't think so.

Captain Hetu: We went to Harvard to visit the class that Bill Thompson was in, of these very senior people, up-and-comers from companies all over the country. I don't remember how many there were in a class, not that many in a class, probably 40 or 60 or something like that. We were up in Boston to do something else, and Bill arranged for the Secretary to come over to Harvard to speak to the senior business school people. They brought in other classes of postgraduate students and so forth, all very senior people, to hear the Secretary. It was, I remember, a large auditorium. I don't know, a couple of hundred people certainly, in the place.

Zack, his son was a freshman at Harvard, undergraduate, of course. The Secretary said, "I want to call ahead and get Zack to come over and go to the speech with us." And so he did. When we came into the back of the auditorium, it was wintertime, I remember. I was in blues and bridge coat and aiguillettes and all this stuff. And Zack was there in typical hippie, is what we called them then, I guess, hippie, long hair. I don't remember whether he had a beard, but scruffy clothes, a lumberjack shirt on or something, and blue jeans and kind of work shoes, and the hair down over his collar.

I remember, and I'm embarrassed to this day that I felt that way, but I was sort of taken aback and thought, "Oh, this kid is not going to come in, certainly in with the Secretary into this auditorium." And Chafee, I remember, hugged him. They hadn't seen each other for a while, and put his arm around him, and you have to remember, this auditorium was seated. Everybody was in the place, and they were all waiting for us to arrive, and there were six seats in the front row or something. We marched down that aisle and Chafee with his arm around his son, okay.

I have never forgotten that. You know, there was not even a glimmer of his being ashamed of his—not that anybody would be ashamed of their kid, but say, "Oh, no, you should have gotten a hair cut, Zack, and put on a tie." Nothing, zero. He just gave him a hug and put his arm around him and walked all the way down the aisle with his son, talking to him. We could sort of hear, "Who's that?" And the first thing John did when he got up to give his speech was introduce his son. Said, "Some people with me today and first of all, my son, Zack, who's an undergraduate freshman, just started in September here at Harvard, and Commander Hetu." I don't know if I was a captain then or not. But he introduced the people with him. Bill Thompson who was part of our party.

Anyway, that was sort of a Chafee story that I always like to tell, because he was very proud of his kids and his family, and that was a very good object lesson for me. I thought, "Why would you ever even think what you thought?" I was embarrassed that I had even thought for an instant that I was kind of embarrassed by this kid, I guess.

Paul Stillwell: And awfully glad you hadn't articulated it out loud.

Captain Hetu: Well, I wouldn't have, but I'm glad I didn't, yes, right. Say, "You're not going to take that kid with you, are you?" Well, that was Chafee, though, that was kind of a Chafee story. He was a nice man, very loyal to his family. Very frugal, as I said. I think we used to laugh, he still wore the same belt with his suits that he had worn in college, and very proud of the fact. The belt was a mess, all cracked, but he was proud of this: "Well, I wore this belt when I went to Brown," or wherever he went.* We bought him a new belt for Christmas and sort of upset him a little bit. But he took it in good sense. But he wore the same shoes and about three suits, I think, all the time I was there.

He used to go crazy when we'd go on these trips. I mean, we went on an almost around-the-world trip where we went to Vietnam and we went to England. I mean, we went sort of around the globe, like a three-week marathon trip, boy, seeing just about everything: the fleets, Seventh Fleet. We, as military people, had to take damn near every uniform we owned, you know: whites, greens, blues, civilian clothes.

Paul Stillwell: Khakis.

Captain Hetu: Khakis, shorts, brown shoes, white shoes, blue shoes, black shoes. I'm trying to remember the first stop, where we went to the hotel, and there was the baggage that had gone off the plane. There was this huge mountain of baggage in the middle of

---

* Chafee received his bachelor's degree from Yale in 1947 and law degree from Harvard in 1950.

the hotel's lobby waiting for us, and he was furious, really got upset. Said, "That's just unbelievable. People are going to think we're this big entourage and dah, dah, dah."

I think by then Thor Hanson was the aide, and Thor tried to tell him, "Mr. Secretary, you arrive and somebody takes your suit off and presses it, and you're all set to go, and you can wear the same thing. We have to change uniforms and have white shirts and khaki shirts and greens."

"Well," he said, "when we go back aboard the plane, I want you all to repack your bags so that you come off with one bag at each stop." One-bag Chafee. So we had to go back aboard, and we all had hang-up bags and all kinds of stuff and thought, "Jesus." So I remember taking turns of repacking our bags on the floor of the plane for the next spot; then you'd go aboard and you'd have to repack for the next stop. We were spending all the time in the air repacking our bags so we could go off with one bag. But he was a nice man. He was fun to be with.

We flew up to Buffalo. They were opening a new terminal, as I recall. Rockefeller was then the governor of New York, and they were buddies.[*] They were pals from the presidential campaign. Interesting that Chafee got the job, because he and Rockefeller were friends. But, anyhow, one of my jobs generally was the trip coordinator, and I had called ahead and talked to the governor's aide and told him when we were coming and how we were coming. We flew in an old A-3 then, which was a dreadful airplane.[†] You had to get in it up through the bottom. They had steps that dropped down where the bomb bay was, and that's how you got in this noisy airplane.

Anyhow, we got on the plane, and there was a Democratic congressman from New York that found out we were going up there and called the office and wanted to ride with us. I can't remember who that might have been. Does Stratton sound right?

Paul Stillwell: Yes. He's a naval reservist, Sam Stratton.[‡]

---

[*] Nelson A. Rockefeller, a Republican, was governor of New York from 1959 to 1973.
[†] The Douglas A3D Skywarrior first entered fleet squadrons in 1956 as a carrier-based heavy bomber. It was reclassified as the A-3 in 1962.
[‡] Samuel S. Stratton, a Democrat from the state of New York, served in the U.S. House of Representatives from 3 January 1959 to 3 January 1989. He served on active duty as a Naval Reservist during World War II and eventually became a captain in the reserve.

Captain Hetu: Right. I think a Democrat, and he called the office and wanted to ride with us. Well, of course, we had to let him come along. This was a noisy airplane, this was a twin jet; it was pressurized but that's about all. I said to Chafee, "Well, I talked to the governor's aide just before we left, and the governor will meet you at the airport with a car and so forth."

He said, "He won't be at the airport.

I said, "Oh, yes, sir, he will. I talked to his aide, who said that they would meet us on arrival."

He said, "Bet you a quarter."

I said, "Okay." So we got to the airport, and the limousines were out there and everything to take us to the hotel. The governor's aide came over and said, "Mr. Secretary, I'm so sorry, the governor got called away at the very last minute on a very important matter, and he'll have to meet you at the hotel. He wanted to come meet you, blah, blah, blah, blah." And Chafee did this number, put his hand out . . . [Laughter]

Paul Stillwell: To collect his quarter.

Captain Hetu: . . . to get the quarter, and I gave him his quarter. We got in the car, and Stratton went off in another car and we went off to the hotel. I said, "Okay, I think I've been had here. Did you talk to him before we left? I think you got that quarter under bad circumstances here."

He said, "No, no, no. I knew that Stratton and Rockefeller are not pals and that no way was Rockefeller going to be out to this airport and have the press take a picture of him greeting Stratton arriving for this ceremony. Because Stratton's here to try and get a piece of the action on this new building, see, for the Democrats. Rockefeller wasn't going to be out meeting him at the airport."

Paul Stillwell: So his political instincts were exactly on target.

Captain Hetu: Absolutely. He said, "I knew there was no way he'd be at the airport."

I said, "Oh, I still think you've beaten me out of a quarter," and he laughed. But we went to the hotel, and Rockefeller was waiting for us, as I recall, in the suite. And Rockefeller was then running against Goldberg, I think, for governor of New York. Goldberg had been the U.N. ambassador, and Chafee was then getting serious about running in Rhode Island.

Paul Stillwell: What year would this have been?

Captain Hetu: Seventy-two, maybe. I was getting ready to leave the suite. Chafee had introduced me to Rockefeller. There were two, I think, double beds in the suite, and they both sort of laid down and I fixed them a drink. I said, "Well, sir, I'll make my exit, diplomatic exit."

Chafee said, "No, no, no." He said, "Sit down. You might learn something here," and did I ever. [Laughter] You know, I probably learned more in that hour of those two guys sitting there talking about their campaigns and what they were going to do and so forth, about how politicians think and so forth than I could have learned in a year of postgraduate school.

Paul Stillwell: What were some of the lessons?

Captain Hetu: Gosh, I would be hard pressed, I guess, to give you examples. I was struck by how detail oriented they were, and just like this not meeting this guy at the airport, about how very detail oriented politicians are in the way they think.

Paul Stillwell: And probably how calculating they are of the effects of everything they do.

Captain Hetu: Absolutely. Absolutely. For instance, one of the things I remember they said, "Stratton will be at the reception." I think we went and did the opening of this thing and then back to the reception. And I remember Rockefeller saying, "Well, you know, John, there will be press at the reception, photographers and stuff."

John laughed and said, "Well, I guess it'll be a good picture of you and Stratton shaking hands."

He said, "I will not get more than five feet close to that guy." I don't think he called him guy. And he didn't. I watched that at the reception, and I watched them skirt around, and Rockefeller never got within shooting distance of the congressman. They never had their picture taken together.

But they worry about things like that. I guess they were just talking about some of the issues of the day—school bussing was a big issue in those days—and how to deal with those issues. I guess I also learned that politicians are not always true to their own feelings on some of these things. They are very much influenced by what the electorate thinks, and I guess that's probably what a politician's supposed to do, to represent the majority or whoever he thinks is going to elect him.

Paul Stillwell: But presumably there are also there are matters of principle that they would not compromise.

Captain Hetu: Yes, that's right. I could be proven wrong here, but I remember this being an issue in Rhode Island which was discussed in some of the back-room political conclaves that Chafee always let me sit in on. When he would even meet with the party people up in Rhode Island, he let me sit in on the meetings just to hear how those things were done. Some issues he would not make a public stand on. He would say whatever the people decided was what he would support. I thought that wasn't a bad way to do it, I guess.

Sort of I had my own personal opinion, but I'm not going to—you know, school bussing, of course, was, I guess, an ethical, moral issue, but it wasn't so much like abortion, I don't think, you know, life-and-death sort of thing.

Paul Stillwell: In the year 1969, while you were still out in Vietnam, Secretary Chafee came very much into the public eye with the resolution of the Pueblo situation.* Were there any after effects of that during your watch?

Captain Hetu: No, no. I don't remember any backlash.

Paul Stillwell: Well, he really took it out of the public eye by halting any further prosecution of Commander Bucher.

Captain Hetu: Yes. Just stopped it dead. John Warner did something similar later on with the POW problem; I remember that.† He did almost the same sort of thing. Took him a little longer to decide it. No, I don't remember any Pueblo backlash when I was there.

Paul Stillwell: Well, you mentioned the name of Kent Lee during our last interview. He moved to the Secretary's office. What was your relationship with him in Washington?

Captain Hetu: Kent came to be head of OPA, Office of Program Appraisal.‡ I was in the E-ring, but on the inner side of the E-ring. So my window looked into his window. Our offices were certainly different in size, so I decided I better get over there and let him know I was there. I had never met him. I think I told you that he had put me really on report, not officially but in a back-channel message to Com7thFlt, and so forth about lack of judgment and so forth of bringing this, I don't know what he called her, woman, out to the Enterprise.§ So I went over to see him, since I was on the Secretary's personal staff, and he was on the staff as well.

So I thought, "I better go over and clear the air on this, not be ducking this guy. I can't be ducking him for two years." So I went over and went in, and I can't recall now

---

* Commander Lloyd M. Bucher, USN, was commanding officer of the Pueblo at the time of her seizure. A court of inquiry in 1969 recommended that he be court-martialed for loss of the ship, but Secretary Chafee decided not to carry out the recommendation, saying that Bucher had suffered enough.
† POW—prisoner of war.
‡ Lee was then a rear admiral. He discussed this tour of duty in his Naval Institute oral history.
§ This incident is covered in Hetu's previous interview.

whether I was a captain or not. I probably was. But, anyway, I went in and I said, "Admiral, I'm Herb Hetu and I'm the Secretary's public affairs officer. I just wanted to come say 'hi' to you. And we share windows sort of and will be working together.

He said, "Hetu? Hetu?"

I said, "Weather girl."

He said, "I know that name."

I said, "Weather girl, Vietnam. Weather girl."

He said, "Ah ha, you're the guy on Det Charlie that sent the weather girl out."

I said, "That's right. That's right. I'm the guy. You got me."

So we laughed about it. He was pretty good about it. I mean, he had a sense of humor, and we didn't really talk too much about it; there wasn't very much to say.

Paul Stillwell: Did you have other dialogue with him as part of your job?

Captain Hetu: Not very much. They did the program appraisal, and I didn't get very much involved in that kind of stuff. We saw each other often at the meetings with the Secretary and so forth, but didn't have a lot to do with each other personally, no.

Paul Stillwell: Some years back I interviewed Captain Andy Kerr, who was a lawyer for four different SecNavs during the 1960s.

Captain Hetu: Yes, I know Andy.

Paul Stillwell: He described the position of the personal staff as more reactive than proactive, saying that really the problems that got to the Secretary's office were the intractable ones, because if there had been a solution, somebody would have figured it out at a lower level. How did that fit in with your perceptions?

Captain Hetu: That sounds pretty good. I shared the suite with a lawyer, Merlin Staring, when I first went there, a wonderful guy, who became JAG.* And John Jenkins, who also became JAG later on.†

Paul Stillwell: Well, did that rationale also work in the public affairs area, that you were reactive?

Captain Hetu: Yes, I think so. We didn't get out ahead on too many issues. One of my jobs was to keep close touch with the Chief of Information, to find out what was going on down there, what they were working on. We talked daily. I mean, that was part of the job, as I saw it, because the Secretary's office is really, in a sense, isolated from the Navy, the mainstream Navy, you know.

Paul Stillwell: Well, were you, in any sense, the Chinfo rep in the Secretary's office?

Captain Hetu: Oh, yes, without question, sure. And, of course, it was important to keep that liaison going with the Chief of Information, and I dealt with the Chief of Information and with the CNO's office. This was especially important with Zumwalt and Warner, who didn't see eye to eye on very much, and to not be a spy or anything of that nature, but to keep the lines of communication open so that we didn't become isolated up there.‡ I think that could easily happen, and I always felt I had to do the outreach. In other words, I didn't sit in the Secretary's office confident that people in the uniforms thought they were going to keep me informed of everything was going on. I don't think they would purposely isolate you, but they didn't think about you, unless you kept yourself going to the meetings and hiking down to Chinfo's office very often and just dropping by and going to some of his meetings, having lunch and so forth. It was an important part of the function, I thought.

---

* Captain Merlin H. Staring, JAGC, USN. As a rear admiral he served as the Navy's Judge Advocate General, 1972-75.
† Commander John S. Jenkins, JAGC, USN. Later Judge Advocate General from 1980 to 1982.
‡ Admiral Elmo R. Zumwalt, Jr., USN, served as Chief of Naval Operations, 1 July 1970 to 29 June 1974.

Paul Stillwell: Well, what was a typical day for you in the Pentagon on that staff?

Captain Hetu: Early to rise, would get to the office probably no later than quarter to 7:00. The press briefers then worked for the Secretary of the Navy's public affairs officer. These were the Chinfo junior officers that gave the press briefing and the CNO and SecNav briefings in the morning, ten-minute press summary. These kids would come in, I don't know what time they came in, 2:00 o'clock in the morning, midnight, something like that, to start reading the papers and put together their briefing. Then they would have it on my desk about 6:30, 7:00, something like that. I think the first briefings were usually at 8:00. So we would go over the briefing and just make sure that it made sense, and they would have the clips with them so that I could take 15, 20 minutes to run over the briefing and make sure it reflected what the story really said.

That was an interesting job. These were all sort of bright young guys; it was fun to work with them. They would work all night and then shoot their wad in ten minutes, so it was a tough job. But it was an important job, a very vital job. I guess I was not in the Secretary's office, I was in the CNO's office when Rivero ordered people not to report anything Jack Anderson reported.* He didn't want his name mentioned in the briefing. In fact, I'm sure it was Jack Anderson. We had to go in and see the admiral and try diplomatically to impress upon him that it was very important to know what the enemy was saying, and this was a classic case of head in the sand: "I don't want to hear what that son of a bitch has to say."

Paul Stillwell: That was when Admiral McDonald was CNO?

Captain Hetu: Yes. And we talked to Admiral Rivero and got him to rescind that order. Said, "You know, we're not trying to aggrandize this guy. We're trying to tell you what he's saying so that you can be prepared from the Hill and all the other places that do read him. That's the purpose of the briefing, not to make these guys heroes. It's to impart information."

---

* Admiral Horacio Rivero, USN, served as Vice Chief of Naval Operations from 31 July 1964 to 17 January 1968. His oral history is in the Naval Institute collection. Jack Anderson is a syndicated newspaper columnist, long noted for his muckraking style.

Okay, so then I was finished with that by about 7:00. I would go to one of the briefings, I guess it was the second briefing. There was one at 8:00 and one at 8:30, I think. One for the really senior people and one for the not-so-senior people.

Paul Stillwell: Moderately senior.

Captain Hetu: Yes, two and three stars. And then start working on the daily schedule, which was incredibly busy. We were always getting ready to go on trips. We were writing speeches. He did a lot of press interviews; Chafee liked to do interviews, and as a politician, recognized the importance of doing them. So he did quite a few interviews. When he did an interview we prepared him very well. A person that senior doesn't have a hell of a lot of time to sit down and do his own study. That's why we were there.

Paul Stillwell: You would prep him with possible questions and recommended answers?

Captain Hetu: Yes, no problem, no job. And a background on the newsman, if he didn't know them, or even if he did. We would do a research of what he had written in the last three years, let's say, and what his bent was on any particular issue, what his reputation was: straight-shooter, watch yourself, don't go off the record with this guy, you know.

So we had to know the issues, we had to know the people we were talking to, and we had to know how to diplomatically get information in a hurry from around the Navy Department. People were very anxious to help us, and so when you got some of these answers you wanted to make awfully sure that they were factually correct. So we would draft answers and then run them through the people who knew the operators. And they were good about that.

My staff used to do that, the chief and the lieutenant, Steve Pfeiffer. Steve was relieved by a guy that's now an admiral.[*] I can't remember his name; I'll think of it. He had a strange name. Anyhow, we kept ourselves very busy, and I was trying always to keep myself up to date with what was going on at Chinfo and to liaison with the CNO's

---

[*] Captain Hetu may have been thinking of Lieutenant Thomas F. Marfiak, USN, who was Pfeiffer's predecessor in the job. He subsequently became a rear admiral and, after retiring from active duty in 1999, became the chief executive officer of the U.S. Naval Institute.

public affairs officer and talk to Jack MacKercher who was down in the Chairman's office.* You were just working your trap line and also getting down to the newsroom to rub elbows with the newsmen, keep up your contacts with these guys and let them know you're around, that you're available to answer questions.

Paul Stillwell: Were there any cases where you were trying to get a story out, and you used that method to do so?

Captain Hetu: Yes, certainly to get our point of view across. People liked Chafee, and he liked to do one-on-ones, and he was good at it. You asked me that, and now I'm trying to think of an example. I guess it was when I was in the CNO's office. I get those two jobs cross-wired sometimes, when they had that terrible fire up at Great Lakes and then the admiral was burned to death and his wife.

Paul Stillwell: There was one when Admiral Yeager was killed.†

Captain Hetu: Yeager, Red Yeager.

Paul Stillwell: That was in the '60s.

Captain Hetu: Yes, that's when I worked for CNO. That's one time that I was able to really turn off—AP was hot on that case, and they had found out that Yeager's wife, I think, had MS. I'm not sure, but she had a debilitative disease.

Paul Stillwell: I think she was an invalid, yes.

Captain Hetu: What they found out as a result of the fire was that they had hospital corpsmen in the admiral's quarters 24 hours a day taking care of his wife, and they were going to make a big hoo-ha about that. I remember Fred Hoffman was the AP guy and I

---
* Captain John C. MacKercher, USN.
† Rear Admiral Howard A. Yeager, USN, died at Great Lakes, Illinois, on 11 March 1967 while serving as Commandant of the Ninth Naval District.

got all the facts and talked to the people and I said, "I've got to know the truth; you've got to tell me the truth. Don't tell me what you want the newsman to say, tell me the truth and then let me decide how to use the truth."[*]

Anyway, I'm digressing but we got Fred Hoffman in and told Fred and said to Fred, "I will tell you exactly what was going on up there, that the admiral's wife was in the hospital. She's an invalid, she was in terrible shape, and he was going to see her two or three times a day at the base hospital, which he was certainly entitled to, and it was debilitating. They were using up a room; the staff at the hospital was diverted to her. The admiral was using half of his time running back and forth to the hospital worrying about his wife. It was their judgment that it was easier and more beneficial to everybody to have these corpsmen come and take care of her at the quarters, do it in her own house, where the stewards would do the cooking and so forth. But you have to make that call. I mean, I'm giving you the facts. This is what happened, and I'm not trying to put any value judgment on it; I'll let you do that. But if you really think that you want to pillory this guy who is now dead, there's not much you can do to him except hurt the Navy and hurt this guy's career."

Paul Stillwell: Well, I think he died trying to save her, didn't he?

Captain Hetu: That's right. Yes, they found that, as I recall, there had been an electric extension under a carpet that had worn through from years of friction, and that's what caused this fire in this old wooden place in Great Lakes. It went up, I guess, like a tinderbox. Yes, Yeager went back in or was in and tried to get up the stairs or something to save her and died in the—I'm not so sure that he hadn't gotten to her and was carrying her when they both died—I think. That sticks in my mind.

So I said to Fred, "You know, this guy was a hero when he was on active duty, and he was a hero in death. Is it that important to you to write this story? So what?

Paul Stillwell: What was the outcome?

---

[*] Fred S. Hoffman was a longtime Pentagon reporter for the Associated Press and later the number-two spokesman for the Defense Department.

Captain Hetu: He didn't write it. And Fred and I remain friends until this day. Fred's still around.

Paul Stillwell: Well, that again is like the CBS example; it's a case of mutual respect.

Captain Hetu: Yes, and tell the truth. Just tell the truth. Just say, "Here it is, and you make your own judgment call. I'm not telling you not to write the story. I wish you wouldn't, but if you want to write it, write it, but here's the real facts. At least have the common courtesy and decency to write it straight and let the readers make up their minds."

Back to Chafee.

Paul Stillwell: Well, any more things that would happen during the course of a day?

Captain Hetu: Oh, the day, yes, the day-to-day. I may have said this earlier, but we had to impress on the staff—I would tell the chiefs and people that would come to work there, "You are not the Secretary of the Navy, I am not the Secretary of the Navy, and don't ever forget that, because it's easy to come here from a fleet job or from some command, and the treatment you get here will be extraordinary. When you call and say the Secretary's office, you get people's attention." The Ollie North, "This is the White House."[*] They find out that people respond and don't really hear whether you're a chief or a commander or what you are. All they hear is "Secretary's office."

It was not unusual for me in preparing trip books. When we would go on trips, I was the trip coordinator and would put together the briefing books for the trip. If we were going to go visit a shipyard, we'd do a little briefing paper on the shipyard. My challenge always was to try and get people to give us brief briefing papers: "I don't want three loose-leaf books. We don't have time to do that, and the Secretary won't have time. What we need is three or four pages max about the issues and the history and so forth."

---

[*] Lieutenant Colonel Oliver North, USMC, got involved in the Iran-Contra scandal in the 1980s while serving on the National Security Council staff in the White House.

I would generally call, if there was an aide, usually the administrative aide or aide to the OP or bureau, like BuPers or the Bureau of Yards and Docks, I guess, was still in existence then.[*] Very often I would either get a call back or a visit from some two- or three-star admiral saying, "Well, so the Secretary's going to see So-and-so or go visit the Second Fleet [or wherever it was going to be]. Well, dah, dah, dah, what can we do?"

And I'd say, "Well . . ."

Paul Stillwell: Just do what I asked.

Captain Hetu: Yes, admiral line. But that could get to you if you didn't keep your head on straight. These guys were not there to see me. They didn't give a damn who Herb Hetu was; they were there to make sure the Secretary got good service from their particular part of the operation. But I used to tell my people that, "Don't let that ever go to your head and don't ever abuse it because some day you're going to be going back out to work somewhere else and . . ."

Paul Stillwell: People will remember.

Captain Hetu: That's right. People remember a lot. "You can make a lot of friends here, but you can also misuse your position and make a lot of enemies, and you don't want to do that."

Paul Stillwell: Well, were there probably a fire drill or two during the course of a day as well?

Captain Hetu: Oh, yes. Occasionally, if something went wrong. I had more fire drills probably with Warner than I did with Chafee. When Warner was the Under Secretary, he was invisible. He didn't want to do anything. I mean, if you saw the John Warner I saw, and the John Warner of today—I mean, they were two different people. John Warner, the Under Secretary, was married to Kathy Mellon, the Mellon Mellons, Pittsburgh Mellon

---

[*] In 1966 the old Bureau of Yards and Docks became the Naval Facilities Engineering Command.

Mellons, and he was deathly afraid of kidnapping of the children and just maintained a very low visibility, didn't want to do speaking, public engagements, nothing.

Traditionally, this job worked for both the Secretary and the Under Secretary, and to some extent, the Assistant Secretaries, if they needed help or advice or something. Didn't write their speeches, but we helped them. I had nothing to do with Warner. Virtually the only thing I had to do with Warner when he was the Under Secretary was when he and Kathy Mellon decided to divorce, he called me in and asked me how I thought he should handle the divorce announcement. I said, "Well, I think you ought to put out a two-sentence, one-sentence statement. Let me do that for you, and then do nothing. You have no obligation to tell anybody about your personal life.

He said, "Oh, great. Would you write that?"

I said, "Yes, sure will." I forget what I wrote. It was a one-sentence straightforward, you know, something, "Under Secretary Warner regrets, [or I don't know it said regrets], he's divorcing or is being divorced or he and his wife are divorcing by mutual consent. The Secretary will have nothing else to say on this matter." It was that simple, which was not very hard to do. But he thought I was a genius, I guess, because—I don't know genius, but he thought I was smart, because we did put it out and we got no queries. Nobody cared that much, not the defense writers. This was a society story more than it was something. The guys in the newsroom at the Pentagon could care less about the Under Secretary of the Navy getting divorced. So when Chafee left—

Paul Stillwell: Well, before we move on, I'd like to talk about the naming of Admiral Zumwalt as CNO, because that certainly got a lot of play on Chafee's watch.

Captain Hetu: Yes. I wasn't terribly involved in that, knew it was going on, and I think Chafee was, to the best of my recollection, very supportive of that, that he liked Zumwalt. He had known him in Vietnam.

Paul Stillwell: Well, I got the impression he was the main instigator in bringing Admiral Zumwalt in.

Captain Hetu: Well, I think that's probably true, but I wasn't part of it, so I don't know. Chafee liked young people and liked young ideas. He was a very physically energetic guy, and I know he liked Zumwalt. I knew he liked him in Vietnam and liked all the forward-looking things that he was doing. And Chafee was a liberal Republican, as I told you about the environmental stuff. So he was all for women in the military and so forth, all the things that were done then.

Paul Stillwell: There was considerable backlash to the Z-grams and various of Zumwalt's reforms.* Did any of that splash into the Secretary's office?

Captain Hetu: Really, yes, but Chafee was very supportive. The great problems arose after Warner came in. I think it was probably when Admiral McDonald was CNO that the offices were reconfigured so that the CNO's office and the Secretary's office connected.

Paul Stillwell: I think so, because he and Secretary Nitze had a good relationship.

Captain Hetu: Yes, and they actually made a walk-through so that they didn't have to go out in the hall and go all the way around and make a big production out of visiting each other. They could go through the back hallway and talk to each other. Zumwalt's problems with Warner, I think, were caused more by frustration than by really a difference of policy. Warner was a procrastinator. It took him a long time to make a decision, with lots of discussions with lots of people. This was not Zumwalt's way of doing business, and that caused them a lot of personal animosity. I mean, Zumwalt would just get so frustrated that he would bubble over occasionally, and I wished that I was not in the room to hear the CNO and the Secretary talking to each other in pretty straightforward terms.

---

* Z-grams were consecutively numbered policy directives from Chief of Naval Operations Zumwalt that attempted to deal with such issues as enlisted rights and privileges, equal opportunity, and Navy families. Junior personnel viewed them much more favorably than did their seniors. See U.S. Naval Institute Proceedings, May 1971, pages 293-298.

I can remember, I guess, it was when Zumwalt sent out one of his first Z-grams about dress code and women. He got tired of waiting for Warner's chop on it, so he finally just sent it out and said, "The hell with him; it's going." Put out his first OpNav notice or whatever they called it, remember the Z-grams, they called them. That caused a lot of consternation when Warner found out that it had gone out.

So there was a lot more difficulties with Warner and Zumwalt, and I think they've sort of, at this stage in life, 1996, have pretty much kissed and made up. I think Zumwalt supported Warner for the Senate.

Paul Stillwell: Well, it was also a measure of the opposition, which was Ollie North.

Captain Hetu: Yes. He supported him against Robb and in the primary here against North. So, when Chafee left he went off to run for the Senate the first time, where he got roundly defeated and went back to practicing law for a couple years.

Paul Stillwell: Well, you probably want to mention something about your farewell party for him.

Captain Hetu: Oh, yes. They had a very, very nice black-tie farewell party for him at the Farragut House across from the White House. It was a very nice evening, and I used to do something that Chafee liked a lot. When we had senior people get transferred, I used to do a picture book, we called them, because we always had a lot of pictures taken every place we went. I would get what I thought were funny poses or people with strange looks on their faces and write captions for the pictures, and we always did a picture book for whoever left. He thought those were great. Chafee had a great sense of humor, and luckily liked my brand of humor; everybody doesn't necessarily.

So for the going-away we produced large pictures. We did a picture book, but we blew them up and we had them on the walls all over the place, which was great for the cocktail hour, and he loved them. I still have one of those around here someplace. But he still had it in his office. I was up to his office in the Senate not terribly long ago, and he still has it on his table. Thor Hanson, who was the aide, and I did a Gallagher-Sheen routine which broke the place up. We were obviously in our mess dress blues, and we each took sort of a striped summer suit and straw hats, which had bumper stickers on them saying "Sailors have more fun" across the top of the hats, and we did this Gallagher-Sheen routine.

We had written the script, and the Navy combo that was there, we had practiced with them, and so they knew what was coming. But nobody else did, and it was really a surprise. This wasn't a stodgy gathering by any means, but it was all the senior military people, the Chairman of the Joint Chiefs, lots of admirals, and assistant secretaries and congressmen and so forth, so a pretty high-powered audience from the Navy's point of view. When Thor and I got up in our straw hats and started doing this Gallagher-Sheen routine, why, it brought the house down. I still have the pictures and stuff, which I've shown you. You can't do that in this, but I'll read you the first verse. This just gives you the feeling of it.

Paul Stillwell: Sure.

Captain Hetu: I started off by saying: "Oh, Mr. Hanson, oh, Mr. Hanson, I've been reading in the latest magazines that the gent we call boss will be soon to us a loss. Can you tell me what this information means?"

Then we did a rat-ta-ta-ta and: "Well, Mr. Hetu, Mr. Hetu, what you read, my friend, is really au passe for the SecNav's plans are firm, and it's rumored Pell will squirm."

"On the level, Mr. Hanson?"

"Positively, Mr. H."

Then we'd do our little dance around the stage, and we had about eight or ten of those that we had written, and had great fun, and Chafee loved it—good party.

Warner was there. He had not yet been named. As I recall, it took some months before they named Warner. They looked high and low for a Secretary, and it was getting up on the election time, and I think nobody really wanted to come in and do it for two years. I don't say that John Warner got it by default, but he was not the first choice. I can't remember some of the people who were in the running at the time, but everybody turned him down, so Warner was named Secretary and when he was, he asked me to stay on, I think largely because of this one-line press release that I had written for him.

Then it was a totally different ball game. It was great fun. It was great fun with Chafee, but they were two different kinds of people. As I recall, John Chafee was pretty good about making decisions and very smart and very politically savvy, attuned. He liked to speak, and he was very gregarious. Warner came in, and he had done hardly any public speaking and was very timid. And if I do say so, I guess I was the guy who first introduced John Warner to the joys of public speaking and dealing with the media. He had never, ever done this before, and, of course, now you wouldn't know that, but he was very timid and very backward.*

I remember our very first news conference. It was in Newport. He was speaking at the war college. We were up there for a visit in Newport in any case, and we had a very small news conference, not very many people. The Providence papers came and one or two television. Press availability—there probably weren't more than ten people in the room. I was getting John ready for this, and we had gone over the issues, and I can't remember what some of the issues were, and the local issues. I guess Stan Turner was there then and had caused some problems, and he had reorganized the place and all this stuff.†

Paul Stillwell: Very dramatically so.

Captain Hetu: Indeed. So I said to Warner, "Now, you know, a good thing to do in news conference, particularly a small one like this, is go out and shake hands with everybody and sort of break the ice. Just don't walk up to the podium. Just walk around the podium; there aren't that many people in the room. Shake hands, 'I'm John Warner, and who are you?' Sort of gets everybody down a level and so forth."

So he did that, and he went around and went to one of the TV cameramen, and the cameraman said, "Mr. Warner, I'm Bill Blotz, and I'm the cameraman from Channel 5."

Warner said, "Well, I was a TV cameraman myself once," and walked away.

---

* At Captain Hetu's funeral in 2003, Senator Warner delivered a polished eulogy, entirely without notes.
† Vice Admiral Stansfield Turner, USN, served as president of the Naval War College from 30 June 1972 to 9 August 1974.

I was doing a take—"You were what?" We did the news conference; it was pretty uneventful except that John would take about 20 seconds after every question to consider his lawyerly answer. We didn't make a lot of news and didn't expect to. But he needed some work, which we did later on.

Afterwards, of course, these people from the station are going, "The Secretary said he was a cameraman, what channel did he . . .?"

I said, "I don't know. I'll have to get back to you on that."

"Okay."

So afterwards I got him aside and said, "You say you were a TV cameraman. Where?"

"Oh, I worked for, [I think, it was the school paper or something], I took pictures."

I said, "You mean with a still camera?"

"Yes, yes."

I said, "That's not a cameraman."

"Oh, you know, close enough."

I said, "Well, we've got to talk about these things; that's not close enough. Now I've got to get back to these people and sort of do a toe dance and tell them, 'Well, you misunderstood and, dah, dah, dah. I think what the Secretary said was "I used to take pictures or something" and the cameraman must have misunderstood or, dah, dah, dah.'" That worked pretty well. But that was one of John's—was always trying to bring himself to the—but I'd say, "Yes, but you've got to be real careful about stuff like that."

We did a lot of sort of in-house rehearsing for news conferences after that, and I would get two or three other people in the room, and we would prep him. I mean, sit down and ask him questions and get him so that he was comfortable in giving good, short, quick answers, and he turned out okay. He does it all right now.

Paul Stillwell: Well, he's a master at it now.

Captain Hetu: Yes, I'll say. But for a guy who didn't like to—people wouldn't believe that, I'd tell them that then.

But he and Zumwalt didn't get along very well, and that was, I guess, the time probably when I most exercised the business about keeping the Navy side and the Secretary's side public affairs-wise in tandem, because it was pretty well known by a lot of people that the CNO and the Secretary didn't see eye to eye on a lot of stuff. That can be a disaster, if you ever let that go publicly and let it affect the day-to-day operations of the two offices. So the staff had to work doubly hard to keep things on track, and the executive assistants had to be very careful.

Paul Stillwell: Well, you've mentioned Hanson in connection with Chafee's departure. What was he like to work with on a day-to-day basis?

Captain Hetu: Oh, Thor has got one of the great senses of humor. Well, of course, we still remain friends to this day, and he was very, very smart. Thor was also a Rhodes Scholar and sort of a protégé of Stan Turner's, and that's probably largely why he got the job, I suppose, helped—he relieved Stan. A very, very bright guy, and Thor is a very outgoing fellow. He, of course, stayed on for a while with Warner and had hoped to get a major command out of that job. Generally the EA to the Secretary and the EA of the CNO are probably shoo-ins for admiral, with very few exceptions. One was one of ours, Bob Miale, who really, I thought, took a hosing.*

Anyway, I remember Thor was leaned upon heavily to take command of the naval station at Pearl Harbor, which was a great disappointment to him. I think he had hoped to go out and get a cruiser or something comparable and some sort of a sea command which would segue into admiral. A Navy base was not something that somebody in that job looked forward to.

Paul Stillwell: Well, Admiral Zumwalt was trying to make a point, though, that shore command was essentially equivalent.

Captain Hetu: Exactly, exactly. This was part of the Zumwalt program to say there weren't enough ships to go around, and it should not mean because you didn't get a ship

---

* Captain Robert E. Miale, USN.

command or a major sea command that you weren't going to make flag. And he twisted Thor's brain, I think, to tell him that, "You are going to be high visibility coming out of the Secretary's office." And he wanted him to take the job. I don't know that he couldn't have taken it, but Zumwalt said, "I really want you to take this job, because it will let people in the fleet know that we mean it, and that it's a workable solution." I don't know whether he told him he would make admiral or not. I don't think anybody can tell you that with any certainty.

So Thor went out to Pearl Harbor, and, of course, I knew he would be an innovative CO, which he was, and he made admiral. In fact, he made three stars before he retired. He was relieved by a CNO-to-be, Carl Trost.[*] And Trost is a very bright guy.

Paul Stillwell: And engaging, as well.

Captain Hetu: Yes, nice guy, yes, I liked him a lot. He had a good sense of humor for a guy who was a brilliant as he was. And we had John Poindexter there with Thor.[†] John was the administrative aide, as commander. I also have great, wonderful memories of John. Poindexter was a very bright, hard working unflappable—that's not a great job. I mean, I guess it's a great job to an administrative aide to the . . .

Paul Stillwell: As a stepping-stone.

Captain Hetu: . . . Secretary as a commander, but it's really a glorified flag secretary job. He's the guy that keeps track of the papers, and it's not a glorious job, but an important job, to be sure. I never heard John complain about the hours. God, he was there when I got there, and he was there when I left.

Paul Stillwell: Were you surprised by the grief he came to later?

---

[*] Captain Carlisle A. H. Trost, USN. He later served as Chief of Naval Operations from 1986 to 1990.
[†] Commander John M. Poindexter, USN.

Captain Hetu: Oh, yes, I sure was.* Interestingly, Steve Pfeiffer was then in the office. I told you about Steve, and then Steve left the Navy and went to law school and ended up working for Fulbright and Jaworski, which is why that was John's law firm when he got in trouble, through Pfeiffer. How these things come back.

Yes, I was terribly surprised. I had known John, I thought, pretty well. We got together socially, not every day or every month but fairly often. Got to know his wife, who also had a wonderful sense of humor and I had sort of a ribald sense of humor, probably, and she thought I was funny.

Paul Stillwell: She's a minister, I think.

Captain Hetu: Yes, she is. She's an Episcopal minister. But John is really a man for all seasons. He's very accomplished with his hands, in the sense he's a carpenter and refinished their TV room and stuff like that while he was in this job. I mean, I don't know when he did it. He must have not slept at all, but I can remember going to his house when were in the Secretary's office and him being so proud of this new room that he had finished. I have trouble with one or two nails, and I said to him, "When did you do this? You never leave the office. I thought you slept there." But he's really something.

Paul Stillwell: There's sort of a natural selection process on people who get to high levels, that they frequently do have a great deal of stamina.

Captain Hetu: Yes. I was greatly surprised. I still don't believe that John Poindexter did anything knowingly wrong, that he did whatever he did to protect the boss.

Paul Stillwell: Out of loyalty then.

---

* Vice Admiral John M. Poindexter, USN, was Assistant to the President for National Security Affairs during the Reagan Administration. He got caught up in the Iran-Contra problems of the mid-1980s and reverted to rear admiral on 4 March 1987. He testified in the summer of the year, along with Oliver North and others, in the congressional hearings on Iran-Contra.

Captain Hetu: Absolute loyalty. He was exonerated, I guess, but—well, not really exonerated, but he was—[*]

Paul Stillwell: In a backhanded sort of way.

Captain Hetu: Yes. After I had retired, of course, when all this came down and John was in the White House and I had done some—I was counselor to five presidential commissions, and saw John occasionally when I was working out of the White House—out of the old Executive Office building, but I spent time in the White House. And he was so loyal, to a fault. After this all came down, I had a call from his law firm one day to ask me if I would come over. John had suggested that I might want to provide them with some public relations advice. I was then working at Hill and Knowlton and I said, "Well, I'll do it, but I cannot take money, and it'll have to be a private thing. The firm can't be mentioned.

But I remember going over. I didn't spend very much time. I spent a couple meetings with these high-powered lawyers who wanted me to review some news releases on some of the things they were doing, which were dreadful. And I told them so. They didn't like it very much, but I wasn't getting paid. They were long and laborious news releases and they were of the—they didn't know how to release them. They didn't know how to get them into the hands of the news people, and it was really amateur night. I was struck that a firm this prestigious had no conception of how to deal with the media, none, or how to write a release.

Paul Stillwell: Sounds as if they were submitting legal briefs.

Captain Hetu: Oh, yes, and also they spent hours trying to change words, and I used to say to them, "It's not going to appear in the media the way you're writing it." If you want to buy a page in the Post, we can do that, but this has got to make sense, and you've got to be able to answer questions about it and defend the words you're using. You can't just

---

[*] Admiral Poindexter was found guilty of obstruction of justice, conspiracy, and destroying evidence during the Iran-Contra scandal. The charges were later thrown out on appeal.

throw a news release out the window and expect to read it in The Washington Post the next day the way you've written it.

After they had worked so hard on this thing and had spent a lot of high-powered time, I said to them, "Why do you want to do this anyway? My really bottom line advice to you is don't do this. I don't know why you're doing this. I know you're trying to get your side out on it." The issue then was the Fifth Amendment and what the Fifth Amendment is, why you're able to take it, that it doesn't mean you're guilty. I said, "First of all, nobody's going to print this, nobody's going to print it the way you want it to be printed. You're opening up a Pandora's box. You're making it another story. They're all looking for a lead, and you're giving it to them, and you're not willing to discuss it and why don't you just throw this away?"

This is what I found to be terribly naive—they said, "Well, we also think that if we could get John's feeling out to the press, if we could get the press to pick up on this theme that we're talking about with the Fifth Amendment, that we would get the White House to concur in what John's saying, that they'll stand up and support him."

I said, "Boys, I don't know what you're smoking, but it must be Grade A. The White House is not going to even admit that you're alive over here. They're so glad that Poindexter's getting skewered and the White House is not, they're not going to help you. Don't look for them to even—not for a flicker of recognition." And they were surprised by that.

Paul Stillwell: You'd become pretty politically astute yourself by then.

Captain Hetu: I guess so, but I was surprised that these guys—and I was talking to vice presidents and senior people. "Really? You don't think the White House . . . ?"

I said, "Not a chance, not a chance. No, they're not going to do anything unless they get subpoenaed and dragged kicking and screaming into this thing. They don't want to be any part of this thing, no way."

Paul Stillwell: Did they wind up putting it out?

Captain Hetu: No. Subsequently, long after this, I worked on the Tower Board, which was the Iran-Contra Board and remembered this story.* But it's so funny, in a town like Washington to find these guys in such a high-powered law firm to be so terribly naive politically and media-wise.

Paul Stillwell: How did Admiral Poindexter react to all that public scrutiny and so forth, and the burden of it, as well?

Captain Hetu: You know, I never talked to him very much during the whole thing going on. He was sort of isolated, and I took him and went to lunch with him afterwards at the Army-Navy Club, I remember. In fact, John Jenkins and I went to lunch with John Poindexter and had a nice, long leisurely lunch and talked about how he was bearing up. It was a personal disaster for this guy. He should have been the Chief of Naval Operations. He was on the fast track, and I think it was a terrible thing to give him that job, national security adviser. It's a terrible job to give somebody that's not politically sensitive.

I was interviewed for the book about John.

Paul Stillwell: The Nightingale's Song.†

Captain Hetu: Yes, several times, because I knew three or four of the players in the book. I met other people like John Poindexter who were—Stan Turner, being one, and this is not degrading Stan or John. They were brilliant thinkers and Stan Turner, for instance—I worked for him later at the CIA for four years, but also knew him in the Secretary's office—was a syllogistic thinker, as I used to like to say from my old Jesuit background. That, you know, if A is true and B is true, therefore, C is acceptable or is right. That's the way they thought, and that's the way Stan was, but terribly street naive, terribly street naive. There's that other input to the syllogism when you're in the political arena. You've

---

* John G. Tower, a Republican from Texas, served in the U.S. Senate served from 15 June 1961 to 3 January 1985. He was chairman, President's Special Review Board (Tower Commission) in 1987.
† Robert Timberg, The Nightingale's Song (New York: Simon & Schuster, 1995). The book tells the story of five Naval Academy graduates—Oliver North, Bud McFarlane, John Poindexter, John McCain, and Jim Webb—who had varying degrees of involvement in the Iran-Contra affair.

got to say, "A is true and B is true, but will it work or will it sell? Sometimes it just won't work. I remember when Stan was getting ready to leave the CIA when Reagan was elected.* He really thought that he had a very good chance of being kept on by Reagan, and I told him at the time, "Stan, you don't stand a chance, not a chance."

"Well, he said, "you know, the President-elect was very impressed with my briefing, and his staff was very cordial and wanted to know a lot about the way the agency works and the intelligence community and stuff."

I said, "Stan, this is a political issue. There isn't a way in hell that they're going to keep you on this job." I think when he was told that Casey was coming he was devastated.† It was the first time in Stan Turner's life that he had ever been fired. He was devastated.

Paul Stillwell: Well, that's not really a firing.

Captain Hetu: Oh, no, but he took it like that.

Paul Stillwell: I see.

Captain Hetu: It was a failure. I mean, he might dispute that. I don't know, you talk to him, but I had to hold his hand almost and say, "Stan, you know, that's political, you were bought . . .

Paul Stillwell: It's the end of the term.

Captain Hetu: Yes, yes. You're just like being the CNO or something here, it's the end, exactly, it's the end of the tour. You're out. That doesn't mean you didn't do a good job.

Paul Stillwell: What was Captain Turner like to work with in the Secretary's office?

---

* Ronald W. Reagan served as President of the United States from 20 January 1981 to 20 January 1989. He was in office during the Iran-Contra affair.
† William J. Casey served as Director of Central Intelligence/Director of the Central Intelligence Agency from 28 January 1981 to 29 January 1987.

Captain Hetu: Just Mr. Efficiency, I remember. He wasn't there a terribly long time. We were there a short time together, just months. You know something silly that I remember about working with Stan Turner. It really is silly, but I was really impressed by this. I mean, sort of impressed. We all have out baskets and so forth, and Stan used to use sharpened wood pencils. When he would get the place where it was no longer as sharp as he wanted it, he'd just throw it in his out basket.

I'd sit there and watch him do that, and he'd write on and on, and he'd throw it in the out basket. I didn't ask him why; I just observed. His secretary would come in and scoop all these pencils up, take them in the other room and sharpen them and bring them back and put them—he had a holder with 50 pencils in it. And I thought this said something. It wasn't that he was demeaning this woman; it was that sharpening pencils just was—

Paul Stillwell: Wasted time.

Captain Hetu: Absolutely, yes. That always impressed me. I thought, I'd like to just some day just throw my pencils in.

Paul Stillwell: Well, he soon was with Admiral Zumwalt, involved in his Project 60 initiatives.*

Captain Hetu: Yes. He was going to be an admiral; there wasn't any question about that.

Paul Stillwell: Well, and a conceptual thinker as well.

Captain Hetu: Yes. He had a lot of courage, Stan Turner. He is not universally liked, I don't think, by the Navy because—certainly the aviators don't like him. Other people don't like him because of his innovations at the war college. He made waves wherever he

---

* Project 60 was a program drawn up in the first 60 days of Admiral Zumwalt's first 60 days as Chief of Naval Operations to serve as a plan for the remainder of his four-year tenure.

went, but for the good, I think. We're not doing other things, but I worked for him for four years at the CIA, too, and got to know him even much better there, and he didn't make a lot of friends at the CIA.

Paul Stillwell: Well, especially because they had their ways of doing business, and he wanted to change that.

Captain Hetu: Yes, yes. And sometimes he wasn't as diplomatic as he might have been in doing that. Yes, he went into a culture that was deeply ingrained; that's really hard to change.

Paul Stillwell: Well, one thing that was a constant during that early '70s period was the racial issue, and it really come to a boil with the carrier mutinies and the oiler Hassayampa.[*]

Captain Hetu: Oh, boy.

Paul Stillwell: How did that impact in Washington?

Captain Hetu: Well, I don't want to tell stories that would sound racist, because I'm not. But we had a black Assistant Secretary of the Navy, Johnny Johnson, who was a retired Marine warrant officer, nice man, very nice man.[†] I don't want to make any judgment calls about whether he was up to the job. I mean, it was clearly a—the fact that he was black in those days certainly had something to do with his being assigned the job. He had a Marine son that died on the operating table at Bethesda, I remember, while he was the Assistant Secretary, which was a tragedy. Some sort of mistake was made by the surgeon or something, I don't remember.

---

[*] Racial disturbances broke out in the carrier Kitty Hawk (CVA-63) on 12 October 1972; in the oiler Hassayampa (AO-145) on 16 October 1972; and in the carrier Constellation (CVA-64) on 3 November 1972. See Captain Paul B. Ryan, USN (Ret.), "USS Constellation Flare-up: Was it Mutiny?" U.S. Naval Institute Proceedings, January 1976, pages 46-53.
[†] James E. Johnson, Assistant Secretary of the Navy (Manpower and Reserve Affairs).

I remember being at a meeting with Johnny Johnson one time. We were talking about racial issues and he started off. It was sort of a free-for-all discussion, and Johnny said, "Well, I'll tell you one thing, if I was black there's one way we would do it." And the whole room stopped and sort of—everybody had the same idea on the tip of their tongue, yet nobody said it, "If you were black . . . " But it was kind of—

I've got to tell you one quick story. Bob Miale came in after Trost to be the executive assistant. Bob Miale and I had been friends since we were ensigns, and he was an operator, not a public affairs officer. He had done wonderful things in the Navy, had commands and all sorts of good jobs—well thought of, smart guy. He didn't make admiral, which was, I think, almost entirely because he worked for Warner, although it didn't hurt Trost. I think it was Monday morning that they used to have a meeting of all the assistant secretaries, the CNO, VCNO, and the DCNOs. That was probably enough to fill up the room, but all of the room full of people, and Miale and I would sit in the corner taking notes. Miale the executive assistant and I was the PAO, of course.

We were both captains, and the thrust of this one meeting was they had two buildings that were coming up for naming at the Naval Academy at the same time. I think it was the engineering building and maybe the science building. Does that sound right?

Paul Stillwell: Well, there was a library that got named after Nimitz and a Rickover Hall.[*]

Captain Hetu: Well, this was the issue, was first of all to name a building after Rickover. He was not yet dead, we didn't think—some people thought they just changed his reactor every—that he had long since died. [Laughter] But anyway, the two issues being discussed at this meeting which were of some importance was, (A), whether we should name a building after Rickover while he's still alive. This was before they started naming ships after live people. And, secondly, having gotten over that hurdle, yes, which building should we then name? Would it be more appropriate to name the science

---

[*] The main offices of the Engineering and Weapons Division are located in Rickover Hall. The building is also the home of three of the Division's academic departments, Aerospace Engineering, Mechanical Engineering and Naval Architecture and Ocean Engineering.

building? Was he a scientist or was he a whatever? So they were doing it, and Miale and I were back in the corner making some notes to ourselves and giggling. We had come up with a solution to this problem, but nothing that we would stand up and mention. So Warner saw Miale and me back there, like two little school kids in this room full of admirals and secretaries giggling. He stopped the meeting, which Warner would do; he was kind of crazy and would do these iconoclastic things.

He stopped the meeting, and he said, "Captain Miale, Captain Hetu."

"Yes, sir?"

You two back there look like you might have some solution to this problem."

We said, "Oh, well, no, sir, we were thinking of a solution, but we don't think it would really—no."

He knew that we were playing grab-ass back in the corner, and he said to me. "Captain Hetu, what is your solution? I just want you to tell us what it is."

I said, "Well, sir, it's true that we're going to have women midshipmen at the Naval Academy, is that not true?"

He said, "Yes, yes, so how would this tie in with this?"

"Well," we said, "we thought what you ought to do is build a women's dormitory and call it Hyman Hall."

Paul Stillwell: Oh, gee. [Laughter]

Captain Hetu: Well, Warner didn't get it for about—there was sort of this dead silence, like bong, you know, kerplunk. And then it computed; he finally registered, women's hall, Hyman Hall. He started laughing and the whole room—everybody was waiting for him to laugh. That silence lasted about a year and a half. [Laughter] I thought, "Doesn't anybody get it?" [Laughter] Anyway, he laughed and everybody laughed and we moved on, and I guess they named the engineering building. They didn't use our idea. But there were some light spots.

That was also the time when the Russian submarine operation was going on.

Paul Stillwell: <u>Glomar Explorer</u>.*

Captain Hetu: <u>Glomar Explorer</u>. And I can't remember what Zeke's name was, this guy Zeke, who was a Naval Academy graduate but was a civilian, and he kind of appeared one day and then appeared often. I did not know about the <u>Glomar</u>; there was no reason for me to know about that and I had no need to know at all. But Zeke would come in and out of the office. I didn't know who he was, they just said, "Oh, he's up from OpNav. He's from the research and development people or something." I didn't learn until years later, when I was at CIA, and ran into Zeke who Zeke was. Zeke was running the <u>Glomar</u> operation, and, of course, Warner was deeply involved.

The big policy decision that he got enmeshed in was when the POWs put one of their people on report, a naval aviator.

Paul Stillwell: For collaboration with the enemy.

Captain Hetu: Yes. Well, that he had talked with the enemy. That was a case that Warner had to decide, and that was not unlike the <u>Pueblo</u> case. John Jenkins was deeply involved in that, and it was a case of, do you satisfy the Navy and the POWs' community by trying this guy and putting him up and then dragging all this and the Navy and everybody through the dreadful experience of a court-martial? He may be found not guilty. Was it really a court-martial offense? Did he really do what he said, or was it the pressures of being in confinement that things get blown out of proportion. All this sort of thing was talked about. He finally decided, after a lengthy period, but after a lot of soul searching and talking to a lot of people, he brought Admiral—the POW Medal of Honor winner.

---

* The <u>Glomar Explorer</u>, a ship with a large concealed opening in the bottom, was built for operation by the Central Intelligence Agency for the purpose of recovering a Soviet submarine. The Golf-class diesel-powered ballistic missile submarine sank 750 miles northwest of Oahu, Hawaii, in 1968. In August 1974 CIA technicians raised the submarine about halfway to the surface from a depth of three miles. The submarine then broke apart and fell back to the ocean floor. Word of the operation became public in February and March 1975 as a result of news media reports. The cover story for the <u>Glomar Explorer</u> was that she was recovering manganese nodules from the seabed.

Paul Stillwell: Stockdale.*

Captain Hetu: Stockdale, and talked to all these people at some length. Stan Turner, by the way, and Stockdale were classmates, and Sybil Stockdale used to come into the office a lot.† Stan Turner really was very close with Sybil all during the time that the admiral was in captivity and helped her. She was very active in the POW wives, and Stan was very helpful to her. I remember that, and I remember I was mighty impressed because he worried about her a lot and took care of her.

Paul Stillwell: Well, really, the POW wives before that had been urged to be quiet, and she made it an activist cause.

Captain Hetu: Yes, that's right, and she was very smart and bright, and Stan was very helpful and got the Secretary's backing and all that. Anyway, Warner made the decision in favor of dismissing the charges, and I think there was probably some back-alley maneuvering. I think the fellow retired quietly. It was a tough one, though. I remember John was very—it took a lot out of him. That was a real decision that finally only he could make, and in the final analysis, John Warner had to say yes or no. I mean, he could waffle and jump around only so long.

I remember there were two major decisions being made, one a shipbuilding decision and one was an airplane decision, Grumman and the F-14.‡ I'm trying to remember who the shipbuilding people were, but there were two meetings going on simultaneously. One on the shipbuilding side, one was the aviation. John was walking back and forth between the meetings, which is what he did best.

Paul Stillwell: Well, Litton had all those claims, Litton and some of the other shipyards.

---

* Captain James B. Stockdale, USN, eventually a vice admiral, had been a prisoner of war in North Vietnam from September 1965 to February 1973. He was subsequently awarded the Medal of Honor for his heroism while in prison.
† Both were in the Naval Academy class of 1947.
‡ Grumman F-14 Tomcat fighters first entered training squadrons in late 1972.

Captain Hetu: It may have been Litton. Yes, that sounds right. But John had infinite patience and would drag these meetings out forever. When he was the Under Secretary, he did the Law of the Sea Conference with the Soviets and drove the Soviets mad.

Paul Stillwell: Well, he signed that Incidents at Sea Agreement in '72.*

Captain Hetu: That's right. John was late for all the meetings with the Soviets, which drove them crazy. I guess I didn't realize that they are very punctual and, by God, when the meeting starts at 1:00 o'clock, it starts at 1:00 o'clock, and he would come wondering in at 10 after, 15 minutes after. He drove them crazy and also with penchant for changing documents. I mean, I saw that in my time working for him in the Secretary's office—and then I subsequently worked for him at the bicentennial—of changing things forever, speeches. It was a dreadful experience. He would change things, and he'd rewrite and rewrite and rewrite.

He drove the Russians crazy, and I guess that's one of the reasons, they say, that we came out of the law of the sea thing so well, because he wore the Russians down, and nobody thought that was possible. But, anyway, I remember this meeting went on and on and on. They had to decide something about the Grumman contract, and it went on and on and on and on. I was not in the meeting, but I was outside and there was an admiral whose name was Swoose Snead.†

Paul Stillwell: Yes, he was the F-14 project officer.

Captain Hetu: Yes. Who, I guess, the story goes, in ultimate frustration after going through these things and they'd redo it, and then Warner would go to the shipbuilding meeting and then he'd come back and he'd redo it again, and they were going nuts. And Snead, I'm told, at one point said, "For Christ's sake, Mr. Secretary, I don't care what you

---

* U.S. and Soviet officials signed the Incidents at Sea agreement in Moscow in May 1972. See John Erickson, "The Soviet Naval High Command," U.S. Naval Institute Proceedings, May 1973, pages 66-87, and David F. Winkler, Cold War at Sea: High-Seas Confrontation Between the United States and the Soviet Union (Annapolis: Naval Institute Press, 2000).
† Rear Admiral Leonard A. Snead, USN, served as project manager, F-14/Phoenix missile, Naval Air Systems Command, 1971-74.

do, but do something. We're going crazy in here." [Laughter] I don't know whether he ever made any other stars after that—and I guess he spoke for everybody. Warner would really drive you crazy with his procrastinating.

Paul Stillwell: Did Watergate have any impact in the SecNav's office?

Captain Hetu: No, only that, of course, Warner was there because of Nixon. John Warner had been the head of Young Republicans for Nixon. That's how he got the Under Secretary's job as a sort of nice reward. I don't know that he was close with Nixon, but he was close with pretty much some of those people. That's how he ended up with the bicentennial job after SecNav.

Paul Stillwell: Did the Yom Kippur War of 1973 have any impact in SecNav's office?*

Captain Hetu: None that I'm aware of, no. I was aware of it, certainly, but I don't think it changed anything that we were doing, no.

Paul Stillwell: Well, it was an operational thing.

Captain Hetu: Yes. I was trying to remember another Warner story that—I don't know, I had a good Warner story on the tip of my brain and I can't—

Paul Stillwell: Well, I hope it comes back.

Captain Hetu: Well, let's go on. It was travel, something that we did on travel.

---

* The Yom Kippur War started on 6 October 1973. Egyptian and Syrian forces began major coordinated ground offensives against Israeli positions, seeking to improve territorial claims in the wake of the Six-Day War of 1967. Supported in part by weapons supplied by the United States, Israeli forces counterattacked and drove back the Arabs. A cease-fire finally took effect on 25 October.

Paul Stillwell: Talking about Chinfo, it was during that era that the first public affairs specialist became Chinfo as a flag officer instead of deputy. Any comments on that development?

Captain Hetu: Yes, Bill Thompson. That happened when Chafee was there. Zumwalt and Thompson had been in the Secretary's office with Nitze, and they had had the same relative relationship that I had with Stan Turner. Bud went off and got his third star as Vietnam as ComNavForV, it was widely suggested that because of that relationship was one of the reasons Bill got selected, which was, to my mind, fine. It was our first guy, so what's the difference?

There was a guy, a Navy captain then, Walt Ellis, who worked down in the Assistant Secretary of Defense Public Affairs office.[*] I had worked for Walt years and years before in Chinfo. Walt was a tough guy and a good practitioner but not very well loved, I guess, you'd say. He wrote a letter to the Secretary of the Navy, taking issue with the fact that—Walt just died about a year ago; I don't wish to say bad things about the dead.

But, anyway, he wrote this letter to Chafee, very critical of the fact that Thompson had been selected and pointed out that he had much more experience than Thompson and that he, Walt Ellis, was much more qualified and deserving for the job. I thought it was a dreadful letter and implied, very strongly, that there had been some collusion going on and that because Thompson had worked for Chafee and been a friend of Zumwalt that it was all politically engineered, which, you know, impugned the integrity of the board and the honesty of the Secretary and so forth. Walt was a good writer, and it was a well-constructed letter, but it was pretty damn damaging. So I wrote a reply, and Chafee didn't want to send a reply. I said, "I think you have to. I mean, this guy has really taken on your honesty and the CNO and everybody else." He had sent copies to God and everybody, to the Secretary of Defense and everybody else. "My God, you can't let this thing do that, hold that."

So I wrote a reply, which I think was a pretty good reply, and Chafee finally did agree that it made sense and talked, I think, to Zumwalt, who agreed that it was probably

---

[*] Captain Walter J. Ellis, USN, a public affairs specialist.

a good thing. We didn't want to do anything to hurt this guy necessarily, but he clearly wasn't going to make admiral. Anyhow, we wrote the letter back and sent copies to everybody that Walt had sent his letter to. And the reason I tell this story is that Ellis—I didn't see him, and I was going down a day or two or later after he had gotten the letter, I never heard from him. But I was walking down that E-ring passageway on the way, I think, to the athletic club one afternoon. I saw Ellis come out of the Assistant Secretary's office heading in my direction, and I thought, "Oh-oh." He knew damn well who had written the letter.

So we approached each other like High Noon, and we got about three paces, without ever stopping.* Walt got about three paces in front of me and he said, "Good letter."

I took about one step, and I said, "I had a good teacher." [Laughter] We both just kept going and both chuckled. He was a good player. He knew that he had taken his shot, and he got a shot in return.

Paul Stillwell: What was the thrust of the reply?

Captain Hetu: Oh, that really I took him on on the business of the integrity and honesty, that it's one thing to not agree with the guy's qualifications; that's one point. You can make that point if you wish, and that's a personal opinion. But when you start accusing the CNO and the Secretary of being cahoots with the selection board, you're getting on dangerous ground. You're getting on very dangerous ground, and that's the reason I thought he had to be taken on, not let him get away with it. If he had just written and said, "I think I'm better," you'd say, "Well, okay."

Paul Stillwell: Somebody else thought differently.

Captain Hetu: Yes, the selection board didn't agree with you, but anyway.

---

* High Noon was a 1952 movie, starring Gary Cooper and Grace Kelly, about an Old West gunfight.

Paul Stillwell: Do you have any philosophical ideas on the relative merits of having a line officer or a public affairs specialist in the Chinfo billet?

Captain Hetu: Well, I served under both, some good line officers and some not so good, and I think that you've got to have a public affairs officer in that job. When you get a line officer in there, or an aviator line officer, submariner, or whatever, it takes them a year to click in, to really. Generally, they were chosen because they were outgoing, liked people. All the misconceptions about public relations were why these guys were picked because they were the Dog Smiths of this world. Great guy, Dog Smith.* Henry Miller, people like that who were, I suppose, great aviators and rah, rah for the Navy, but had no conception of what public affairs was all about in dealing with the media and what role public affairs has in formulating policy and policy decisions, had not a clue.†

Paul Stillwell: Well, the rationale was to get an operational fleet understanding into that office, and perhaps there are other ways to achieve that.

Captain Hetu: Yes. Well, I think that there is a well-established track now for public affairs officers. One thing they now, and I'm sure for many years now, have had to have three or four years of operational experience before they're even permitted to try to change their designators. Although Kenny Pease, Kendall Pease, the current Chief of Information, was a 1650 right out of the Naval Academy, worked for me in his first tour, in fact, in Vietnam. I think I've said that before.

He got it because of a physical problem. I think he had a knee that he wrecked playing football, but he certainly turned out okay. No, public affairs officers now do a lot of sea time and usually staff time, I suppose, but still they're at sea, and they come up through the drill just like legal officers.

---

* Rear Admiral Daniel F. Smith, USN, served as the Navy's Chief of Information from August 1960 to August 1962.
† Rear Admiral Henry L. Miller, USN, served as the Navy's Chief of Information from April 1966 to October 1968. His oral history is in the Naval Institute collection.

Paul Stillwell: That's right. You have a lawyer as the Judge Advocate General, and you have a doctor as the Surgeon General.

Captain Hetu: Yes. I think it's finally been accepted that public affairs is a profession. As I told you earlier, I was surprised when I got a master's of science in public relations. But it is a science, and it is a way of life; it's a profession.

Paul Stillwell: Well, typically you've cited the line officers who were in SecNav's office went to very good billets. Did you seek another Navy job after being in the SecNav's office?

Captain Hetu: No. I would have very much liked to have been Chinfo, and that's probably one of the disappointments in my life, that I wasn't. I was never up for selection. I had retired undefeated, but I think I probably had, in some humility, all the tickets punched. I'd been in the CNO's office, I'd been in the Secretary's office, and I had my Vietnam tour, and I had a fleet. I had all the jobs that you're supposed to have and did, I guess, pretty well.

They offered me a job to take over the internal communications command, or whatever they were calling it then. It was brand-new command. Navy Internal Relations Activity. They gave you a command button, I think. That was what Bill Thompson wanted to give me, and I guess the deputy's job wasn't open, or I don't remember whether Cooney was in it by then or not. Anyway, I couldn't think of very many jobs that I wanted after all the jobs I'd had. I would have stayed if I thought I would have gotten a job that would have at least given me a good shot at Chinfo. I didn't think NIRA did, although I was dissuaded of that and, again, nobody can promise you anything. Zumwalt even got me in when he heard I was retiring and asked me to reconsider and stick around.

Again, no promises, but I thought it was very nice of him to do that. He said, "The Navy doesn't want to lose you." Anyway, John Warner left, and President Nixon named him the head of the Bicentennial Administration. In fact, they were getting rid of the Bicentennial Commission, which had floundered and floundered and bumped along and dumped that and created a whole new administration, a new congressional bill to create the administration and make John Warner the first administrator, first and only administrator and have him run the bicentennial.

We were on an airplane going to London, I think, having a drink on the airplane and John Warner said, "Herb, I haven't told anybody this or very many people or whatever, but the President has asked me to take the bicentennial administration. What do you think?"

My knee-jerk answer was, "Wow, why would you want to do that? My God, it seems to me to be a loser." This was before Watergate, and I said, "You're Secretary of the Navy, got your own plane, you're traveling, it's an important job, it's fun, interesting, and you're going to go to the bicentennial that's a mess and try to pull that thing together. If you succeed it'll be Nixon's success and if you fail, you're the one that's going to be holding the brown bag." I said, "I think it's a no winner, but . . ."

John had a strong sense of history, really, and he said, "Well, I think it's important, and I think the country needs this, dah, dah, dah." And he said, "I think I'm probably going to do it."

I said, "Well, enjoy, good luck." I guess we got back, and a couple weeks later on a Saturday morning he called me in the office and said, "I would like you to go with me to the bicentennial."

I said, "Oh, I don't think so, I don't think that's what I really want to do."

"Well, what are you going to do?"

I said, "I don't know, probably retire and do something, but I'm not sure."

He said, "Well, think about it."

I thought about it over the weekend, and I thought, "Well, you know, I have done every job I wanted to do except Chinfo, and it doesn't look like that's on the horizon. It does give me an opportunity to do something very unique." John was going to make me an assistant administrator, handle communications for the bicentennial. I thought, pretty good segue, so I did. I left; I went over on active duty for a couple months and then retired and walked into a super-grade job. I was his executive assistant there for several months until he got himself organized, and then I pulled in my chit and said, "I want to be the assistant administrator for communications. You promised."

He said, "Okay," so that's what I did.

Paul Stillwell: Did you feel any pangs, taking off the uniform after more than 20 years?

Captain Hetu: Yes, I did. When I decided to retire, John Warner was gone, but he said, "You know, I can still orchestrate whatever you want. If you want a review at the Navy Yard or whatever, I'll be sure that you get one."

I said, "No, I don't want to do anything like that, nothing, zero."

Yes, it was tough. The day I went to turn in my green ID card, I went with just my wife and my family to the Navy yard.[*] I forget, some second class or something cut it up in front of me and broke my heart and took my pictures for my retired card. And that was my retirement.

By the time I retired, I guess, Dave Cooney had been selected while I was over at the bicentennial.[†] And they, several months after, had me over for lunch. They took me up to the Pentagon cafeteria, which was my farewell lunch, and took me back to the Chief of Information's office, where they gave me a plaque like that, only that's not it because they had misspelled my name, which I thought was very appropriate. I wanted the plaque, but they sort of pulled it out of my hand and then gave me a new one.

You know, there was no bitterness certainly. I loved the Navy. My God, the Navy had given me such a wonderful career, I'd do it again in a heartbeat. I had wonderfully interesting jobs and met friends who are still friends. Harry Padgett, Jack Garrow, Bill Thompson. I mean, we're still pals. What a way to spend a life. I've always said to people, "If you get a job, there's got to be at least three elements. It's got to be something important in your mind that you're doing, something where you can really make a contribution to the organization you're with and that that organization is an important organization, and the third element is that it's got to be fun. If one of those elements is missing, then you'll probably be unhappy." That was the Navy throughout. I always felt I was working for something, a terribly important organization. I was doing an important job and it was fun. I mean, what else is there?

---

[*] A green ID card signifies that one is on active duty; cards for retired personnel are gray.
[†] Rear Admiral David M. Cooney, USN, served as the Navy's Chief of Information from February 1975 to August 1980.

Paul Stillwell: That's like a classic definition of job satisfaction.

Captain Hetu: Oh, yes. And all of them were that, from the time I was an ensign through my absolute last minute in the Navy, just terrific.

Paul Stillwell: Well, maybe you can hit some of the highlights on the civilian jobs you've been in since then.

Captain Hetu: Oh, yes, well, quickly. The Navy prepared me, of course, and I left the Navy and went immediately to the bicentennial, a very unique, interesting job with John Warner. We traveled all over the world together. It was complicated by the fact that the President resigned, so we had to change directions for the bicentennial, change philosophies, if you will. That the founding fathers had created quite a marvelous country and laid down a very, very solid blueprint that the President resigned.[*] We didn't have a revolution, the military didn't have a coup, the stock market didn't crash. We had an orderly transfer of power. The country moved on and we had a lot to celebrate. That was our philosophy, and I think it worked.

I was getting ready to leave the bicentennial. I stayed on after Warner left and helped to write the final report, which was a five-volume report on the bicentennial. I was just finishing that up when Stan Turner got named to the CIA and called me and asked me if I would like to come to the CIA and start a classic public affairs office. He said, "They don't have one. They have a guy doing the job, but they've never had a professional, and it's been always an ad hoc position."

I went happily to the CIA, had a wonderful four years there with Stan Turner. Again, was able to create, like I had done at the bicentennial, an office, create it, built it.

Paul Stillwell: And create a public affairs plan.

Captain Hetu: A plan, yes, in both places I did a plan. I had an extraordinary time at the CIA. I stayed on a little while after Stan left and worked with Casey. I worked for

---

[*] Richard M. Nixon resigned on 9 August 1974 and was replaced as President by Gerald R. Ford.

Casey; I didn't work with him. Our philosophy was diametrically opposed. I didn't want to stay anyway. I told Stan I didn't want to stay. Even if Carter had been reelected, I didn't want to stay for eight years; four was enough.[*] I probably would have stayed, but I don't know.

Casey and I came to a disagreement of minds, although Bobby Inman was there by then and offered me a couple other jobs to get me to stay, which I thought was very nice, and very pleasant of the agency.[†] He told me that people there thought that I was a professional and that they would like to have me stay and do something else. Offered me the assistant IG job or run the EEOC office.[‡] I said, "I don't think either of those are things I would do very well or with my heart. They lack at least one of the elements of my—they wouldn't be very much fun for me."

So I started my own PR firm with another guy named Dick Luckstadt, and we were pretty successful. This was 1981 and not a great time for businesses, but we started a firm downtown, and we were pretty successful. We did okay. After about two years we were bought by Hill and Knowlton, which was then the number-one PR firm in the world. That was a mistake by us. The synergism wasn't there that was promised, that they would give us the small accounts they didn't want, and they'd take the big ones we couldn't handle and all that, never happened. People were scared to death to talk to you. They didn't want to lose an hour on their account, so that didn't work very well at all.

So Dick and I bought our names back after about two years for $1.00 or $25.00 or whatever it was and decided to get out of there. We had made some money when we sold our firm, but it was a dreadful experience, and it's not worth going into here, about all the pressures and so forth. Dick, my partner, wanted to start the firm up again, and I didn't want to do that; I had had enough. And serendipity, Carl Byoir and Associates, the second-largest PR firm in the world was then looking for somebody to run their Washington office, for a lot of reasons, and I got the job. Carl Byoir had been in Washington for many years and had never made a profit. They knew they needed a Washington office, but they weren't quite sure why.

---

[*] James E. "Jimmy" Carter, Jr., a Naval Academy graduate in the class of 1947, served as President of the United States from 20 January 1977 to 20 January 1981. He and Stansfield Turner were classmates.
[†] Admiral Bobby R. Inman, USN, had a long career in the intelligence field, capped by service in 1981-82 as Deputy Director of the Central Intelligence Agency.
[‡] IG—inspector general; EEOC—Equal Employment Opportunity Commission.

So, anyhow, in the year I was there, turned it around and edged into the black, probably by about $1.25, but we did ease over the line, which was part of my contract, if I would do that. After about a year, Hill and Knowlton bought Carl Byoir worldwide, not just because of me. And so there I was back in Hill and Knowlton, where I didn't really want to be. Hill and Knowlton had done a complete change in leadership in that year, which was usual in PR operations. So I went into a whole new company, but I didn't like it any better. I'm not made for living your life in 15-minute increments and having to charge somebody for 57% of your time or you get a rocket from the front office saying, "You're not being billable." I couldn't stand it. So I was dreadfully unhappy my second tour in Hill and Knowlton. I didn't mind Carl Byoir because I was in charge and I could kind of pick and choose what I wanted to do, and I enjoyed that.

Anyhow, the Aerospace Industries Association was looking for somebody at that time. They had a new president after 25 years, and they wanted to build a new team and have a new thrust to public relations. The aerospace industry had taken some bad hits—waste, fraud, and abuse—and coincidentally the whole industry had pretty much a change of leadership from the old World War II fighter pilots to the new MBAs and younger people. They wanted a proactive team, and Don Fuqua was the head of that, newly retired congressman from Florida.* Anyway, he hired me, and I went in to start a whole new public relations office and write a plan and had a good run there, nine years, which I never thought I'd do in my lifetime.

Interestingly, back before AIA, during my public affairs time, I got hooked up with five presidential commissions, which were very exciting. I started off with the MX Commission, or the Scowcroft Commission, met a lot of nifty people along the way on these commissions.† This was as a counselor or an independent counselor, usually from my PR firm. The second was the Kissinger Commission on Central America, worked with Henry Kissinger for a long time.‡ That was really something interesting to do and there were some marvelous, interesting people on that Commission. That's where I met

---

* Don Fuqua, a Democrat from Florida, served in the House of Representatives from 3 January 1963 to 3 January 1987.
† Lieutenant General Brent Scowcroft, USAF (Ret.), served on the President's Advisory Committee on Arms Control, the Commission on Strategic Forces and the President's Special Review Board, also known as the Tower Board.
‡ Henry A. Kissinger was the President's national security adviser, 1969-73 and later served as Secretary of State, 1973-77.

Ollie North. Ollie traveled with us and spent a lot of time, because he was a Central America buff, as we later learned. So he spent a lot of time at the Commission and also traveled with us to Central America.

Then from there I did the Packard Commission, the year-long study on the Defense Department with Mr. Packard, the Hewlett-Packard Packard, former Deputy Secretary of Defense.* And, again, a bunch of heavy hitters on there, Frank Carlucci and Woolsey and people of that ilk.† I mean, you really got to see some interesting people in operation; it was fascinating. Then the Challenger, I was on the Challenger Commission, which was examining the accident.

Paul Stillwell: William Rogers ran it.

Captain Hetu: Yes, Rogers. And then lastly worked on the Tower Board, which wasn't a commission, what they call a commission, it was the Tower Board, Iran-Contra. Worked for John Tower, Ed Muskie, and Scowcroft again.‡ In fact, the executive director of the Tower Board was the same guy who had run the Packard Commission. So, you know, all the stuff that goes around, comes around. Rhett Dawson, who had worked for Tower up on the Hill, been the staff director for Tower—he and Scowcroft recommended me to Tower to be the public affairs person because I had worked with both of them before. Anyway, I went into the—it was sort of a green table, and there was Muskie and Scowcroft and I knew Scowcroft was on my side and, of course, Rhett Dawson. And Rhett told me before that he was just going through the motions, "He's going to trick you a little bit and see how you react. Tower's a little pixie, so stay on your toes."

I said, "Okay." I didn't know Muskie at all. But, anyway I went in, and there were three pretty heavy hitters sitting there. So Tower started off, and he was looking at

---

* David Packard served as Deputy Secretary of Defense from 1969 to 1971. He was a co-founder of Hewlett-Packard Company and over the course of years held a number of positions, including chief executive officer and chairman of the board.
† Frank C. Carlucci served as U.S. Secretary of Defense from 23 November 1987 to 20 January 1989. R. James Woolsey served as Under Secretary of the Navy from 9 March 1977 to 7 December 1979. He was later Director of the Central Intelligence Agency.
‡ Edmund S. Muskie, a Democrat from Maine, served in the U.S. Senate from 3 January 1959 until his resignation 7 May 1980, to become Secretary of State, a post held 1980-1981.

my biography. He's sort of a little very prissy little guy, not prissy, very all together, and he said, "Well, I see you were a Navy captain."

I said, "Yes, sir."

He said, "If I gave you this job, do I have to call you 'captain'?"

I said, "Only if I can call you 'Chief.'" And I thought, "Boy, oh, boy," and he started to laugh.

He said, "How'd you know I was a chief?"

I said, "I was there the day that John Warner gave you your hat."

He said, "I'll be damned. Were you?"

I said, "Yes. You got promoted in the reserve to chief boatswain's mate. I was there that day, and I was handling the press. You probably didn't see me."

He said, "I'll be damned. I was a chief boatswain's mate." And we started talking about Chief boatswain's mate and, dah, dah, dah. Rhett Dawson looked down the table and gave me the old signal—you got it.

Paul Stillwell: Thumbs up.

Captain Hetu: So that was kind of funny, and Tower was a terribly interesting man to work for and a very, very interesting guy. If he had been Secretary of the Defense, I don't know, I might have—who knows? He had talked to me about going to the Defense Department, but then he didn't get it.* He got pilloried in the Hill.

Paul Stillwell: Any memories of working with Kissinger?

Captain Hetu: Oh, yes, Kissinger was a terribly interesting character. He just intimidated everybody virtually. I was only working for him temporarily, and he was his own master public relations man. I mean, this guy knew how to—could he work a crowd or what? I saw him masterfully handle news conferences, and he loved the attention. We went on a five-day trip to Central America, and we went to six countries in five days, wild trip. In

---

* On 9 March 1989 the U.S. Senate voted, 53-47, against confirming former Senator John G. Tower as Secretary of Defense. The vote was in response to allegations of his drinking and womanizing.

each country we would have an arrival press conference at the airport and then one on departure.

The press was, I mean, incredible; these were major news conference, and they'd bring a lot of people. We had a whole contingent from the United States following us around—all the networks, and then the local man. And he would say to me, "You know, I don't like to do this."

I would say, "Yes, sir, I know."

I can't remember what airport we landed and the press was just—you could see them when we were taxiing up. He called me up and said, "I told you I didn't want all these press out there. You know I don't like all this attention."

I'm thinking, "Yes, right."

He said, "How can we not do this? How can we not have all these press out there? Why do I have to be subjected to these questions?

I said, "Well, there's only one solution I know of right now."

He said, "What's that?"

I said, "Would you mind wearing a bag over your head when we leave the airplane?"

He sort of looked at me. He had a way of looking at you with a dead glare like you'd just been erased from existence, and then he started to laugh. He said, "Ho, ho, ho, I guess you're right." He was funny; he was interesting to work for.

These commissions gave me an opportunity to sit in these meetings with very heavy hitters, people who were very senior people, and to watch the dynamics of all these commissions and see how they would come together as one body to work on a central problem. It was terribly interesting to watch this dynamic and how it worked almost the same in each commission. It took me back to my days in OCS, how when we got into OCS in these small cells that we worked in, how we became instant friends, and we were all shooting for the same goal, and there was an instant camaraderie.

Paul Stillwell: Or in boot camp when the chief pulls you together.

Captain Hetu: Exactly. It was sort of like that. I used to have that feeling, these people, many of them, most of them knew each other because they were on that same sort of level, but it was wonderful to watch the byplay, and Strauss was on the Kissinger Commission.* He was a Democrat, and he was the protagonist and he used to drive Kissinger crazy. And just to watch these two guys and they were both smart guys but very different ways of dealing with things. Strauss is a Texan and he said what he felt, and he said it loud and he'd drive Kissinger crazy. Interesting group of people.

Paul Stillwell: Well, to wrap this up, maybe we could talk about the evolution of your family over time, the switch in wives during that period and also what has become of your children.

Captain Hetu: Yes. I got married right off the Salem to sort of a hometown sweetheart. We had gone with each other through college, and she went to a separate college, but we dated pretty much throughout college. Then she went to fly for American Airlines as a then stewardess, now flight attendant. I have a daughter who's a flight attendant now for American. I came off the ship with orders to Chinfo, and we got married between those jobs and moved to Washington together as a young couple. Moved into an apartment that a guy from the Salem had had who had gone before me.

Had five children; had the first three within two years. We were Catholics, and we didn't know how to get the machine stopped. That was before the pill or any of that which was acceptable to the Catholic Church. Anyhow, we had three for our third wedding anniversary, which, I'm sure, impacted the marriage. We, as you know, moved around a lot, and we didn't have a lot of money and we had a lot of kids. We ended up, we had five children.

Let's see, Mike was born in Bethesda, Debbie was born prematurely at the Tripler after we got to Honolulu and Susan, our third born, was born in Tripler Army Hospital in Honolulu. Then we went to California, where Patty, our fourth was born in Pasadena, at St. Luke's Hospital. There was a naval hospital at Long Beach, but it was really too far

---

* Robert Strauss held a number of positions over the years, including serving as U.S. ambassador to Russia, 1991-93.

away. Then lastly, Jacqueline was born here at Fort Belvoir. We would have gone to Bethesda, but there was no bridge then and it was a long trip. Belvoir was a lot closer; we lived in Vienna.

I think our kids moved around to Honolulu, not all of them—there were only three of them, they were little teenies then. But Puerto Rico, London, around the country, and I had several short tours which took their toll, I think. Not on the kids—I think the kids all turned out quite well. But we had some short tours, you know, a ten-month tour in Los Angeles after leaving Honolulu. A one-year tour at Boston University, a ten-month tour at San Juan, 14-month tour with CNO, 16-month tour in London. You know, that's got to impact.

My first wife Peggy was a wonderful mother. She raised these kids, to a great extent without me because I was always either in a high-activity job—even when we were together I was working weekends and evenings and traveling and so forth, so it was tough, it was tough for her, tough for the kids to move. I think they all came out of it very well, the children. I mean, I'm pleased. We have five squared-away kids. They are all drug free and—

Paul Stillwell: Productive citizens.

Captain Hetu: Yes, they're all successful, and so they all turned out well, and I think that's in large tribute to Peggy, who did a wonderful job with the kids. She and I, unfortunately, grew apart; it was after we got out of the Navy. It was after really probably during my CIA days, and it had nothing to do with the CIA. I worked long hours there, but I didn't travel very much. I did take a couple trips there, one to South America for a month under cover, which I didn't tell you about, but that was pretty interesting.

We just grew apart, and I guess people change. I changed and she changed. Nothing dreadful happened, at least from my point of view in the sense that she didn't do anything terrible, didn't steal money or end up with a boyfriend or anything like that. We just grew apart, and the love went away—from my side in any case—and so we separated in 1981. We tried for four years to see what we could do about that and went to counselors and so forth. It just wouldn't work, and in '85 we finally got a divorce.

Then I didn't remarry again until three years ago. Met a woman whom I didn't even know. I mean, she had moved here from Kansas so I didn't even know Kathy in the Peggy days at all or at any time. She moved in next door to me in the townhouse in Old Town, and that was it.*

Paul Stillwell: Something clicked.

Captain Hetu: Something clicked, big time, and we got married. I retired from the Aerospace Industries Association in December of last year, '95, started my own sort of consulting business, and I'm busier now that I ever thought I would be. I have done jobs for a couple public relations companies in town. One for the Jefferson Group. I did a job for Kaman Aircraft. I'm working now on a project for Capital Line, a public relations agency for The Citadel, getting them ready for the Supreme Court decision on women in single-gender military stated-supported colleges.

And I'm back at the CIA, I'm happy to say, which will be almost a full-time job soon, as the director of the CIA 50th anniversary program office, getting them ready for their anniversary next year. And that's where I am.

Paul Stillwell: Well, could you just mention briefly where your children are now and what they're doing?

Captain Hetu: Yes. Mike is the oldest. Michael, and the only son, is manager of an auto parts warehouse. He has been into automobiles since he was old enough to stand up, I guess, and loved automobiles and has done very well, master mechanic and running a warehouse, doing very well. Mike, I think, tried college when he got out of high school, largely to please me, and it didn't take very well and we sort of agreed to agree that, come on, I said, "You know, you only go around once and you don't have to go to college. You

---

* Old Town is a section of Alexandria, Virginia.

ought to do what you like to do." He loves working with his hands, and he's awfully good at it, and he's much happier being that.

Debbie is the next child. Mike just turned 40, Debbie's 39, will be 40 shortly. She went to Virginia Tech, and she then went to dental hygienist's school after she got her degree and was a dental hygienist for a while. She married a fellow my age, Jack Eckert, who was a nifty, great guy, and I won't tell you the whole story behind that, but that was an interesting choice for her to make. Well, I knew that Jack was not a youngster, but then we met, and we met downtown at the Ritz Carlton Hotel for a drink after work one day. When I saw Jack, I knew that he was not a youngster, but Jack's in terribly good shape, much better shape than I am and looks younger than I do, fortunately. But I knew he was not her age, and so we started to chat and Jack, I remember, trying to do the icebreaker, said, "Well, I understand you were in the Navy."

I said, "Yes, I was."

He said, "Well, I was in the Navy, too, but I was enlisted."

I said, "I was enlisted too."

"Oh, were you?"

I said, "Yes."

He said, "Well, when were you?"

I said, "Well, I went through boot camp in 1948."

He said, "So did I." [Laughter] Bingo. I saw Debbie's jaw drop. We had pretty much established our relative ages with that. Anyway, Jack's turned out to be a wonderful husband, good guy, and terrific husband. They're very happy and now living in Sunset Beach in North Carolina, right near Myrtle Beach.

Number-three child is Susan, who's 38. Debbie and Susan are what we call Irish twins, born within 11 months of each other, so there's a month each year where they're the same age. Susan has been for, gosh, 15, 16 years, a flight attendant for American Airlines. She married another flight attendant, male, she met in the airline. Gary was in the restaurant business and sort of went into the airlines like some of us would go in the Navy. That's where they met and they got married oh, 15 years ago at least. They're happily married, living in Dallas. He's a wholesale liquor distributor, and she still flies for the airlines. They have two children, 14, and let's see—13 and 11, 13 and 12. I don't know, they keep changing.

Paul Stillwell: Yes, they do.

Captain Hetu: They're happy and doing well. I talk to them often. I don't see them as often as I'd like. Number-four child is Patricia. Patty went to Embry Riddle Aeronautical University and was a pilot and still flies. She's a flight instructor on weekends to keep her time up, and during the week she works the government, works for the Air Force as a civilian pilot. Unfortunately, Patty married a guy she met at Embry Riddle, who was from here, but they didn't know each other here. In any case, he is a pilot for U.S. Air, and they were married for about six years or so, and then they have just recently divorced. I say unfortunately, it's too bad; I hate to see that happen, but she's better off.

Oh, I should go back and mention, Mike has two children as well, two girls, they're a little younger, seven and four, and Susan has the two older girls and then my youngest daughter, Jackie, who was born at Fort Belvoir, is married to another Embry Riddle graduate whom she met through her sister. He is a pilot, but he's not an active pilot. He works at the CIA as a research and development chief; he's a branch chief. He's on a fast track, doing very well, indeed, like a GS-15 at age 32 or something, and they have two boys, two small boys, two and five, I think.

So the kids are all doing well; they're all in their houses and well taken care of and straight and happy and healthy. So I've had a wonderful, wonderful life. Had a good first wife and great second wife. That's too bad, but that's what happens in life. It's sometimes more important to make a change than it is to go forward unhappily. I don't want to get into that.

Paul Stillwell: Well, I'm most grateful to you for sharing this wonderful life, not only with me but with people who will be probably reading it years into the future.

Captain Hetu: Well, I never thought I'd talk this long, and I probably didn't say very much.

Paul Stillwell: Well, you did indeed, not only explaining what a public affairs professional does but also giving the examples that illustrate it so well.

Captain Hetu: Well, it's a terribly interesting way to live your life; it's an interesting profession. You live largely by your instinct and wits, sharpened by your professional knowledge and experience, I guess, but it's a wonderful way to make a living, I think.

Paul Stillwell: Thank you very much.

Captain Hetu: Thank you.

Index to the Oral History of
Captain Herbert E. Hetu
U.S. Navy (Retired)

Air Force, U.S.
    In the late 1950s ran a liaison office in Hollywood, 94

Alcohol
    In the early 1950s crew members of the heavy cruiser Salem (CA-139) drank on liberty, 32-34, 41-42
    In the late 1950s actress Felicia Farr spilled a drink in Hetu's lap, 100
    Consumed in Saigon, South Vietnam, in the late 1960s by officers of Seventh Fleet Det Charlie, 222-225
    Heavy drinking by members of a Soviet scientific team in Antarctica in the early 1970s, 251-252
    Americans drank scotch and wine in Antarctica in the early 1970s, 253-254

Allied Forces Southern Europe (CinCSouth)
    In the early 1970s Vice Admiral William Mack was slated to become CinCSouth but got aced out for political reasons, 128-129

Anderson, Admiral George W., Jr., USN (USNA, 1927)
    As Chief of Naval Operations in the early 1960s, 236-238

Anderson, Jack
    Syndicated columnist who was a thorn in the Navy's side in the late 1960s, 265

Antarctica
    In 1972 Secretary of the Navy John Chafee and a number of politicians made a junket to Antarctica, 250-255

Antisubmarine Warfare
    Goblin on the Doorstep was an early 1960s film about Grumman's ASW aircraft, 125-127

Army, U.S.
    In the late 1950s ran a liaison office in Hollywood, 94
    In the mid-1960s Army officers stationed in Puerto Rico played a prank on their Navy counterparts, 164-165
    Was not completely cooperative in April 1969 in providing caskets for dead Navy men, 211-212

Astronauts
    Foul-up in the mid-1960s in pinning special wings on the Navy's early astronauts, 185-187

Australia
    Chief of Naval Operations David McDonald visited in 1967 on the 25th anniversary of the Battle of the Coral Sea, 171-173

Australian Navy
    In June 1969 the aircraft carrier Melbourne collided with the U.S. destroyer Frank E. Evans (DD-754), 227-234

Banner, USS (AGER-1)
    In the late 1960s was a sister ship of the ill-fated Pueblo (AGER-2), 213-214

Bay of Pigs, Cuba
    Failed invasion in April 1961, 119

Bicentennial, U.S.
　　Work in the mid-1970s of the Bicentennial Administration, 295-296, 298

Bigley, Commander Thomas J., USN (USNA, 1950)
　　In the mid-1960s served as an aide to Chief of Naval Operations David McDonald, 180, 182, 184

Boston, Massachusetts
　　In the early 1940s was the homeport for the heavy cruiser Salem (CA-139), 44-45
　　Postgraduate study in public relations at Boston University, 1964-65, 143-152

Boston University
　　Hetu's postgraduate study in public relations in 1964-65, 143-152

Bouchet, Barbara
　　Actress who appeared in the 1965 movie In Harm's Way, 136-137

Brett, Captain Robert B., USN
　　In the late 1960s served as the public affairs for Chief of Naval Operations Thomas Moorer, 189

Brown, Lieutenant Commander Nicholas, USN (USNA, 1956)
　　In the late 1960s served as aide to Admiral John McCain, CinCUSNavEur, 194

Buckley, James L.
　　In 1972 Secretary of the Navy John Chafee and a number of politicians, including Senator Buckley, made a junket to Antarctica, 250-255

Buckley, William F.
　　Writer who joined Secretary of the Navy John Chafee's junket to Antarctica in 1972, 250-255

Budgetary Considerations
　　Impact of Secretary of Defense Robert McNamara and his Whiz Kids in the early 1960s, 123

Bufkins, Commander Russell L., USNR
　　Served in the mid-1950s in the Navy's Office of Information, 51
　　In the mid-1960s as Tenth Naval District public affairs officer, 158

Bulkeley, Rear Admiral John D., USN (USNA, 1933)
　　In 1964 cut off the supply of Cuban water to Guantanamo Naval Base, 162-163

Burke, Admiral Arleigh A., USN (USNA, 1923)
　　As Chief of Naval Operations 1955-61, 55-58, 60

Butts, Captain John L., Jr., USN
　　Served in the late 1960s as chief of staff to Admiral John McCain, 205, 208, 241

C-130 Hercules
　　Used by U.S. military people in Antarctica in the early 1970s, 251-252

Caldwell, Rear Admiral Henry Howard, USN (USNA, 1927)
　　Served 1963-65 as Commandant of the Tenth Naval District, 158

Campbell, Rear Admiral Norman D., USN
　　Naval aviator who took postgraduate work in public relations in the mid-1960s, 144, 146

Campbell, Rear Admiral Robert L., USN (USNA, 1924)
   Was Commander Service Force Pacific Fleet, 1958-61, 85-87

Caribbean Sea Frontier
   Operation in the mid-1960s of the public affairs office, 157-160

Cartozian, Lieutenant Commander Haig O., USNR
   In the late 1960s served with the U.S. Military Assistance Command Vietnam, 219

Castillo, Captain Edmund L., USN (Ret.)
   Navy public affairs specialist and longtime friend of Hetu, 72

Central Intelligence Agency
   Bay of Pigs fiasco in April 1961, 119
   Admiral Stansfield Turner as Director of Central Intelligence, 1977-81, 282-283, 298-299
   Hetu's public affairs work at the agency, 1977-81, 114-115, 154, 238-239

Chafee, John H.
   Served 1969-72 as Secretary of the Navy, 62, 241-264, 266-267, 269-275, 292-293
   Political career and its considerations, 244-245, 247, 255, 258-261, 273
   Personal and working styles, 247-250, 255-257, 266-267, 269-275
   Children of, 249, 256-257
   Trip to Antarctica in 1972, 250-255
   Meeting with New York Governor Nelson Rockefeller in Buffalo, 258-261
   Interviews with news media people, 266-267
   Farewell party when he ended his tenure as SecNav, 273-274

Chertavian, Lieutenant Armen, USN (USNA, 1951)
   In the late 1950s commanded the small oiler Genesee (AOG-9), 82-83

Chinfo
   See: Information, Navy Office of (Chinfo)

CinCSouth
   See: Allied Forces Southern Europe

Clarey, Captain Bernard A., USN (USNA, 1934)
   In the late 1950s commanded the fleet oiler Hassayampa (AO-145), 84

Coast Guard, U.S.
   In the mid-1960s operated HU-16 aircraft in Puerto Rico, 159

Coghlan, Lieutenant Commander Francis E., Jr., USNR
   Former child actor who worked in the Navy's Hollywood office in the late 1950s, 95

Collisions
   In June 1969 the aircraft carrier Melbourne collided with the U.S. destroyer Frank E. Evans (DD-754), 227-234

Commercial Ships
   The Soviet-chartered cargo ship Marucla was involved in the 1962 Cuban Missile Crisis, 116-117

Congress, U.S.
   In the early 1970s Representative Samuel S. Stratton made a trip to Buffalo, New York, with Secretary of the Navy John Chafee, 258-261

In 1972 Secretary of the Navy John Chafee and a number of politicians made a junket to Antarctica, 250-255

Cooney, Rear Admiral David M., USN
Public affairs specialist who served as the Navy's Chief of Information, 1975-80, 116, 295, 297

Cooper, Jackie
Work as a television actor in the 1950s and 1960s, 98-99

Coral Sea, Battle of the
Chief of Naval Operations David McDonald visited Australia and New Zealand in 1967 on the 25th anniversary of the battle, 171-173

Craighill, Rear Admiral Richard S., USN (USNA, 1932)
Served 1965-67 as Commandant of the Tenth Naval District, 158, 160-161, 167

Creighton, Captain Liles W., USN (USNA, 1927)
In 1953-55 commanded the heavy cruiser Salem (CA-139), 28-29

Crenna, Richard
Work as a television and movie actor in the 1950s and 1960s, 97-98, 100-101

Cuba
Guantanamo Bay was the site of refresher training in the early 1950s for the heavy cruiser Salem (CA-139), 29-30, 34
Bay of Pigs fiasco in April 1961, 119
Work of the Navy press desk and the news media during the 1962 Cuban Missile Crisis, 111-113, 115-119
In 1964 Rear Admiral John Bulkeley cut off the supply of Cuban water to Guantanamo Naval Base, 162-163

Cuban Missile Crisis
Work of the Navy press desk and the news media during the 1962 crisis, 111-113, 115-119

Deep Freeze, Operation
In 1972 Secretary of the Navy John Chafee and a number of politicians made a junket to Antarctica, 250-255

Defense Department
Work of the Navy press desk in the early 1960s, during the Kennedy Administration, 55-58, 110-123
Impact of Secretary Robert McNamara and his Whiz Kids in the early 1960s, 123

Dooley, Lieutenant Thomas A. III, USNR
Doctor who did people-to-people work in the 1950s in Vietnam, 60-61

EC-121
Navy intelligence plane shot down by North Korea in April 1969 and lost with all hands, 209-214

Eastern Airlines
In the mid-1960s a postgraduate class at Boston University produced a public relations plan for the airline, 148-149

Ellis, Captain Walter J., USN
Public affairs specialist who wrote a letter of complaint in the early 1970s when he was not selected as the Navy's Chief of Information, 292-293

Enlisted Personnel
    Hetu's Navy enlisted service in 1948-49, 9-17
    Role of enlisted journalists in Navy public affairs programs, 88-91

Enterprise, USS (CVAN-65)
    In 1969 received a visit from a buxom weather woman stationed in South Vietnam, 226-227

F-14 Tomcat
    Grumman files financial claims against the Navy in the early 1970s on the F-14 project, 290-291

Farr, Felicia
    Actress who was in Hollywood in the late 1950s, 100

First Fleet, U.S.
    In June 1963 put on a sea power demonstration for President John F. Kennedy, 138-139

Forbes, Lieutenant Commander Bernard B., Jr., USN (USNA, 1945)
    In the late 1950s was aide to Admiral Felix Stump, 79-80

Ford, Glenn
    Work as a movie and television actor in the 1950s and 1960s, 98-99

France
    In the early 1950s the heavy cruiser Salem (CA-139), the Sixth Fleet flagship, was based at Villefranche, 31-32

Frank E. Evans, USS (DD-754)
    Destroyer cut in two in June 1969 in a collision with the Australian aircraft carrier Melbourne, 227-234

Gammell, Lieutenant Clark M., USN (USNA, 1955)
    In the late 1950s, as a Navy public information officer, appeared in an episode of the "Perry Mason" program, 96-97

General J. C. Breckinridge, USS (AP-176)
    Transport that took Hetu and his family to Hawaii in 1956, 66-67

Genesee, USS (AOG-8)
    Small oiler that was publicized by the Pacific Fleet Service Force in the late 1950s, 82-83

Glenn, Commander Hardy, USN
    Navy public affairs specialist in the 1960s, 125-126, 137-139

Glomar Explorer
    Ship that attempted in the early 1980s to recover a lost Soviet submarine, 287-288

Great Britain
    In the late 1960s CinCUSNavEur was based in London, 190-191, 194

Great Lakes, Illinois, Naval Training Center
    Site of recruit training and hospital corpsman school in the late 1940s, 10-14, 93
    Death in March 1967 of Rear Admiral Howard Yeager, the commandant of the Ninth Naval District, 267-269

Greece
    The heavy cruiser Salem (CA-139) provided disaster relief following an earthquake in August 1953 in the Ionian Islands, 42-44

Grumman Aircraft Corporation
    Early 1960s film about the company's ASW aircraft, 125-127
    Financial claims against the Navy in the early 1970s on the F-14 project, 290-291

Guantanamo Bay, Cuba
    Site of refresher training in the early 1950s for the heavy cruiser Salem (CA-139), 29-30, 34
    In 1964 Rear Admiral John Bulkeley cut off the supply of Cuban water to Guantanamo Naval Base, 162-163

Gunnery-Naval
    Practice in the early 1950s by the heavy cruiser Salem (CA-139), 35-36

HU-16 Albatross
    In the mid-1960s the Coast Guard operated HU-16s in Puerto Rico, 159

Haiti
    In the early 1950s visited by the heavy cruiser Salem (CA-139), 33-34

Hanson, Captain Carl Thor, USN (USNA, 1950)
    In the early 1970s was executive assistant to the Secretary of the Navy, 233, 258, 273-274, 277
    Commanded the naval station at Pearl Harbor and was subsequently selected for flag rank, 277-278

Harris, Commander Brayton R., USNR
    In 1969 provided public affairs support after North Korea shot down an EC-121 intelligence plane, 209-214
    Unusual career pattern, 215

Harvard University, Cambridge, Massachusetts
    In the early 1970s Secretary of the Navy John Chafee visited the university, where his son was a student, 255-257

Hassayampa, USS (AO-145)
    Large oiler that was publicized by the Pacific Fleet Service Force in the late 1950s, 84

Hawaii
    Work of the Navy public information offices in the area in the late 1950s, 67-79, 81-85
    Hetu's liaison role on the movies The Enemy Below and South Pacific, 73-79
    Life for a Navy family in the late 1950s in Hawaii, 102-105

Henkin, Daniel Z.
    In the late 1960s was Deputy Assistant Secretary of Defense (Public Affairs), 199-200, 211-212

Henry W. Tucker, USS (DD-875)
    In the spring of 1969 recovered remains of lost crewmen from an EC-121 aircraft, 210-214

Hess, Colonel Dean, USAF
    Pilot who was the subject of a 1957 movie that starred Rock Hudson, 94

Hetu, Captain Herbert E., USNR (Ret.)
    Civilian employment in accounting and newspaper work, 1-3, 63-65
    Naval Reserve experience, 2, 25, 65
    Active duty as a supply officer in World War II, 4-7, 9-10

Hetu, Captain Herbert E., USN (Ret.)
    Parents, 1-7, 9-10, 20, 49, 63-65
    First wife Peggy, 46, 59, 66-67, 94, 107-108, 127, 145, 157, 165, 191, 205, 207, 221, 304-306, 308
    Second wife Kathy, 306, 308
    Children of, 59, 66-67, 95, 102-103, 107-108, 143, 145, 153, 157, 159, 191, 221-222, 304-308
    Growing-up years in the 1930s and 1940s, 2-10
    Education, 6-9, 17-20, 69, 143-152
    Navy enlisted service in 1948-49, 9-17
    Commissioned in 1952 through Officer Candidate School, 21-27
    Served 1952-54 in the heavy cruiser <u>Salem</u> (CA-139), 27-48, 90
    Served 1954-56 in the Navy Office of Information, 46, 49-55, 59-61
    In 1956 augmented to the regular Navy and converted to the public information designator, 58-59, 65
    Served 1956-58 in the Pacific Fleet information office, 59, 67
    Served 1958-59 in the Service Force Pacific Fleet information office, 81-92
    Served 1959-60 in the Navy Liaison Office in Hollywood, 93-101, 106-107
    Served 1961-62 in the Navy press office of the Defense Department, 107, 110-115
    Served 1962-64 as head of Chinfo's audio-visual branch, 124-142, 235-240
    Postgraduate study in public relations at Boston University, 1964-65, 143-152
    Served 1965-66 with the Tenth Naval District in Puerto Rico, 157-167
    As PAO for CNOs David McDonald and Thomas Moorer in 1966-67, 166-189, 267-269
    As PAO for CinCUSNavEur John McCain in 1967-69, 190-209
    Special project in April 1969 after an EC-121 intelligence plane was shot down, 209-214
    In 1969 served in Seventh Fleet Det Charlie in South Vietnam, 5-6, 215-234, 243
    Served 1970-74 as the Secretary of the Navy's public affairs officer, 155-156, 240-278
    Retirement from active duty in 1974, 297
    Work in the mid-1970s for the U.S. Bicentennial Administration, 295-296
    As public affairs officer at the Central Intelligence Agency, 1977-81, 114-115, 154, 238-239, 298-299
    Post-Navy career in public relations firms and various government commissions, 280-282, 299-304, 306

Holmberg, Lieutenant Colonel William C., USMC (USNA, 1951)
    In the mid-1960s served as an aide to Chief of Naval Operations David McDonald, 184-186

<u>Holmes County</u>, USS (LST-836)
    Christened by Hetu's mother in 1944, later served off Vietnam, 5-6

Homosexuality
    Doctor Thomas Dooley, a best-selling author, quietly left the Navy in the 1950s when his homosexuality was discovered, 60-61

Hope, Bob
    Comedian who participated in a 1967 going-away luncheon for Chief of Naval Operations David McDonald, 188

Incidents at Sea Agreement
    The United States and Soviet Union signed this agreement in 1972, 290

Indian Navy
    In the early 1950s had ships in the Mediterranean, 40

Information, Navy Office of (Chinfo)
Name of the office changed late in World War II from public relations office, 153
Colorful Chief of Information, 1955-57, Rear Admiral Whitey Taylor, 49-50
Populated in the mid-1950s by public information specialists, 47-51
Work in the mid-1950s of the book and magazine branch, 51-55, 59-61
Pubic affairs role in the early 1960s and relationship with the Defense Department, 120-121
Work in the early 1960s of the audio-visual branch, including the growing emphasis on television, 124-142
Relative merits of having the job of Chief of Information held by a public affairs specialist rather than an unrestricted line officer, 294-295

Intelligence
In April 1969 North Koreans shot down a U.S. Navy EC-121 intelligence plane, 209-214

Ionian Islands
The heavy cruiser Salem (CA-139) provided disaster relief following an earthquake in August 1953, 42-44

Iran-Contra
Rear Admiral John Poindexter's involvement in the investigation in the mid-1980s, 278-282
Investigated in the 1980s by a board headed by Senator John Tower, 301-302

Italy
In the early 1950s the heavy cruiser Salem (CA-139) visited Naples and Venice, 32-33, 38

Japan
In April 1969 the destroyer Henry W. Tucker (DD-875) delivered bodies of crew members from a Navy aircraft to Sasebo, 210-214

Jenkins, Commander John S., JAGC, USN
In the early 1970s served in the office of the Secretary of the Navy, 264, 282, 288

John Carroll University, Cleveland, Ohio
Hetu attended in the late 1940s and early 1950s, 9, 17-20, 69

Johnson, James E.
In the early 1970s served as Assistant Secretary of the Navy (Manpower and Reserve Affairs), 285-286

Joseph P. Kennedy, Jr., USS (DD-850)
Role during the Cuban Missile Crisis in late 1962, 116-118

Kelley, General Paul X., USMC
Future Commandant served in the heavy cruiser Salem (CA-139) in the early 1950s, 31-33, 41, 43

Kennedy, President John F.
Work of the Navy press office during the Kennedy Administration, including the 1962 Cuban Missile Crisis, 55-58, 110-122
Visits to fleet ships in 1963, 137-141
Assassination in Dallas in November 1963, 140
Navy film of Kennedy's November 1963 funeral, 141-142

King, Rear Admiral Jerome H., Jr., USN
In 1966-68 served as executive assistant to the Chief of Naval Operations, 180, 183-184, 186-189
In 1969 presided over the inquiry into the collision between the aircraft carrier Melbourne and the destroyer Frank E. Evans (DD-754), 228-234

Kissinger, Dr. Henry A.
   In the 1980s headed a commission on Central America, 300-304

Kitty Hawk, USS (CVA-63)
   Visited by President John F. Kennedy in June 1963, 138-139

Korea
   See: North Korea

Korth, Fred H.
   Served 1962-62 as Secretary of the Navy until ousted by the Kennedy Administration, 154

Kully, Commander Sheldon, USN
   In the spring of 1969 commanded the destroyer Henry W. Tucker (DD-875) when she recovered remains of lost crewmen from an EC-121 aircraft, 210-214

Laird, Melvin R.
   Served 1969-73 as Secretary of Defense, 244

Leave and Liberty
   For personnel in the Mediterranean and Caribbean in the early 1950s, 31-37

Lederer, Captain William J., Jr., USN (USNA, 1936)
   Navy public information specialist also noted as an author and speaker, 52, 58, 68-71

Lee, Rear Admiral Kent L., USN
   In the late 1960s commanded the aircraft carrier Enterprise (CVAN-65), 226-227, 262
   In the early 1970s headed the Secretary of the Navy's Office of Program Appraisal, 262-263

Lemmon, Jack
   Work as a movie actor in the 1950s and 1960s, 99-101

Liberty, USS (AGTR-5)
   Washington, D.C., reaction to the June 1967 attack on the ship, 180-181

Logan, Josh
   Directed the 1958 movie South Pacific, 74-79

London, England
   In the late 1960s CinCUSNavEur was based in London, 190-191, 194

Lumpkin, Captain Pickett, USN
   Longtime Navy public affairs specialist who was a mentor to Hetu, 50, 55-58, 67, 71-74, 79-80, 85, 93, 104-105, 107, 110-111, 120-123, 197

MacBain, Commander Merle, USN
   After World War II became one of the Navy's early public information specialists, 49-50

Mack, Vice Admiral William P., USN (USNA, 1937)
   Served 1963-66 as Chief of the Navy's Office of Information, 125-127, 132-133, 236-237
   In the early 1970s was slated to become CinCSouth but got aced out for political reasons, 128-129

MacKercher, Lieutenant John C., USN
   A Navy public affairs specialist who in 1961 transferred from California to the East Coast in a memorable trip with Hetu, 107-110

Malta
    Visited by the Sixth Fleet flagship, the heavy cruiser Salem (CA-139), in the early 1950s, 39-40

Marine Corps, U.S.
    Marine detachment of the heavy cruiser Salem (CA-139) in the early 1950s included future Commandant P. X. Kelley, 31-33, 43, 47-48

Marquez, Commander Octavio J., USN (Ret.)
    Enlisted journalist who became an officer and public affairs specialist, 88

Marucla, SS
    Soviet-chartered cargo ship that was involved in the 1962 Cuban Missile Crisis, 116-118

McCain, Admiral John S., Jr., USN (Ret.) (USNA, 1931)
    Served 1965-67 as Commander Eastern Sea Frontier and adviser to the United Nations ambassador, 203-204
    Served in 1967-68 as Commander in Chief U.S. Naval Forces Europe, 190-208
    Personal style, 192-198, 203-204
    Was well known for his lectures on sea power, 196-197
    In early 1968 he and his wife viewed films of their son John as a POW in North Vietnam, 201-202
    Served 1968-72 as Commander in Chief Pacific, 204-206, 210
    In 1969 corrected a too-low ranking on Hetu's fitness report, 241-242

McCain, Lieutenant Commander John S. III, USN (USNA, 1958)
    In the late 1960s was filmed by French television while a prisoner in North Vietnam, 200-202

McCallum, Commander James L. P., USN (USNA, 1935)
    In the early 1950s was executive officer of the heavy cruiser Salem (CA-139), 30-31, 41-43, 46

McCool, Lieutenant Commander Richard M., Jr., USN (USNA, 1945)
    World War II Medal of Honor recipient who later became a Navy public information specialist, 51

McDonald, Admiral David L., USN (USNA, 1928)
    As Chief of Naval Operations in the mid-1960s, 166-189
    Visited Australia and New Zealand in 1967 on the 25th anniversary of the Battle of the Coral Sea, 171-173
    Relationship with Secretary of Defense Robert McNamara, 176-178
    Did not want to serve as CNO, 178
    Opposition in 1967 to reactivating the battleship New Jersey (BB-62), 178-179
    Reaction to the June 1967 attack on the intelligence ship Liberty (AGTR-5), 180-181
    Gave personal awards sparingly to subordinates, 182, 188-189
    Going-away party arranged by his staff, 187-189

McLemore, Commander Albert S., USN
    In June 1969 was the commanding officer of the destroyer Frank E. Evans (DD-754) at the time of her collision with the Australian aircraft carrier Melbourne, 228, 233

McNamara, Robert S.
    Impact of Secretary of Defense McNamara and his Whiz Kids in the early 1960s, 123
    Relationship with Chief of Naval Operations David McDonald, 176-178

Medical Problems
    Eye surgery at the Philadelphia Naval Hospital in the late 1940s, 15-16

Melbourne, HMAS
    Australian aircraft carrier that in June 1969 collided with the destroyer <u>Frank E. Evans</u> (DD-754), 227-234

Miale, Captain Robert E., USN
    In the early 1970s served in the office of the Secretary of the Navy, 277, 286-287

Military Assistance Command Vietnam, U.S.
    In the late 1960s ran "5:00 O'clock Follies" briefings for the news media, 218-219

Missiles
    Concern in the early 1960s about a possible leak of information on Polaris use, 55-58

Moorer, Admiral Thomas H., USN (USNA, 1933)
    As Chief of Naval Operations in the late 1960s, 179-180, 189

Mountbatten, Admiral of the Fleet, Lord Louis, Royal Navy
    In the early 1950s gave an excellent briefing on a NATO exercise, 39-40

Movies
    Navy liaison work for the 1957 film <u>The Enemy Below</u>, 73-74
    Navy liaison work for the 1958 film <u>South Pacific</u>, 74-79
    Hetu's work in 1959-60 in the Navy Liaison Office Hollywood, 93-101, 106-107
    Navy liaison work for the 1960 film <u>Wackiest Ship in the Army</u>, 99-101
    Early 1960s film <u>Goblin on the Doorstep</u> about Grumman's ASW planes, 125-127
    Navy film of President John F. Kennedy's November 1963 funeral, 141-142
    Navy liaison work for the 1965 film <u>In Harm's Way</u>, 102, 132-137

Music
    In the 1960s the Tenth Naval District had a popular steel drum band, 161

Naples, Italy
    Visited in the early 1950s by the heavy cruiser <u>Salem</u> (CA-139), 32-33

NATO
    See: North Atlantic Treaty Organization (NATO)

Naval Academy, Annapolis, Maryland
    Naming of new buildings in the early 1970s included Rickover Hall, 286-287

Naval Forces Europe, U.S.
    Admiral John McCain's role in 1967-68 as commander in chief, 190-208
    Admiral Waldemar Wendt in 1968-71 as commander in chief, 205-207
    Relationship in the late 1960s with the Royal Navy, 202-203

Naval Forces Vietnam, U.S.
    Role in country in Vietnam in the late 1960s, 216-217

Naval Reserve, U.S.
    Hetu's father drilled with the reserve before and after World War II, 2

Naval War College, Newport, Rhode Island
    Vice Admiral Stansfield Turner as president in the early 1970s, 62

New Jersey, USS (BB-62)
    Opposition in 1967 by Chief of Naval Operations David McDonald to the ship's reactivation, 178-179

News Media
    Time magazine coverage of an August 1953 earthquake in the Ionian Islands, 43-44
    Relationship in the mid-1950s of publishers with the Navy's Office of Information, 51-55
    In Hawaii in the late 1950s, 72-73, 82-83
    Relationship in the early 1960s with the Defense Department, 56-56, 110-122
    Work of the Navy press desk and the news media during the 1962 Cuban Missile Crisis, 111-113, 115-119
    CBS television coverage of the 1963 loss of the submarine Thresher (SSN-593), 235-240
    Interaction with Chief of Naval Operations David McDonald and his PAO Hetu in the mid-1960s, 170-171, 173-176, 183
    Coverage of the death in March 1967 of Rear Admiral Howard Yeager, 267-269
    Interaction with CinCUSNavEur John McCain and his PAO Hetu in the late 1960s, 192, 200-202
    In the late 1960s Lieutenant Commander John McCain was filmed by French television while a prisoner in North Vietnam, 200-202
    Coverage of the Vietnam War in the late 1960s, 218-220
    Columnist Jack Anderson was a thorn in the Navy's side in the late 1960s, 265
    Coverage in 1969 of the inquiry into the collision between the Australian aircraft carrier Melbourne and the U.S. destroyer Frank E. Evans (DD-754), 228-234
    Interaction with Secretary of the Navy John Chafee in the early 1970s, 266-267
    Interaction with Secretary of the Navy John Warner in the early 1970s, 275-276

Ninth Naval District, Great Lakes, Illinois
    Death in March 1967 of Rear Admiral Howard Yeager, the district commandant, 267-269

Nixon, President Richard M.
    In 1974 appointed John Warner head of the Bicentennial Administration, 295-296

North Atlantic Treaty Organization (NATO)
    NATO naval exercises in the Mediterranean in the early 1950s, 39-40
    Naval exercises in the Caribbean in the mid 1960s, 161-162
    In the early 1970s Vice Admiral William Mack was slated to become CinCSouth but got aced out for political reasons, 128-129

North Korea
    In April 1969 North Koreans shot down a U.S. Navy EC-121 intelligence plane, 209-214

Observation Island, USS (EAG-154)
    In November 1963 President John F. Kennedy was on board to see a Polaris missile test, 139-140

Officer Candidate School, Newport, Rhode Island
    Training program in 1952, 21-27

P-3 Orion
    Land-based patrol plane used in late 1962 to transport news media representatives to the scene of the Cuban Missile Crisis, 116-118

Pacific Fleet, U.S.
    Work of the public information office in the late 1950s, 67-80

Padgett, Captain Harry E., USN (Ret.)
    Longtime Navy public affairs specialist and friend of Hetu, 142-143

Pease, Rear Admiral Kendall M., Jr., USN (USNA, 1968)
    In the late 1960s did public affairs work in Seventh Fleet Det Charlie in Saigon, 223-227
    In the 1990s served as the Navy's Chief of Information (Chinfo), 294

Pfeiffer, Lieutenant Steven B., USNR
    Served 1973-74 as a special assistant in the office of the Secretary of the Navy, 246-247, 266, 279

Philadelphia Naval Hospital
    Treatment of patients in the late 1940s, 15-17

Philippine Islands
    In 1969 Subic Bay was the site of the inquiry into the collision between the Australian aircraft carrier Melbourne and the U.S. destroyer Frank E. Evans (DD-754), 228-234

Poindexter, Rear Admiral John M., USN (Ret.) (USNA, 1958)
    In the early 1970s served in the office of the Secretary of the Navy, 278
    Involvement in the mid-1980s in the Iran-Contra investigation, 278-282
    His wife is a minister, 279

Polaris Missile Program
    In the late 1950s Commander Ken Wade trained Rear Admiral William Raborn on making public appearances on behalf of the program, 105-106
    Concern in the early 1960s about a possible leak of information on Polaris use, 55-58
    In November 1963 President John F. Kennedy was on board the tracking ship Observation Island (EAG-154) to see a Polaris missile test, 139-140

Powell, Dick
    Work in the late 1950s as a movie director, 73-74

Preminger, Otto
    Director of the 1965 film In Harm's Way needed Navy cooperation, 132-137

Prisoners of War
    In the late 1960s Lieutenant Commander John McCain was filmed by French television while a prisoner in North Vietnam, 200-202
    Concern in the early 1970s over what to do with U.S. prisoners who had collaborated with their North Vietnamese captors, 288-289

Public Relations
    Hetu's role on board the heavy cruiser Salem (CA-139) in the early 1950s, 37-38, 42-45, 47-48
    Work in the mid-1950s of Chinfo's book and magazine branch, 47, 49-55, 59-61
    Work of the Pacific Fleet public information office in the late 1950s, 67-80
    Hetu's role in connection with various movies and television programs, 73-79, 102, 132-137
    Work of the Pacific Fleet Service Force public information office in the late 1950s, 81-93
    Role of enlisted journalists in Navy public affairs programs, 88-91
    Work in the early 1960s of the Defense Department information office, 55-58, 110-123
    Postgraduate study in public relations at Boston University, 1964-65, 143-152
    In 1965-66 by the Tenth Naval District in Puerto Rico, 157-167
    For CNOs David McDonald and Thomas Moorer in 1966-67, 166, 267-269
    For CinCUSNavEur in the late 1960s, 190-208
    Public affairs support in April 1969 after North Korea shot down an EC-121 intelligence plane, 209-214
    Role of Seventh Fleet Det Charlie in Saigon in 1969 in providing public affairs support during the Vietnam War, 215-227
    Involvement in 1969 with news coverage of the inquiry into the collision between the Australian aircraft carrier Melbourne and the U.S. destroyer Frank E. Evans (DD-754), 228-234

In the early 1970s for Secretaries of the Navy John Chafee and John Warner, 243-292
In the mid-1970s of the Bicentennial Administration, 295-296, 298
For the Central Intelligence Agency, 1977-81, 114-115, 154, 238-239
Hetu's post-Navy career in public relations firms, 280-282, 299-304, 306

Pueblo, USS (AGER-2)
Impact of the ship's January 1968 capture on Navy public affairs, 199-201, 262

Puerto Rico
Was the base in the mid-1960s for the Tenth Naval District and Caribbean Sea Frontier, 157-167
Local culture of the Puerto Ricans, 163-164

Racial Issues
Unrest on board Navy ships in the early 1970s, 285-286

Radio
In the late 1950s the Pacific Fleet information office produced a program called "Across the Blue Pacific," 68-69

Rainey, Lieutenant Commander Charles W., USNR
In the early 1950s was the Sixth Fleet public information officer, 42-43

Recruit Training
At Great Lakes in the late 1940s, 10-13

Rhode Island
As Secretary of the Navy, 1969-72, John Chafee paid attention to politics in his home state, 244-245, 247, 258-261
A news conference in the early 1970s in Providence involved Secretary of the Navy John Warner, 275-276

Rickover, Admiral Hyman G., USN (Ret.) (USNA, 1922)
The naming of new Naval Academy buildings in the early 1970s included Rickover Hall, 286-287

Rivero, Admiral Horacio, Jr., USN (USNA, 1931)
In the mid-1960s served as Vice Chief of Naval Operations, 190, 265

Rockefeller, Governor Nelson A.
Meeting in Buffalo, New York, in the early 1970s with Secretary of the Navy John Chafee, 258-261

Rodgers, Captain George F., USNR
In the late 1960s served as Sixth Fleet public affairs officer, 208-209

Royal Navy
Relationship in the late 1960s with Commander in Chief U.S. Naval Forces Europe, 202-203

Saigon, South Vietnam
Role of Seventh Fleet Det Charlie in 1969 in providing public affairs support, 215-227

Salem, USS (CA-139)
In the early 1950s deployed to the Mediterranean as Sixth Fleet flagship, 27-28, 31-33, 36-44
Refresher training at Guantanamo, 29-30
The Marine detachment in the early 1950s included future Commandant P. X. Kelley, 31-33, 41, 47-48
Gunnery practice, 35-36
Public relations, 37-38, 42-45, 47-48

Provided relief following an August 1953 earthquake in the Ionian Islands, 42-44
The ship was homeported in Boston in the early 1950s, 44-45
Daily shipboard newspaper, 90

Sasebo, Japan
In April 1969 the destroyer Henry W. Tucker (DD-875) delivered bodies of crew members from a Navy aircraft to Sasebo, 210-214

Schifferdecker, Lieutenant (junior grade) Arnold P., USNR
Served in the early 1960s in the Navy's Office of Information, 124

Schumm, Captain Brooke, USN (USNA, 1927)
In 1952-53 commanded the heavy cruiser Salem (CA-139), 28-30

Schwab, Commander Herbert S., USN (USNA, 1933)
In the early 1950s was the Sixth Fleet legal officer, 41

Service Force Pacific Fleet
Work of the public information office in the late 1950s, 81-93

Seventh Fleet, U.S.
Role of Det Charlie in Saigon in 1969 in providing public affairs support during the Vietnam War, 215-227

Sharp, Captain Erwin A., USN
In the late 1960s served in the public affairs office of CinCUSNavEur and later for the Joint Chiefs of Staff, 191-192

Ship Handling
Refresher training in the early 1950s for the heavy cruiser Salem (CA-139), 29-30

Shore Patrol
In the early 1950s from the heavy cruiser Salem (CA-139), 33-34

Sixth Fleet, U.S.
In the early 1950s the heavy cruiser Salem (CA-139) served as flagship, 27-28, 31-33, 36-44

Slawson, Commander Ralph L., USN
In the late 1960s was public affairs officer for the Seventh Fleet, 209, 227

Snead, Rear Admiral Leonard A., USN (USNA, 1947)
In the early 1970s was project manager for the F-14 Tomcat, 290-291

Solomon, Lieutenant Commander Bernard S., USNR
In the early 1950s was the public information officer for the First Naval District, 44-46

South Pole
In 1972 Secretary of the Navy John Chafee and a number of politicians made a junket to Antarctica, 250-255

South Vietnam
Navy doctor Thomas Dooley did people-to-people work in the 1950s, 60-61
Role of Seventh Fleet Det Charlie in Saigon in 1969 in providing public affairs support, 215-227

Soviet Union
In the early 1970s maintained a scientific station named Vostok in Antarctica, 251-252

Soviet Navy
    Emergence as a power in the late 1960s, 196-200, 202
    In April 1969 recovered debris after North Koreans shot down a U.S. EC-121 intelligence plane, 210, 214
    U.S. effort in the early 1970s to recover a Soviet submarine with the <u>Glomar Explorer</u>, 287-288
    Signed the Incidents at Sea agreement in 1972, 290

Stadelhofer, Lieutenant Commander Robert R., USN
    Naval aviator who served in the early 1960s in the Navy's Office of Information, 124

Stafford, Commander Edward P., USN (Ret.)
    Served in the early 1970s as a speechwriter in the office of the Secretary of the Navy, 245-246

Steere, Captain Richard C., USN (USNA, 1931)
    In the late 1950s was chief of staff to Commander Service Force Pacific Fleet, 91-92

Stierman, Commander Joseph William, USN
    Public affairs specialist who in the late 1960s ran Seventh Fleet Det Charlie in Saigon, 209, 215-216, 222

Stockdale, Captain James B., USN (USNA, 1947)
    In the early 1970s, while he was a prisoner in North Vietnam, his wife made active efforts to publicize the cause of POWs, 288-289

Stratton, Representative Samuel S.
    Trip to Buffalo, New York, in the early 1970s with Secretary of the Navy John Chafee, 258-261

Stump, Admiral Felix B., USN (USNA, 1917)
    Served as Commander in Chief Pacific, 1953-58, 67-68, 70, 72-73, 79-80
    Wife of, 80

Subic Bay, Philippine Islands
    In 1969 was the site of the inquiry into the collision between the Australian aircraft carrier <u>Melbourne</u> and the U.S. destroyer <u>Frank E. Evans</u> (DD-754), 228-234

Sylvester, Arthur
    During the Kennedy Administration served as Assistant Secretary of Defense, 110-112, 114-115, 132

Taylor, Rear Admiral Edmund B., USN (USNA, 1925)
    In 1955-57 was the Navy's Chief of Information, 49-50

Taylor, Captain Joseph Z., USMC
    In the early 1950s commanded the Marine detachment of the heavy cruiser <u>Salem</u> (CA-139), 32-33, 43, 48

Television
    Contacts in the late 1950s with the Navy's liaison office in Hollywood, 95-99
    In the early 1960s networks began developing film archives of Navy material, 129-131
    In the early 1960s NBC started allowing the Navy to show the "Victory at Sea" series, 131-132
    CBS coverage of the 1963 loss of the submarine <u>Thresher</u> (SSN-593), 235-240

Tenth Naval District, Puerto Rico
    Operation in the mid-1960s of the public affairs office, 157-167
    In the 1960s had a popular steel drum band, 161

Thompson, Rear Admiral William, USN
    In 1969 was replaced by Hetu as public affairs officer for the Secretary of the Navy, 240-241, 243-246
    In the early 1970s was a graduate student at Harvard, 256-257
    Served 1971-75 as the Navy's Chief of Information, 122, 292, 295

Thresher, USS (SSN-593)
    CBS television coverage of the 1963 loss of the submarine, 235-240

Tower, Senator John
    In the 1980s headed a board that investigated the Iran-Contra affair, 301-302

Training
    Boot camp at Great Lakes in the late 1940s, 10-13
    Hospital corpsman school in the late 1940s, 13-14
    Officer Candidate School in Newport in 1952, 21-27
    Refresher training in the early 1950s for the heavy cruiser Salem (CA-139), 29-30

Trost, Admiral Carlisle A. H., USN (USNA, 1953)
    Future CNO served in the early 1970s in the office of the Secretary of the Navy, 278

Turner, Admiral Stansfield, USN (USNA, 1947)
    In the late 1960s-early 1970s worked in the office of the Secretary of the Navy, 62, 241-242, 277, 283-285, 289, 292
    In 1972-74 was president of the Naval War College, 62, 275
    Served 1977-81 as Director of the Central Intelligence Agency, 154, 282-283, 285, 298-299

Uniforms-Naval
    In the mid-1960s, as Chief of Naval Operations, Admiral David McDonald made a few personal modifications to the uniform, 175-176

Vietnam War
    USS Holmes County (LST-836) took part in the war, 5-6
    In the late 1960s Lieutenant Commander John McCain was filmed by French television while a prisoner in North Vietnam, 200-202
    Role of Seventh Fleet Det Charlie in Saigon in 1969 in providing public affairs support, 215-227
    Concern in the early 1970s over what to do with U.S. prisoners who had collaborated with their North Vietnamese captors, 288-289

Villefranche, France
    In the early 1950s the heavy cruiser Salem (CA-139), the Sixth Fleet flagship, was based here, 31-32

Wade, Captain Kenneth W., USN
    Longtime Navy public affairs specialist, 102, 105-106, 183
    In 1966 informed Hetu of his selection for commander, 165-166, 168-170

Warner, John
    Served 1969-72 as Under Secretary of the Navy and 1972-74 as Secretary of the Navy, 129, 264, 270-277, 286-292, 302
    Personal and working style, 270-273, 275-276, 289-291
    Signed the Incidents at Sea agreement in 1972, 290
    Work in the mid-1970s as head of the U.S. Bicentennial Administration, 295-296, 298

Wendt, Admiral Waldemar F. A., USN (USNA, 1933)
    Served 1968-71 as CinCUSNavEur, 205-207

Whitney, Lieutenant (junior grade) Craig R., USNR
In the late 1960s did public affairs work in Seventh Fleet Det Charlie in Saigon, 222-224

Wilson, Captain Donald W., USN (USNA, 1936)
In the early 1950s was executive officer of the heavy cruiser <u>Salem</u> (CA-139), 30

Wouk, Herman
Noted author who spoke at the Naval War College in the early 1970s, 62-63

Yeager, Rear Admiral Howard A., USN (USNA, 1927)
Died in March 1967 while trying to rescue his wife from a fire in their quarters at Great Lakes Naval Training Center, 267-269

Yugoslavia
In the early 1950s the heavy cruiser <u>Salem</u> (CA-139) visited Split, 36-37

Zumwalt, Admiral Elmo R., Jr., USN (USNA, 1943)
As Chief of Naval Operations in the early 1970s, 129, 264, 271-273, 277-278, 292-293, 295

www.ingramcontent.com/pod-product-compliance
Lightning Source LLC
Chambersburg PA
CBHW080618170426
43209CB00007B/1459